Last Post over the River Kwai

Last Post over the River Kwai

The 2nd East Surreys in the Far East 1938–1945

Cecil Lowry

Pen & Sword
MILITARY

First published in Great Britain in 2018
by Pen & Sword Military
An imprint of Pen & Sword Books Limited
47 Church Street
Barnsley
South Yorkshire
S70 2AS

ISBN 978 1 52673 691 8

A CIP catalogue record for this book is
available from the British Library.

Typeset in Ehrhardt
by Mac Style

Printed and bound in the UK
by TJ International

Pen & Sword Books Limited incorporates the imprints of Atlas,
Archaeology, Aviation, Discovery, Family History, Fiction, History,
Maritime, Military, Military Classics, Politics, Select, Transport,
True Crime, Air World, Frontline Publishing, Leo Cooper,
Remember When, Seaforth Publishing, The Praetorian Press,
Wharncliffe Local History, Wharncliffe Transport,
Wharncliffe True Crime and White Owl.

For a complete list of Pen & Sword titles please contact
PEN & SWORD BOOKS LIMITED
47 Church Street, Barnsley, South Yorkshire, S70 2AS, England
E-mail: enquiries@pen-and-sword.co.uk
Website: www.pen-and-sword.co.uk

Contents

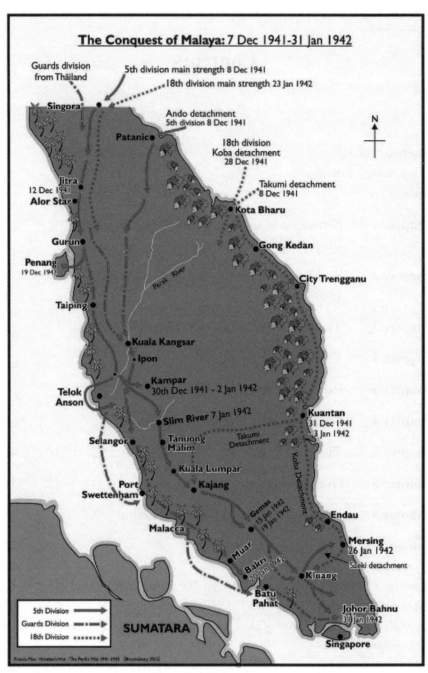

The Conquest of Malaya: 7 Dec 1941-31 Jan 1942

Map of the Japanese invasion of Malaya from December 1941 to January 1942, showing the route of their forces down the Malayan peninsula.

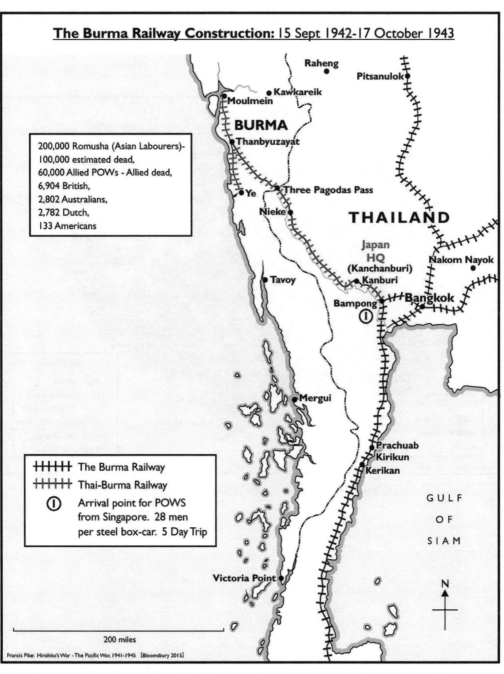

The Burma Railway Construction: 15 Sept 1942-17 October 1943

200,000 Romusha (Asian Labourers)-
100,000 estimated dead,
60,000 Allied POWs - Allied dead,
6,904 British,
2,802 Australians,
2,782 Dutch,
133 Americans

Raheng
Pitsanulok
Kawkareik
Moulmein
BURMA
Thanbyuzayat
Ye
Three Pagodas Pass
Nieke
THAILAND
Japan
HQ
(Kanchanburi)
Nakom Nayok
Tavoy
Kanburi
Bampong
Bangkok

Mergui

Prachuab
Kirikun
Kerikan

GULF

OF

SIAM

The Burma Railway
Thai-Burma Railway
Arrival point for POWS
from Singapore. 28 men
per steel box-car. 5 Day Trip

Victoria Point

N

200 miles

Francis Pike: Hirohito's War - The Pacific War, 1941-1945 [Bloomsbury 2015]

Map showing the route of the Thai/Burma Railway and statistics of the numbers of Asian
labourers and Allied prisoners of war employed.

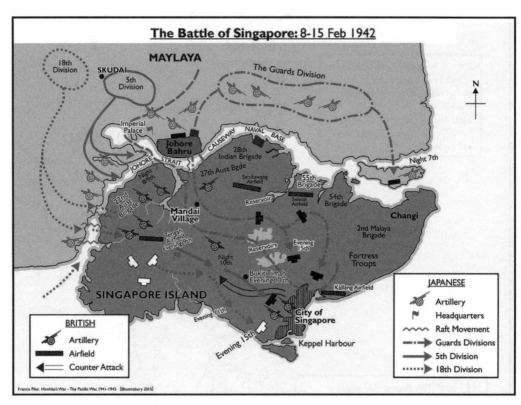

Map of Singapore Island in 1942, showing the Japanese advances.

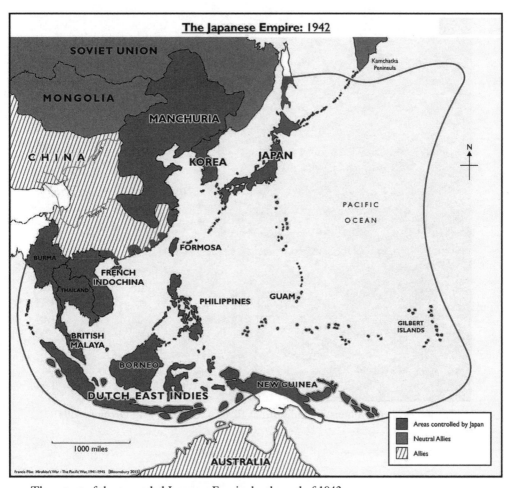

The extent of the expanded Japanese Empire by the end of 1942.

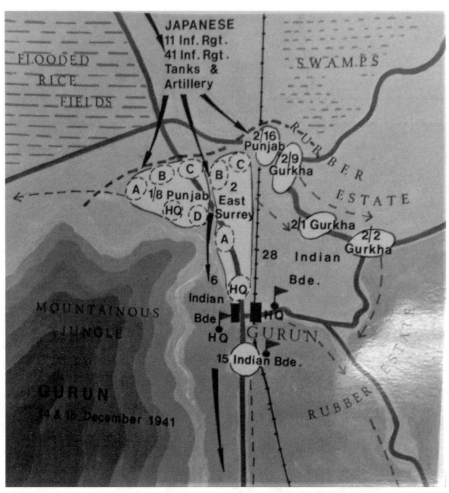

A plan of the Allied positions at the disastrous Battle of Gurun, 14–15 December 1941.

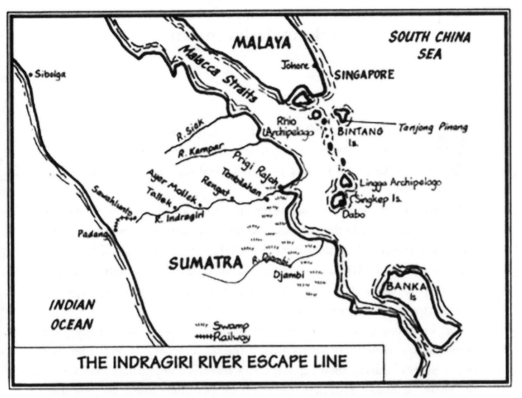

THE INDRAGIRI RIVER ESCAPE LINE

The Indragiri River escape line across Sumatra, set up by the Allies in December 1941 when the situation for forces in Singapore became bleak. Some 2,500 men managed to escape using the route, with around 500 others captured in Padang or en-route.

Acknowledgements

Writing a book is often a lonely and self-centred business. However, as most writers will tell you, there are always people in the background offering you advice and support, and of course they need to be acknowledged.

Firstly, I must thank my long-suffering wife, Liz, for putting up with my addiction to the war in the Far East and the long hours I have 'gone missing' whilst I worked on this manuscript. Secondly, I thank the staff of the Surrey History Centre in Woking, whom I can only describe as 'wonderful', for their help as I spent days trawling through the documents, photographs and manuscripts in their collection.

I'm indebted to the late Sergeant Major Camp of the Surreys, who managed to secrete away his records of the movements of every single man of the Surreys during their captivity. Few records and journals were kept, as the Japanese imposed harsh penalties on any prisoners found keeping them.

Thanks to our good friend Jean Johnston, who meticulously proof-read it and corrected my grammar. To Terry Mantan and Rod Beattie of the Death Railway Museum in Kanchanburi for providing me with a wealth of information on the 2 East Surreys, including the full list of deaths on the Thai/Burma Railway.

Thanks to my good friends Richard Brown and Ken Hewitt for supplying me with information. Richard's dad was a sergeant bandsman in the 2 Surreys and Ken's dad was in the 1 Leicesters, with whom the Surreys amalgamated to form the British Battalion in Ipoh on 20 December 1941. Thanks also to Ray Withnall, for providing me with a mine of information regarding the 2 East Surreys who were sent to Ubon.

Thanks also to Francis Pike, author of the excellent *Hirohito's War* for permitting me to use several of his charts, and to Jim Erickson for his information on the 'Hellships' and PoW camps in Japan.

It would be remiss of me to exclude the later Roger Mansell, whose excellent website is a mine of information. Finally, my thanks to Tony Walton for editing the book.

2 East Surrey Timeline

1881   Regiment formed in India
1885   The Sudan – Mahdist War
1889   Durban, South Africa – Boer War
1915   France – First World War
1924   Jersey, The Channel Islands
1927   Gibraltar
1938   Shanghai, China
1940   Singapore
1941   Jitra, North Malaya
1942   Singapore – prisoners of war
1945   Kingston upon Thames, United Kingdom
1959   Regiment disbanded (became the Queen's Royal Regiment)

Prologue

The inspiration for this book came from my father's experiences with the 2 East Surrey Regiment during the six years they spent in the Far East from 1938–1945. It traces the history of the regiment from 1938 through to their return from the Far East at the end of the Second World War in 1945.

For almost four long years, the men of the 2 Surreys suffered great hardships at the hands of a cruel and brutal Japanese Imperial Army. They bore the brunt of initial Japanese assaults into Malaya on 10 December 1941 and seventy-eight days later, at the surrender of Singapore, only 658 men out of the original battalion strength of 986 were accounted for. Later statistics show that 204 men had died on the battlefields during those fateful seventy-eight days.

Over the next three-and-a-half years in captivity, 156 more East Surrey men were to die of starvation, disease and cruelty in Japanese prisoner of war camps scattered over South East Asia.

As I write this regimental history, there are very few 2 Surrey men left alive to tell their story. I was very fortunate to be able to spend many hours with Corporal John Wyatt at his home in Sydenham whilst researching his book *No Mercy from the Japanese* and to interview Captain Howard, the adjutant of the Surreys, at his home in Guildford. Sadly, both men have since passed away. I was fortunate in obtaining a rare copy of Lieutenant Stephen Abbott's book *And All my War is Done*, a book that outlines in detail his experiences as a Surrey company commander during the Malayan campaign and his years in Japanese PoW camps. I also obtained a copy of Captain John Barnard's book *Endless Years*, which tells the story of the 2 Surrey men's captivity on the Thai/Burma railway between 1942 and 1945.

Winston Churchill dubbed the Malayan campaign and the fall of Singapore as Britain's worst ever military disaster. Following the surrender of the Allied forces on 14 February 1942, 137,000 Allied servicemen, including my father, became prisoners of war of the Japanese.

The Japanese did not permit record keeping, except their own, and went out of their way to destroy all records kept by the Allied military, but several valuable documents survived. The 2 Surrey War Diaries and Quartermaster Sergeant Camp's detailed records of the movements of every man during their imprisonment by careful questioning of every Surrey man he met. When the Japanese made many of their frequent searches, Camp's document was carefully hidden away and was never found. After the war it proved to be of great value for determining the fate of many of the men who did not return and was used as the official basis for pensions and pay awards by the War Office.

A full transcript of Camp's records is available in the Surrey History Centre, Woking. Camp was rather unfairly nicknamed 'Harry the Tramp' by the men, but was held in great esteem by them.

Some regiments, including the Gordon Highlanders, managed to bury their records near to the Kanchanaburi war cemetery in Thailand. These were recovered at the end of the war, which suggests that a variety of tricks were employed by the prisoners to keep records safe.

In 2012, my wife and I visited Singapore, Malaysia and Thailand. In Singapore, we toured the battle sites and gun emplacements where the 2 Surreys spent their final days before captivity, and the Kranji War Cemetery where thirty-three men of the regiment were laid to rest. In Kanchanburi, we had the privilege of visiting the Death Railway Museum and the war cemetery where fifty 2 Surrey men are commemorated, many of whom were exhumed from along the length of the railway and brought back to be interned there. We were fortunate to be taken along the full length of the Thai/Burma railway from Kanchanaburi to the Three Pagodas Pass on the border with Myanmar (formerly Burma) by Rod Beattie, probably the foremost authority in the world on the railway and the Director of the Death Railway Museum.

My father was fortunate to survive his years in the Far East and return home at the end of the war when the Japanese surrendered. Had he joined the 360 men who lost their lives in that conflict I would not be writing this regimental history today.

It can be problematic when writing about historical events, particularly relating to memories and memoirs of individuals, but where possible in this book I have consulted primary sources of information. I acknowledge that some of the facts and figures may not be totally accurate, but this does not in any way detract from the horrors that the men went through. I have done my utmost to verify the statistics, but with events that took place almost eighty years ago, there will always be errors and I apologise in advance for any of these.

An author can do no more than try to see the general picture, finding out details from men who were there or from first-hand accounts from primary sources; where possible I have done this.

This is not an academic book, but a factual account of those eight years spent in the Far East by the officers and men of the 2 Surrey Regiment. Anyone who had a relative in the regiment or anyone with an interest in military history will enjoy reading this book.

Cecil Lowry

Chapter 1

Formation of the Regiment/Shanghai, China 1938–1940

At its formation in 1881, the East Surrey Regiment (known by the nickname of the 'Glasgow Greys' as they had a distinctive grey on their uniform facings) was stationed in the British garrison town of Dinapore in the Indian state of Bihar.

The regiment fought with distinction in the Second Boer War and the First World War, before returning to the regimental depot at Kingston on Thames in 1929.

In 1936, the 2nd battalion trooped the regimental colours at the celebration of Ypres Day at Shorncliffe barracks and the men enjoyed a peaceful few years back home. On 17 November that same year, my father joined the 2 Surreys as a fresh-faced 17-year-old, little knowing at the time what the next nine years was to bring for him.

The following year the regiment was trained as a machine–gun battalion, with all the open spaces around the barracks taken up by small squads undergoing instruction on how to use the Vickers machine gun. Driver training was also stepped up.

Twelve months later, they were ordered to revert to being a rifle battalion. Motor transport was not widely welcomed, as many of the officers were horse lovers and the hunting programme was curtailed due to an outbreak of foot and mouth disease.

At the beginning of 1938, the 2 Surreys, commanded by Lieutenant Colonel Edward Leslie Lowry Acton MC (no relation), were put on alert to move to Shanghai, China. During the early 1930s the Japanese had embarked on a military campaign to set up an empire in Asia. By 1931, they had annexed Manchuria under the pretext of protecting the population from the Russians, thus creating the puppet state of Manchukuo under Pu Yi. This threatened British interests in Shanghai and in the rest of China.

In 1937, skirmishes between China and Japan, particularly the Marco Polo Bridge incident, had turned into bloody, all-out war.

When the Surreys arrived in late 1938, the Japanese were in control of most of the north and east coast of China and up to 400 miles inland. One young Japanese nationalist was reported as saying at that time:

'America and Britain had been colonising China for many years. China was a backward nation ... we felt Japan should go there and use Japanese technology and leadership to make China a better country.'

During the early 1930s, Britain's position in China had deteriorated and it was imperative that the armed forces should uphold law and order to protect British subjects living and working there. The Surreys were to relieve the 1 Seaforth Highlanders, who had been in Shanghai for over a year. The maintenance of a British garrison in Shanghai and Tientsin at that time was thought by the War Office to be a strategic liability, but they were committed to ensure the security of British nationals living there.

Lieutenant Colonel Acton was given explicit instructions from the War Office as to the role of the 2 Surreys in Shanghai, as follows:

'Extract from Army Council Instructions for the General Officer Commanding the British Troops in China: Atten: Lieutenant Colonel Acton – East Surrey Regiment. Dated December, 1937. British Garrisons in Shanghai China. The role of the garrison is, in co-operation with the forces of other interested Powers, the defence of the International Settlement from outside aggression by Chinese forces, and the protection of foreign lives and property within the area covered by the tactical dispositions necessary for the security of the Settlement.

'Tientsin.

'In addition to the duties for which the Boxer Protocol of 1901 provides ... the British Garrison in Tientsin has the further duty of protecting the British Concession. It must be realised that the primary object in the establishment of garrisons in Tientsin, Peking and Shanghai was the defence of British interests against the Chinese,

[but] it may not be militarily practicable or politically desirable to offer the same degree of resistance to encroachment on British interests by other Powers (e.g. Japan).

'In the event of Japanese troops seeking to enter British Sectors of the defences of the International Settlement at Shanghai, they should be asked what are their intentions.

'NOTE: Whilst the French are concerned primarily with their own Concession, the security of that concession is of considerable importance to that of the International Settlement and vice versa. Plans for the defence of the Settlement and of the French Concession therefore require co-ordination.

'Intentions: It should be pointed out, that the British troops are responsible for the sectors which have been allotted to them. If the Japanese admit that their entry is with a view to further operations against [the] Chinese, the British Commander should protest and state that he is referring home for instructions. No forcible opposition should be offered. In Tientsin, although the status of the British Concession differs widely from that of the International Settlement in Shanghai, yet the fundamental principle of avoiding armed conflict is equally applicable. Opposition to any Japanese claim to enter the Concession must not be carried to a point where armed conflict is likely to result. In the last resort, the Japanese should be permitted entry subject to strong protest and notification that the matter is being referred home for instructions.

'Should any question of principle arise which is not covered by these instructions, reference should be made to the War Office, since any precipitate action may have far reaching international repercussions. In the last resort however, force may always be employed against any Power in defence of British lives. Though in peace a political necessity, the maintenance of garrisons in Shanghai and Tientsin is strategically a liability. In the event of war, either in the Far East or elsewhere, it will probably be desirable to withdraw all or part of these garrisons if the military and political situation permits. Except, however, in case of grave and obvious emergency demanding immediate action, these garrisons are not to be withdrawn without reference to the War Office.'

It was under such a delicate situation in China that the 2 Surreys were put on a state of alert.

At 0400 hrs on 1 September 1938 the regiment embarked for Shanghai. They marched the half mile or so from their camp to St Botolph's railway station, boarding a train bound for Southampton where the troopship HMT *Lancashire* was waiting to take them to the Far East.

As the *Lancashire* made its way down the English Channel and into the Atlantic, the men were kept busy with boat drill fatigues, fitness training and weapons training. Crossing the notoriously rough Bay of Biscay, many of the men became sea sick, but once they had passed through the Straits of Gibraltar and into the Mediterranean things settled down on board. The balmy autumn evenings were a delight, and my father said that he enjoyed sleeping on deck under the stars as the ship made its way through the Mediterranean towards the Suez Canal. The only drawback to sleeping on deck, he told me, was that they had to be up out of their covers an hour before reveille, as the Indian crew hosed the decks down around 0500 hrs. If you lingered you were liable to get a drenching from the hoses.

After passing through the Suez Canal the *Lancashire* docked at Port Sudan on the west coast of the Red Sea. There they picked up three officers and 153 other ranks of the 1 East Surreys, making the battalion up to its normal peacetime strength. The first battalion had been in the Sudan for twelve months and was soon to be posted back to the UK, but for these 156 men it was to be China instead of England.

The next port of call was the British protectorate of Aden. The men did not have the opportunity to go ashore as the *Lancashire* quickly refuelled, restocked and headed on towards Colombo, the capital of Ceylon. There they had their first opportunity to go ashore and for two days were able to find their land legs again and enjoy the local amenities.

The next leg of their long journey took them across the Bay of Bengal and down the Straits of Malacca before arriving into Singapore's Keppel Harbour on 29 September, almost a month after leaving England. They arrived on the day of the Munich crisis back in Britain, and their onward journey to Shanghai was postponed in case they were needed back in Britain.

In Singapore, the Surreys were given a good old Irish welcome from the Royal Inniskilling Fusiliers, who were stationed in the colony. I have no doubt my father would have enjoyed a few glasses of his favourite Bushmills Irish whiskey with his fellow countrymen during this short stay there.

After a pleasant two-week stay in Tanglin barracks, the regiment left the island on 12 October onboard the submarine depot ship HMS *Medway* on the penultimate leg of their journey to Shanghai. Five days later the *Medway* docked in Hong Kong's Victoria Harbour, where the Surreys were welcomed by the Royal Scots, the regiment they were to replace. The Royal Scots escorted them to their camp located on a plateau overlooking a Catholic monastery halfway up Mount Nicholson: not really a mountain at all at 1,400 feet, it nevertheless had superb views over the city.

Hong Kong had very few skyscrapers at that time and the men would often sit on the hillside gazing over the panorama towards the harbour. The view was particularly spectacular at night when the lights of the city blazed brightly in a dazzling carpet below them.

For the next four weeks the Surrey men enjoyed the various social and recreational facilities available to them in Hong Kong. The most popular venue was the Cheerio Club, run by the YMCA, where they could obtain excellent meals and great entertainment.

Private Dave Clemens of the 2 Surreys recalled his time in Hong Kong:

'Each Saturday night the Royal Engineers used to run a dance on the 10th floor of the Peninsula hotel. A lot of us used to take the ferry to Kowloon and then get a rickshaw to the hotel. It was always an enjoyable evening.'

After four weeks in Hong Kong and more than two months after leaving England, the regiment set off again on the last leg of their journey to Shanghai, boarding a British India boat, the SS *Santhia*. Originally a cattle boat, the accommodation on the *Santhia* could only be described as 'basic'. The men were housed deep in the holds, where they slept on straw mattresses laid out on the iron decks. The smell was terrible and according to Sergeant Frederick 'Bunny' Austin, 'The food was inedible, a far cry from the conditions on board the *Lancashire*.'

Dave Clemens also recalled that part of the trip:

'We probably fared worse than the cattle. We were housed in holds, palliasses on iron decks to sleep, the smell was terrible and apart from the discomfort, the food was uneatable, but luckily by hitting the tail end of a typhoon in the South China sea, most of us were too seasick to bother with the mess dished up by the crew.'

A great sigh of relief went up from the men when the *Santhia* eventually steamed up the Huangpu River, docking at the Bund in Shanghai on 17 November. On disembarkation, the Surreys were piped ashore by the pipes and drums of 1 Seaforth Highlanders, the only other British regiment in Shanghai at that time. Headed by Lieutenant Colonel Acton on a white horse that magically appeared from nowhere, they marched up the Nanking Road to the Race Club barracks. After a brief rest and some excellent hospitality, including a few 'wee drams' from the Highlanders, they proceeded on up the Bubbling Well Road to the Great Western Road barracks, where the main body of the regiment was to be based. A detachment of two companies under command of Major F.B.B. Dowling MC were based 2 miles away at Jessfield Park.

After settling in, and with winter approaching, the men were issued with fur hats in preparation for temperatures that would soon drop to below freezing. They were also issued with 'whites', a smart tropical linen suit that was to be worn on parade and special occasions.

Shanghai, with the exception of the International Settlement, had been under the control of the Japanese for several months before the Surreys arrived. The Japanese did not occupy the settlement for fear of reprisals from Britain, the USA and France, but they did try to dominate it though acts of terrorism and subversive activities. It was part of the Surreys' task to counter such a threat to the settlement's multicultural citizens.

Shanghai at that time was a city shattered by terrible destruction. As the men gazed across the rooftops, they could see the flattened buildings and burnt-out skyscrapers of a city that was gradually being destroyed. It was a truly cosmopolitan but dangerous city with its lurid vice, savage violence and conspiratorial atmosphere, no place on earth better exemplified the twilight zone between politics and criminality than this Chinese city in 1938. Before the Japanese arrived in 1937 Shanghai had been an extraordinary city, where a type of civil war raged among the various political factions and criminal gangs. Intelligence organizations, police forces and paramilitary units of many nationalities vied with one another for supremacy. It was also a great commercial port, where banking, shipping, opium dens, prostitution, first-class shops, restaurants, hotels and schools all went hand-in-hand with poverty and disease. Espionage, subversion, propaganda and crime came together in a lethal concoction.

The International Settlement formed an entity unique in world politics at the time. It encompassed hundreds of factories, miles of quays and godowns (warehouses), as well as parks and pleasure-grounds, fashionable clubs and hotels and the consulates of the great powers.

By the time 2 Surreys arrived the Japanese had taken over most of Greater Shanghai, along with the industrial section of the International settlement, leaving the residential district to be governed and protected by Britain, the USA and France. They had surrounded it with a barbed-wire fence with their troops checking everyone going in and out. The Surrey men stood cheek by jowl with the Japanese troops, each quite unconcerned by the other's proximity. Whilst relations between the two were formal, they were not friendly. The wire boundary running along the Shanghai-Nanking railway was known as the 'Perimeter', with the Japanese guarding their side of the fence and the British the other. Whilst most of Shanghai had been devastated, the International Settlement was left undisturbed by the Japanese invasion; the men were still able to enjoy the many and varied sporting and social attractions, including several modern cinemas and dance halls. A particularly popular venue for the soldiers was the Shanghai YMCA. The building housed two swimming pools, two gymnasiums, a restaurant, snooker room and bowling alley, all used regularly by the men during their off-duty hours. There were also two roller skating rinks, very popular with the men as they were frequented by lots of attractive local girls. A dance hall on the Rue-Chu-Pao-San in the French sector was also well frequented during off duty hours. Known locally as 'Blood Alley', fights often broke out amongst the many different nationalities that mixed there. The Military Police, along with an ambulance, were continually on patrol outside to deal with the regular disturbances.

Sport also played an important part in life for the Surreys in Shanghai, as indeed it did wherever they were posted. Football took main priority, but hockey, boxing and cross-country running also played a role in the lives of these men posted so far from home.

Five months into the posting, in April 1939, Lieutenant Colonel Acton was recalled to Britain to take up a training role, and Lieutenant Colonel George Edward Swinton took over as commanding officer. Due to the seriousness of the political situation, Swinton was reluctant to speak about the work of his men during their time in Shanghai, but he was always willing to wax lyrical about the sports teams and the prestigious regimental band. Many of the men had been top-class sportsmen before joining the regiment. Private Dave Clemens from Enfield was a long-distance runner who had won many races back home. Prior to the regiment's departure for China, Clemens, a member of Southgate Harriers, won the Essex 20-mile championship and was tipped for a place on the Great Britain marathon team for the 1940 Olympics. These games were scheduled, ironically, for Tokyo, but the outbreak of war with Germany in 1939 put an end to his hopes. (He was however, to run against the Japanese several years later in much different circumstances.)

Clemens wrote home to his family from Shanghai in March 1939:

'It would take too long to tell you everything about Shanghai but everyone should visit it. After a few weeks though I long for the cleanliness of England. The headlines in yesterday's paper says what a big health improvement in February, only 3,557 deaths were recorded, which was 1,324 less than in January. These are all civilian, none are war dead of course those numbers do not include 49 Europeans, our bodies are stronger and have more chance of fighting disease. Hat stealing is a racket here, and so most [of] the men in Shanghai are hatless, some are just lost, some are not on the hat rack when you return or perhaps an ancient and decrepit one is in its place but most of them go through the hat racket gentry. The French concession houses the best bars and the prettiest girls and the biggest fights, mainly among sailors.'

Little did Clemens know at the time that his running career was to be put on hold and that he would not see his family again for another seven-and-a-half years, three-and-a-half of those languishing in a Japanese prisoner of war camp. Running was in Clemens' blood, however, and he managed to complete the London Marathon at the age of 80.

Lieutenant Con O'Neil Wallis was also a top sportsman, having been a rugby international. He won his first cap for Ireland in 1935 and represented the Army for four successive years.

As the sports facilities were in the occupied territory, the men had to constantly cross the divide to make use of them. Just to be troublesome the Japanese would sometimes stop a soldier at their checkpoint and demand to see his cholera pass, often keeping him hanging around for quite some time.

As an occupying force the Japanese treated the Chinese residents of Shanghai very badly. The Surrey men found this very frustrating and were just itching to 'have a go' for such maltreatment of the locals, but this was out of the question due to the tense political situation. Colonel Swinton made several formal complaints to the municipal authorities about the treatment of the local people, but to no avail.

As winter turned to spring, the Japanese began to pursue an even more aggressive policy in Shanghai to try to drive out the British, French and American presence. By June, the Japanese began to erect barricades at the entrances to the British and French concessions in Tientsin, a clear indication of their increased aggression. With around 1,100 British subjects in the city, the situation the Surreys faced was a very muddled one.

Back in Britain with war with Nazi Germany looming, conscription was introduced and the Military Training Act was enacted in May 1939. Males aged between 20 and 21 were to be called up for compulsorily six months' full-time military training before being transferred to the reserve. It was common for men to be called up into their local regiment and of course most Surrey men joined the East Surreys.

When war with Germany broke out on 1 September 1939, Colonel Swinton was kept fully up to date with matters back home, and of course the men were also kept informed as they were concerned for the well-being of their families back in Britain. They were frustrated at being so far from home and unable to help the war effort.

Sergeant Fred (Bunny) Austin said at the time:

'It seemed strange that Europe was engaged in a big conflict and here we were, part of the British Army, enjoying the facilities of Shanghai with no bombings or fighting to worry about.'

Sergeant Austin and his comrades were soon to experience plenty of bombing and fighting of their own as we shall discover later.

Shanghai was militarily indefensible should the Japanese decide to take it over entirely and the British commander, Major-General Frank Simmons, received instructions of what to do in the event of such a takeover:

'British troops will not resist but will allow themselves to be interned, either by the Americans or the French, preferably by the former, since the latter are likely to be involved in operations also.'

Three days after Britain declared war on Germany the Japanese Government demanded that the British withdraw their warships and troops from China. With the situation in China worsening, they had no alternative but to start withdrawing their forces and in October 1939 twenty British warships were withdrawn to Singapore, leaving only HMS *Peterel* to support the 2 Surreys in Shanghai.

Back in camp, the regiment was packed and ready to move out at short notice. The men were disappointed when it soon became evident that a quick return home was not going to happen. They settled down once again to their mundane sentry duties, and life in Shanghai continued as before. The 2 Surreys' regimental band was still in constant demand for dances and concerts, and the men continued to lead a hectic life as they tried to put the war in Europe out of their minds.

During their time in Shanghai, several of the men met Chinese girls and a few were married there. Corporal Arthur Connor, from Ramsgate in Kent, met and married a Russian girl. Lance Corporal Barling married a Chinese girl, but unfortunately he was later killed in action and never got to see his new wife again. Drummer William Quinnell married a Eurasian lady, Ivy Enid Batviau, on 29 June 1940 in Christ the King Church, Shanghai. Mrs Quinnell made her way back to the UK from Shanghai when the regiment was moved to Singapore later that year. Another man is reported to have married an Italian girl in Shanghai, but his name is not recorded.

By the summer of 1940, the situation in Shanghai was becoming even more tense. Japanese sabre-rattling had increased considerably, and their sentries who stood a matter of yards from the Surreys on the other sides of the barricades were far from friendly. Tensions were running high and any false step or act of aggression at the wrong moment might cause an international incident, resulting in world-wide repercussions. The Surreys, however, were well disciplined and no serious incidents occurred.

With the international situation worsening by the day, the men were now confined to barracks. No longer able to protect their own people from the daily aggression of Japanese soldiers, they became even more frustrated and angry towards the Japanese – bordering on hatred. Attacks on British subjects became commonplace, and it seemed likely that British concessions would soon be seized by the Japanese. 'We just wanted to get out there and kick the shit out of the little yellow bastards,' my father reminisced.

In August 1940 the 2 Surreys were finally recalled from China when a most important most secret order was issued to Lieutenant Colonel Swinton.

a) You are now of little military value.
b) The Japanese are out to force a quarrel leading to hostilities.
c) Failure to withdraw now might lead to an ultimate withdrawal in humiliating circumstances.

With their departure imminent, the regimental band staged a final concert in aid of the War Fund, raising over US$3,000, taking their total fundraising during their twenty-one-month stay in Shanghai to over US$48,000. On 21 August the band of the 4th US Marines, with whom they had struck up a friendship, trooped the Surreys down to the docks on their farewell march through the International Settlement. The 2 East Surreys' stay in Shanghai had come to an end.

With the Germans now holding much of western and central Europe, Japan had taken full advantage of Britain's diverted attention and further strengthened its position in China. The Tripartite Pact treaty with Germany and Italy was signed on 27 September 1940.

Chapter 2

Back to Singapore/the Japanese Invasion of Malaya, 1940–1941

The 2 Surreys arrived at Keppel Harbour, Singapore, on 1 September 1940, and were driven in lorries to a temporary camp under canvas at Changi. As they travelled through the city, the men were amazed by the colours of the tropical flowers in the parks, the washing hung out on bamboo poles from the windows of hundreds of shanty houses and the smell of fish drying on the pavements. It was bright and warm, and the air smelled of fresh fruit.

Lieutenant Colonel Swinton said on arrival that:

'Singapore brings more opportunities for solid training – and what is looked forward to with anticipation, greater sporting activities, particularly in hockey. It will take some time for the teams to find their feet of course because of the little opposition we encountered in Shanghai.'

After a month under canvas they were moved into more permanent accommodation in the Chinese High School on Bukit Timah Road.

Singapore at that time was a lively, cosmopolitan, bustling city, probably more so even than London, Calcutta or New York. It was the first global city of the twentieth century. The sea sparkled all around and there were patches of green everywhere – sports grounds, golf courses, parks and gardens abounded.

After settling into their camp, the troops were given the opportunity to enjoy the shops, clubs and bazaars that abounded in Singapore. The New World Club was a particularly popular place. Many of the men took full advantage of the more specific 'hospitality' on offer in the plethora of bars and clubs and any thoughts of an impending war were pushed to the back of their minds as they lapped up the delights of this 'paradise in the east'. The only downside was the poor purchasing power of the Malayan dollar after the excellent exchange rate they had enjoyed in Shanghai.

There was of course a more serious reason why they had been posted to Singapore. The island was crucial for the defence of British possessions in the east, with its huge naval base built at a cost of £25 million over fifteen years lying at its heart.

For the next six months, the 2 Surreys were trained on searchlight and machine-gun operation in the Pasir Panjang sector on the island's south-east coast, before moving on once again up to North Malaya.

On the fifteenth of February, an advance party consisting of D Company under the command of Captain Tony Cater, along with several small details of other companies set off by train for Alor Star. The rest of the regiment followed five days later. From Alor Star, they were transported to their camp at Tanjung Pauh, 12 miles further north and a mere 7 miles from the Thai border. Originally built to house an Indian unit, their camp was situated in a rubber plantation in the middle of the jungle, surrounded by swamps.

Captain W.G. Gingell notes in his report at the time:

'The huts had been erected for an Indian unit and certain alterations to the cookhouse etc. had to be carried out. There was no electric light and therefore no fans; it was extremely hot and unpleasant owing to the bad light. These difficulties were quickly overcome and the troops as always soon settled down to life in the rubber. Everything possible was done to break the monotony, billiard table, table tennis, darts and all kinds of indoor games were introduced and netball courts erected in company areas.'

Football matches were arranged at the RAF football pitch at Kepala Bata, and other pitches were used at the Abdul Hamid College in Alor Star.

The 2 Surreys were still about 200 men short of battalion strength. To make up the numbers, seven officers and 180 newly conscripted other ranks left Glasgow on 11 January 1941 on board the *Empress of Japan* as part of the largest convoy ever to leave British waters during wartime. Although it was a luxury ship, with so many men on board conditions were cramped. Some of the men commented that if they were to pay for such a voyage it would cost about £100, and here they were on a 'freebie'. Little did they know at the time, however, that they were on a 'freebie' heading to hell.

Corporal John Wyatt, one of the conscripted 2 Surreys on board, outlined the journey to Singapore in his book *No Mercy from the Japanese*:

'We eventually sailed on 11 January 1941 as part of the largest convoy ever to leave British shores. The sight was incredible as we left the Clyde, it seemed inconceivable that Britain could ever lose a war with this sort of military strength at its disposal.

'The next few weeks were very boring as the convoy sailed via Iceland, Newfoundland, the West Indies and Freetown before docking in Cape Town. The captain informed us that we would be staying in South Africa's capital for four days and that we would be able to go ashore each day to do some sightseeing and enjoy the pubs and clubs.

'The following morning, we disembarked and as we strolled into the City centre I thought that I had landed in another world. The locals were so kind to us, they bought us drinks, meals and we had a wonderful few days swimming, dancing and generally enjoying the South African hospitality. The war in Europe seemed like a million miles away and for me it gave me the opportunity to write to my family for the first time since I left home. Any mention of our destination or task however was forbidden although by now we were all aware that we were heading for the Far East.

'On leaving Cape Town the convoy split up in smaller groups and the *Empress of Japan* headed north with several other ships up the East coast of Africa. We should have sailed straight across the Indian Ocean to Bombay, but our intelligence had been informed that the German battleship *Deutschland* was sailing somewhere out in the Indian Ocean. It was a much safer option for the small fleet to hug the African coast and head for Mombasa instead.

'We arrived in Mombasa on the twenty-first of February where we spent three days. It was incredibly hot and it was a great relief to cast off our British winter uniforms and don the new tropical kit with which we were issued.

'The three days spent in Mombasa went past in a blur and soon the ship slipped anchor again and we set off across the Indian Ocean towards Bombay. At Bombay, we were once again able to go ashore and visit the markets and nightclubs for eight hours or so before setting sail again on the last stage of our marathon voyage to Singapore. We arrived in Singapore on 11 March.'

To alleviate the boredom of such a long voyage, the men would entertain themselves in a variety of ways, including card games and sport. Despite the cramped conditions, they managed to arrange competitions, boxing being one of the most popular. Private Pugh, a Welsh heavyweight, was the 2 Surreys' star boxer and when he fought he was cheered on by the rest of the men. Unfortunately, he suffered a low punch in one of his bouts, resulting in him being hospitalized when the ship docked in Cape Town. Although still suffering from his injury, he insisted in rejoining the group when the ship left for Bombay.[*]

On arrival into Singapore, the men were fitted out with tropical kit and left the next day in an old wooden Federated Malay States train, arriving at the 2 Surreys camp near Alor Star twenty-four hours later. The journey was uneventful, and the men laughed and joked about what life would be like in Malaya as the train made its way north.

On arrival at Alor Star, Bert Irwin from Egham was given the sad news that his wife had been killed and his daughter seriously injured when a German bomb hit their house. Irwin was devastated by the news and of course being so far away from home he felt helpless but his friends in the regiment gathered round and did their best to cheer him up.

Officers arriving with the conscripts at that time were shocked at the complacency of the troops in Malaya. With the possibility of war looming, the 'spit and polish' attitude, the insistence of exact colours, measurements and turnout was at odds with a regiment preparing for conflict. Lieutenant Abbott describes the situation they encountered on arrival in his book *And All My War is Done*:

---

[*] Pugh was later to die in Kanchanaburi PoW Camp on 17 August 1943. Sergeant Ruoff, who was with him at the time, later wrote that, 'I'm sure Private Pugh died because of his injuries sustained in that bout on board the *Empress of Japan*.'

'We were summoned to the Adjutant's private quarters. Having taken special care with our dress and appearance we presented ourselves. Waiting for our directives on our duties, we were amazed when the Adjutant said in a pained voice:

"Where did you obtain those peculiar ties?" Here all officers wear the regimental tropical tie with informal mess uniform. Was this what we had come so far from home for, from a country that waited for nightly invasion. Had the terrible events of the last eighteen months in Europe passed unobserved in this far corner of the empire?'

The defence of the narrow Kra Isthmus near the Thai border was vital for the defence of Malaya and Singapore should the Japanese invade. This narrow neck of land some 50 miles wide had to be defended against any possible attack through Thailand.

With Britain under threat from an invasion by the Nazis and most of the British armed forces based back at home or in the Middle East, the defence of Malaya was left largely to the Indian Army and the Australian Imperial Force.

The 2 Surreys were attached to 6 Indian Infantry Brigade under the leadership of Brigadier William O. Lay, which in turn was part of 11th Indian Division headed by Major General D.M. Murray Lyon. The only other two British infantry regiments in Malaya at the time were the 1 Leicesters and the Argyll and Sutherland Highlanders.

The Surrey men found it extremely hot in north Malaya. The midday temperatures often reached 35°C in the shade and the reality soon hit them as to what fighting in a hot equatorial climate would be like. Soon after they arrived, real jungle training began in earnest, with the men marching up to 30 miles a day in the tropical heat. Combat exercises in the swamps and paddy fields were thrown in for good measure. It was an exhausting time for the men as my father testified:

'We sweated, toiled and swore in the rubber plantations whilst bivouacking under mosquito nets and wondering whether we would roll over into a king cobra in the night. Leeches, scorpions, snakes and mosquitoes, we endured them all.'

Corporal John Wyatt also recalled:

> 'Quite a few of the lads took ill during training often from snake bites or from the effects of leeches that managed to get in under our puttees. I remember Frank Seymour getting bitten by a python and I ended up in hospital in Ipoh for three weeks with swollen legs and severe cramps.'

With the debilitating conditions taking their toll on the men's health, a rest camp was set up on the island of Penang 65 miles to the south just off the west coast. Groups of about sixty men were sent there for some rest and relaxation on a rotational basis. Penang, the oldest British settlement in Malaya was one of the first holiday resorts in the country and it was a logical place for the men to recharge their batteries after their exhausting jungle training. Food and accommodation were excellent and many of the troops felt that the looming war was just a distant figment of someone else's imagination.

On 24 July 1941, the Japanese occupied French Indochina under an agreement with the puppet Vichy government in France, ramping up the tensions in the British and Dutch possessions in the Far East. With the political situation deteriorating, training was increased to an even higher tempo when the Americans froze Japanese assets, blocking trade between the two countries and holding back vital supplies of petroleum. Australia stopped supplying Japan with scrap metal and Britain blocked the supply of tin from Malaya. It now seemed very likely that the Japanese threat to invade Malaya could soon become a reality.

Should their forces land on the south-east coast of Thailand near Singora and Patani, as was believed likely, it was to be the role of the 11th Indian Division to stop the Japanese advancing overland into Malaya. 'Our job is to stop them in their tracks before they can get a proper foothold in Malaya,' announced Colonel Swinton at one of his briefings to the troops.

It was well known that if the Japanese landed on the Gulf of Thailand, they were likely to invade Malaya down the west coast as that side of the peninsula had an excellent road and rail network all the way to Singapore. The east coast on the other hand was largely underdeveloped, with hills and dense jungle that would make progress difficult.

The town of Jitra was crucial to the defence of Malaya as the west coast railway and trunk road converged there, before running parallel for 48 miles to the road and rail bridges at Sungei Patani. Unfortunately, the Jitra positions were ill-prepared, mainly due to an ongoing conflict between the military and colonial powers in Malaya. The colonial administration was reluctant to draw labour away from vital rubber production and also turned down point blank a request to flood the rice fields on the left flank of the defensive positions, a scheme that would have deterred any flanking movement by the Japanese.

The main road and railway line from the Thai border ran past Jitra just a few miles north of the 2 Surreys' camp where the troops started to prepare a defensive line some 35 miles wide. As well as their heavy training schedule, they worked tirelessly to complete the defences, with only a few days rest and recuperation in Penang to look forward to.

When the defence lines were completed, the 2 Surreys were given the role of the enemy in a mock attack against the rest of the 11 Brigade positions. Ironically, as it turned out, this exercise was almost identical to what happened just a few months later when the Japanese invaded Malaya.

The 2 Surreys were looking forward to 'having a go' at the Japanese after the experiences they had endured a few months previously in Shanghai, where they had been humiliated. Captain Gingell was reported to have said about the Japanese at the time:

'I have seen a great deal of the squint-eyed looking devils and I say without fear of contradiction, that no British Battalion was fitter in every department and more anxious to come to grips with the enemy than the second Battalion the East Surrey Regiment which is not only a very efficient unit (and considered by higher authority as such) but a most happy one, which goes a long way especially in war, to achieve its end.'

The primary aim of 11 Indian Brigade was to hold the Malaya/Thailand border against any invasion, but it was also in the minds of the military. As alluded to earlier, the Japanese were likely to land on the beaches of south-east Thailand. To counter this threat, a plan, code-named Operation

Matador, was hatched to move forces forward into defence positions overlooking the beaches; the 2 Surreys were put on a state of alert to be part of such an operation. The plan was to advance north-east across the border using an armoured train with motorized columns, Bren gun carriers and armoured cars, along with artillery and field company units. The strategic railway junction of Haadyai was to be the first objective, followed by a push on towards the beaches of Singora and Patani, where it was thought the Japanese would land.

Matador, however, was put on hold due to the delicate political situation between Bangkok and London. Thailand was still theoretically neutral and the British government was reluctant to cause an international incident by launching a military force into a neutral country. Any invasion of Thailand by the British before any landings would have given the Japanese international support. Churchill was anxious to ensure that a Japanese invasion force was heading for Thailand before Matador could be launched. Entry into Thailand was only to be made if the Thais requested it or if their neutrality was violated by the Japanese

News filtered through to the 2 Surreys' camp that the Royal Navy's two most prestigious ships, HMS *Prince of Wales* – its newest battleship – and HMS *Repulse*, a veteran battle cruiser, along with four destroyers, had arrived at Singapore on 2 December. The fleet was to have been accompanied by one of the navy's latest aircraft carriers, HMS *Indomitable*, but it had hit a reef off Kingston, Jamaica, and was now in a US dockyard in Virginia for repairs. The loss of *Indomitable* to the naval group was to prove disastrous, as events were later to prove.

Tension began to rise even more in the 2 Surreys' ranks when reports of a large Japanese force in the Gulf of Siam began to filter through as they waited in their allocated positions at Tanjong Pauh for the launch of Operation Matador.

For two days, the men sat waiting in the heavy rain, but the order to advance into Thailand never came as on 7 December, Sir Josiah Crosby, the British Minister in Thailand, sent a telegram to Air Chief Marshal Sir Robert Brooke-Popham – the commander-in-chief of Britain's Far East Command – advising him that:

'British forces should not occupy one inch of Thai territory unless the Japanese go in first. The Thais have a very full conviction of the powers of Japan to do them harm, but, alas they have no faith at all in our power to assist them.'

Crosby had close links to the Thai government and felt that the Thais would oppose any military incursion into their country. He was unaware, however, that the Japanese had been pressurizing them for some time to allow the passage of Japanese troops through their country to invade Malaya and Burma. The Thai prime minister, Phibunsongkhram, well aware of the Japanese military strength, considered it preferable to co-operate with them rather than fight off any invasion. He had convinced Crosby that his country was anti-Japanese and was strongly opposed to any foreign power entering their territory.

At around 1400 hrs on 6 December 1941, the crew of a Lockheed Hudson of No.1 Squadron RAAF (Royal Australian Air Force), flying on a reconnaissance mission out of Kota Bharu on the east coast of Thailand, spotted three Japanese ships steaming west. A few minutes later, a second Hudson also sighted the ships. The crew radioed back to their base and Air Chief Marshal Brooke-Popham was advised of these sightings. He put his forces in Malaya on full alert, and ordered continued surveillance of the convoy. Aircraft were sent up during the night of 6/7 December to monitor the convoy, but no further action was taken.

The following morning, 7 December, a Royal Air Force Catalina flying-boat was shot down by Japanese Zero fighters over the Gulf of Siam and the war in the East had started. Almost simultaneously, the Japanese attacked the American fleet in Pearl Harbor, Hawaii, bombed Wake Island, Midway Island, Luzon, Mindanao in the Philippines, Bataan island and Kai Tek airfield in Hong Kong.

Shortly after midnight on 8 December, a large Japanese force of over 12,000 troops, with 400 vehicles and tanks, landed in Thailand on the beaches of Singora and Patani. By sunrise they were flooding south-westwards towards the border town of Betong near Kroh. Another force landed further north and took over the Kra Isthmus, the narrow neck of land separating Thailand from Malaya.

Back in Singapore, Lieutenant General Arthur Percival, GOC commanding Allied troops in Malaya, called the Governor of Singapore, Sir Shenton Thomas, to tell him the news. Thomas responded with words that were come back to haunt him: 'Well, I suppose you'll shove the little men off.'

Now on full alert, the Surreys' personal kit, including letters from home, was now collected together, crated and sent to Penang for 'safekeeping'. Corporal Denis Gavin remembers the shouts of his colleagues as they prepared to leave their barracks: 'Tokyo here we come' and 'look out, you yellow bastards.'

But by now the opportunity to launch Matador had well and truly gone. The decision to cancel the surge into Thailand was made at 1300 hrs on the morning of the eighth when a message came through to the Surreys' HQ: 'Matador off – man Jitra.' The switch from an offensive operation to going back to man the partly completed and waterlogged defensive line at Jitra, had a damaging psychological effect on the men.

Sergeant Gavin recalls:

'As the Japanese Bull charges ashore, the "Matador" stood still and waited. We were not going to attack anybody. The era of defence had started and, for the last time ever, we moved out of our jungle camp, with the barracks huts already crackling in the flames of the demolition gang. Nothing was being left to chance and if the enemy was to break through our lines, we didn't want to leave a welcoming note. Slowly, and just a bit subdued, we advanced northwards. By nightfall we had dug new trenches, our mortars were set up and our 10lb bombs were stacked neatly in the gun emplacements. We dined royally on stolen chickens and eggs and even had huts to sleep in, as the positions were in the centre of a village from which the inhabitants had hurriedly fled.'

Lieutenant Colonel Swinton received a message the next morning from Brooke-Popham that read:

'Japan's action today gives the signal for the Empire's Naval, Army and Air Forces, and those of their allies, to go into action with a common aim and common ideals. We are ready. We have plenty of warning and our preparations are made and tested. We do not forget at this moment the years of patience and forbearance in which we have borne, with dignity and discipline, the petty insults and insolences inflicted on us by the Japanese in the Far East. We know that those things were only done because Japan thought she could take advantage of our supposed weakness. Now, when Japan has decided to put the matter to a sterner test, she will find out that she had made a grievous mistake. We are confident our defences are strong and our weapons efficient. Whatever our race, and whether we are now in our native land or have come thousands of miles, we have one aim and one only. It is to defend these shores, to destroy such of our enemies as may set foot on our soil, and then, finally, to cripple the power of the enemy to endanger our ideals, our possessions and our peace. What of the enemy? We see before us a Japan drained for years by the exhausting claims of her wanton onslaught on China. We see a Japan whose trade and industry have been so isolated by these years of reckless adventure that, in a mood of desperation, her Government has flung her into war under the delusion that, by stabbing a friendly nation in the back, she can gain her end. Let her look at Italy and what has happened since that nation tried a similar base action. Let us remember that what we have here in the Far East forms part of the great campaign for the preservation in the world of truth and justice and freedom. Confidence, resolution, enterprise and devotion to the cause must and will inspire every one of us in the fighting services, while from the civilian population, Malay, Chinese, Indian or Burmese, we expect that patience, endurance and serenity which is the great virtue of the East and which will go far to assist the fighting man, to gain final and complete victory.'

Unfortunately, Brooke-Popham's confident appraisal of the situation at that time was misplaced, as the 960 men of the 2 Surreys were soon to find out.

Jitra was a poor defensive position for the 11th Indian Division, as most of the defences were grouped around two converging roads. As time was now short, the men sweated and toiled, desperately trying to get defence lines finalized to face the Japanese onslaught. Weapon pits were dug, telephone cables laid and over 1,500 land and anti-tank mines planted, all under heavy monsoon rains. Ammunition had to be transported by hand as, due to the thick muddy morasses, vehicles had great difficulty moving around. Trenches had to be constantly re-dug as they quickly filled with water from the incessant rain, and with little or no protection from the elements the troops spent their nights in rain-soaked uniforms huddled under capes. Nerves were stretched to the limit as they knew that an assault was coming: sentries were posted and patrols were sent out regularly to probe for any sign of enemy infiltration.

Lieutenant Colonel Swinton tried his best to keep up morale, but the situation did not look good for the British and Indian forces just south of the Thai border. They had little or no air support, as most of the Royal Air Force planes had been destroyed by Japanese raids on the airfields of Kepala Batas and Butterworth; those that survived had fled south to Singapore.

Morale within the 2 Surreys' ranks sank even further when they learnt that the *Prince of Wales* and *Repulse* had been sunk by Japanese fighter-bombers off Kuantan. The Royal Navy's two capital ships, along with four destroyers, had left Singapore early on the morning of 8 December, heading north through the South China Sea. Their task was to engage the Japanese troopships heading for the beaches of Thailand and Malaya and to prevent any landings.

The commander of the convoy, Admiral Sir Tom Phillips, had been warned about the lack of air cover, but Philips was 'old school' navy and was convinced that his ships would be able to inflict a heavy defeat on the Japanese. Unfortunately, this stubbornness was to prove his nemesis as both ships were sunk by Japanese aircraft operating out of French Indochina. Phillips, along with 1,870 of his crew, went down with the *Prince of Wales* and the *Repulse* that fateful day, one that was to prove a pivotal point in the opening moves of the war.

As dawn broke on 11 December, the Japanese 5th Division crossed the border into Malaya, and by sunset was engaging the forward positions occupied by the 1 Leicesters. Things were relatively quiet for the 2 Surreys, but when the

Leicesters came under heavy pressure, a section of Surrey Bren gun carriers pushed forward to support them. The strength of the Japanese force was too much for them and they had to retreat, hastily abandoning one of their carriers, leaving inside a detailed map of the Allied dispositions.

The situation was now looking very bleak for 6 Indian Infantry Brigade at Jitra. To avoid complete annihilation, orders came through for them to fall back towards the town of Anak Bukit, 4 miles north of Alor Star. The retreat down Malaya had begun.

Jitra had been a major disaster for 6 Indian Infantry Brigade. A Japanese force of around 600 had driven them back, killing or capturing around 1,400 men and taking great quantities of weapons and equipment. Fifty field guns, fifty heavy machine guns and 300 trucks and armoured cars, along with ammunition and provisions for a division for three months, fell into Japanese hands. It was a rout. Units were scattered all over the area, with poor communications exacerbating the situation. Crucial time, initiative and confidence were lost in a matter of hours. A position, one that should have held out for three months, fell to the Japanese in a mere fifteen hours. According to Japanese statistics, over 3,000 Allied troops surrendered at Jitra, with a loss of only twenty-seven of their own men. This was one of the most incompetently fought battles by Allied units during the Second World War and the most decisive of the Malayan campaign.

The overnight withdrawal for the 2 Surreys along a single road towards the town of Alor Star proved to be chaotic. The weather was exceedingly bad and much more valuable equipment was lost as heavy equipment became bogged down in the clinging mud. Total panic reigned as Bren gun carriers and lorries loaded with stores and ammunition tore down the narrow road at high speed in a long convoy.

During the early hours of the following morning, 13 December, Captain Gingell with his B echelon of ration men, drivers and storemen (including my father) stumbled upon a Japanese patrol just north of Kepala Batas. In the darkness and confusion, they managed to kill all the enemy, as reported in Gingell's personal report on the incident:

'On arriving at Kepala Batas, my small party was shot at by an advance patrol who were obviously trying to get into position to smash up the road where all transports were withdrawing. Fortunately, the patrol of about eighteen was spotted and allowed to come on to about 150 yards and I ordered my party, which had increased to eight and a Bren gunner of the RA[,] to open fire with the result that all were killed. A platoon of Gurkhas went out and ensured no other enemy could get near.'

Later that same morning, Captains Clive O'Neil Wallis and John Kerrich arrived at Alor Star with their C and A companies. Wallis had to leave around sixty men at Anak Bukit as they were too exhausted to continue, instructing them to follow on when they had rested.

On reaching Alor Star, they took up the best available positions along the south bank of the river, covering the bridge and areas either side. When they believed everyone was across, the engineers blew up the bridge to try to halt the Japanese advance. Unfortunately, Lieutenant K.R. Bradley, along with eight Bren gun carriers and around fifty men, were left stranded on the north side of the river. With the Japanese closing in on the town, Bradley had no option but to disarm the carriers and dump them into the river to prevent them getting into Japanese hands. Whilst they were doing this, the enemy attacked in force. A small group of 2 Surreys grabbed a couple of light machine guns and engaged the attacking troops, allowing the rest of the unit to escape across the river in small boats. Lieutenant Leonard Sear, Lance Sergeant John Ferris and Private Jack Whittal were wounded in this skirmish, Sear and Whittal later dying of their wounds. The rest of the men managed to get across the river safely.

By nightfall, the remnants of the demoralized 2 Surreys began to withdraw southwards from Alor Star under heavy enemy fire. They were totally exhausted, having had virtually no sleep for five days and marching for about 30 miles the night before. The terrain was swampy and the men spent hours weaving back and forward along the few paths they could find. Heavy mud sapped the remaining strength from their legs. As they approached a road bridge over the river, mortar bombs began falling all around them and a machine gun suddenly opened up from the direction of the bridge.

Corporal John Wyatt of A Company takes up the story of their retreat:

'Although we had hardly seen any action we were ordered to withdraw from Alor Star and head for a new line just south of the town. This was most demoralizing as we had to abandon all our anti-tank guns as the first section of the withdrawal was along a narrow footpath through muddy paddy fields. It was well after midnight when we reached a canal bank where we had to stumble along up to our waists in muddy water and even swim in some places. By the time we reached the main road heading south we had been wading, nay stumbling along for over 10 hours with hardly anything to eat and I was totally knackered. When we could rest for a few minutes it took a superhuman effort to get going again. Most of our weapons had been dumped except for our trusty Lee Enfield rifles.'

With no troops left to defend it, the crucial airfield at Alor Star had to be abandoned by the RAF, leaving it virtually undamaged with vast supplies of bombs, petrol and stores left behind. The Japanese took immediate control of it, allowing their aircraft to land and refuel on what they called 'Churchill's stores'.

Chapter 3

The Battles of Gurun and Kampar

As the 2 Surreys made their way south from Alor Star, many companies got split up. Their maps only covered the Kedah area, so they were reduced to using maps obtained from local schools. Two platoons of A Company lost their way completely and marched west instead of south, taking about four hours to reach Kuala Kedah on the west coast after trudging through paddy fields, swamps and thick jungle. From there they managed to get a boat that took them to Port Weld in Perak, where they were able to join up with the rest of the regiment at Taiping several days later.

During this frantic retreat, Lieutenant Colonel Swinton broke a leg when he came off the back of a motorcycle ridden by Sergeant Croft during a reconnaissance trip to check out the route south. In great pain, Swinton was evacuated back to Singapore, with Major F.B.B. Dowling taking over control of the regiment.

As dawn was breaking on 14 December, most of the 2 Surreys, other than the two platoons who had escaped by boat, finally arrived at Gurun, where Captain Gingell and his catering crew were waiting with a most welcome hot stew. The men had not eaten a proper meal for two days and were delighted to see the captain and his men, who had been transported by MT (motor transport) earlier.

The village of Gurun, at the foot of the 4,000ft Kedah peak, was an untidy clutter of shacks, shops and Malay houses constructed on stilts over a swamp. It would have been one of the best natural defensive positions in Malaya if the necessary preparation work had been done in advance, but this was not the case when the 2 Surreys arrived. There was to be no respite for the men, who were immediately ordered to start preparing defences. Trenches were dug in the thick mud, coils of barbed wire were laid out and the heavy jungle was cut down to clear paths of fire.

With a Japanese attack expected, B and C companies were posted to the north of the town just off the main road, with Battalion Headquarters located in a hut in the village itself.

Around noon on the fourteenth, Japanese patrols made contact with a 2 Surrey patrol on the Yan crossroads just north of the main defence lines. Two hours later, eleven trucks full of Japanese troops advanced down the road, led by three medium tanks. They were halted for several hours by the guns of 88 Field Regiment Royal Artillery and 80 Anti-Tank Regiment at roadblocks.

As the Japanese advanced towards the village, Brigadier William Oswald Lay, 6 Indian Infantry Brigade's commander, ordered the 2 Surreys to engage them. A small party led by 2nd Lieutenant R.H. Colls attacked with Molotov cocktails, but this brave move failed as the 2 Surreys simply did not have the necessary Boyes anti-tank guns to stop the advance. They were forced to withdraw back to the village under intense enemy fire.

Sleep was almost impossible that night as the Japanese continued to probe the 2 Surreys' defensive positions. By dawn the situation was becoming serious, and by late afternoon the enemy were just a matter of a mile or so to the north. As the men huddled in their defensive positions waiting for the next inevitable attack, they were stunned to see Indian troops of the 1/8 Punjab running back down the road with fear in their eyes.

As dawn broke on the morning of 15 December, eighteen Japanese soldiers on bicycles appeared down the road in front of B Company. They were immediately wiped out by Bren-gun fire. A further twenty-four cyclists appeared several minutes later, but upon seeing the bodies of their comrades strewn over the road they quickly disappeared into the jungle, carrying their bicycles with them.

Shortly afterwards, the 2 Surreys came under heavy fire. Japanese tanks led an attack towards their defensive positions and aircraft began strafing the trenches. Corporal John Wyatt recalls this assault:

'Captain Kerrich, our Company Commander said to us: "we have got to hold on here lads – each man have a cigarette – have your last smoke before the little beggars reach us."'

The Surreys threw everything at the Japanese tanks as they ploughed inexorably towards them, but with a shortage of anti-tank weapons, their line was quickly broken and they had no alternative but to make a hasty retreat once again.

Lieutenant Stephen Abbott writes of this action in his book *And All My War is Done*:

'The main enemy attack started at dawn. John Kerrich, my company commander, was killed in the first few minutes, so were three other chaps. Then the Jap tanks came through. Japanese, British and Indian troops were all mixed up together. The buildings around us were blazing, and the crackle of burning timber mixed with the deafening thunder of the tank guns and the uproar of rifle fire.

'I looked down now at the deep roadside drain where a Sergeant Major, eight men and myself lay – all that were left of my one hundred and thirty strong company [-] and awaited the next enemy assault. When it came, a corporal lying beside me fell asleep whilst working the bolt of his rifle – with the Jap infantry advancing a hundred yards away. I remember hurling a grenade uselessly at an enemy tank a few minutes later.

'I collected the few men who were still alive and ran into the rice field behind the village. As we ploughed our way knee deep through the mud and slime, bullets and shells came at us from all directions. We reached the protective cover of the jungle, and collapsed exhausted in the undergrowth.

'The next 36 hours remain an agonising dream. We had no food, our clothes were in ribbons, and at the end of it most of us were marching in bare feet. We cut our way through jungle, swamps and acres of rubber plantation. I suppose we covered about 25 miles, with only my compass to guide us. It was sheer luck which brought us eventually back to the main road at a point the Japanese had not yet reached. I think we were all proud that we still had every rifle we'd started out with.'

As Abbott and the nine remaining men of his company withdrew, he would not have been aware that the 2 Surrey Battalion Headquarters in a ramshackle hut at Gurun had been overrun and almost everyone there killed. At around 1830 hrs that day, the Japanese surrounded the hut and machine-gunned the flimsy structure at close range, before bursting inside and finishing off the remaining officers with bayonets. Captain Hill, Lance Corporal Smith, Captain Bradley, 2nd Lieutenant Bradford, Captain (Doctor) Thomson, Rev. Rawtensthorne and 2nd Lieutenant Meyers were all killed in the attack. Only three officers escaped with their lives that fateful day: Brigadier Lay had left earlier to visit one of the outlying companies; Captain A.J.H. Martin, the Intelligence Officer, managed to crawl out and make his way to 6 Brigade Headquarters further south and Major Dowling had already left to go to Brigade Headquarters. Dowling was also to lose his life a short while later when the Japanese also overran the Brigade HQ, leaving the battalion without a Commanding Officer. Captain E.A.F. Howard, the adjutant, also escaped with his life, having left headquarters just before the attack.

Captain Howard vividly described to me his escape from Battalion Headquarters on that fateful day over sixty years later when I visited him at his home in Guildford:

'I was adjutant of the 2nd Battalion East Surreys during the regiment's time in Malaya. I was attached to Headquarters during our retreat down the peninsula, watching all the front-line people. At Jitra we were all mixed up but we got as far as Gurun, where we sorted ourselves out and I ended up back in HQ again. My job was to ensure that all four companies had runners linking them with each other and HQ. It is imperative in a mobile war that you have a good system of runners as you cannot have fixed lines. I was sitting in HQ when the companies were out in front waiting to hold off the Japanese. I said to my CO, who was Pat Dowling at the time, "Look I can't sit on my backside in HQ all my life, I need to be up with the boys." Dowling sent me forward to D Company HQ with an order for Tony Cater to counter-attack at 0430 hrs. Tony's Company at that time was temporarily attached to the 1/8 Punjab. It must have been around 0100 hours when I set off up the road towards our forward positions and suddenly I found myself under Japanese fire. Astride the main road on the left-hand side was D Company, in the centre was A Company in reserve and on the right-hand side C Company commanded by Captain Alistair Hill. I walked up the road, as I passed John Kerrich's company I came under Japanese fire again coming straight down the road. I had a runner with me. You don't travel without a runner; it was a silly thing to do. So we got off the road and into a small stream on the left-hand side and proceeded on up to D Company HQ under Tony Cater. It took me about three hours to reach D company, who were in a defensive position around the area. Just below us was a gunner OP [observation point] in which was a gunner officer to direct the guns which were supporting the battalion. Major Andrews, CO of the 1/8 Punjabis, decided that it was too dangerous to send D Company back to Gurun as he thought that they were already cut off. I was very tired by then and Tony sat me down in the bivouac tent and gave me a glass of something or other, and do you know something I fell asleep. When I awoke, I was totally alone. For some reason, they had left me asleep as they made their withdrawal just before dawn. I found out later that they had moved out from their positions westwards towards the Yen coastal road to try and link up with the rest of 11th Indian Division. It was obvious that I was now behind Japanese lines so I managed to crawl away into the jungle and headed in a westerly direction, where I knew I would soon hit the coast. I eventually managed to get across to Penang on a small boat.'

After overrunning 2 Surreys HQ at Gurun, the Japanese pushed quickly on and, as described earlier, destroyed 6 Brigade HQ where most of Brigadier Lay's staff were also killed. Brigadier Lay himself managed to survive this attack by hiding in a nearby house.

The situation for the 6th Indian Division in and around Gurun was now at crisis point. The 2 Surreys had lost most of their officers and it was left to company commanders, and indeed in some cases platoon leaders, to make their own escape from the debacle as best they could. Various small groups managed to get away, heading in several different directions.

After the war, Private Church wrote a detailed account of his attempted escape from the shambles of Gurun:

'I was in a position with PSM Clark, Corporal Mason and Private Paget when we were surrounded by Japs. As we tried to get away along a river we were fired upon and hid in the river banks. We eventually climbed the river banking to look for cover and as we reached the top four Japs appeared. PSM Clark told us to put our hands up and surrender, but the Japs took no notice and opened fire on us[,] killing PSM Clark, Corporal Mason and Private Paget. I was wounded in the hand and shoulder but managed to survive by feigning dead. When the Japs had gone, I crept into the jungle where I wandered around for almost a week before stumbling into a Kampong [village] near Gurun Railway station.

'There I was looked after by some Tamils but a few days later three Jap soldiers arrived and I was taken prisoner. They took me to Alor Star prison where my wounds were attended to by a local surgeon from the hospital. Later I was transferred to Taiping jail.'

Several men under the command of Lieutenant Bateman and Captain Hill made their escape from Gurun, trekking through the jungle for hours and eventually reaching Kampung Lasah in the state of Perak. At Lasah, Hill flopped down totally exhausted, unable to go any further. He urged the rest of the group to leave him and push on to safety, but two of his men, Corporal Nall and Corporal Saunders, volunteered to stay with him for a day or so in the hope that he might recover enough to be able to press on. Unfortunately, Hill was in such a bad way that Nall and Saunders had no choice but to abandon him to his fate. Captain Hill's body was never found.

Nall, writing about this event after the war, said:

'Although Captain Hill's condition was deteriorating further with the passage of time, he bore himself with dignity throughout and neither sought nor expected preferential treatment by virtue of his rank – a good example of fortitude to all of us. I naturally regretted having to leave him but with the dilemma confronting us, we had no alternative.'

The rest of the group managed to reach Taiping, some 60 miles to the south, after a struggle through thick jungle.

Meanwhile, the remnants of D Company, under Captain Tony Cater, made their way westwards through the hills, eventually reaching the coast on 17 December. There they commandeered a boat and rowed to the island of Penang. The Japanese had already occupied the island but Cater managed to get his company away in two boats.

Landing on a small island, they stole some civilian clothes from a house to avoid detection, abandoned the boats and took over a junk owned by a Chinese man. They sailed for a week before eventually being picked up by a British gunboat and taken to Malacca.

Another small group of 2 Surreys, after trekking across country, also made it to Penang. They landed near a monastery on Christmas Eve, where the monks suggested that they 'chuck it in' as the Japanese were swarming all over the area. Reluctantly agreeing, they surrendered and were taken to Penang jail where they remained for six weeks before being transferred to Taiping jail.

Around thirty 2 Surrey men were captured during the shambolic escape from Gurun, with most of them ending up in Pudu jail in Kuala Lumpur, a prison that eventually was to hold around 1,200 Allied prisoners of war.

Whilst smaller groups got split up, the main party of 2 Surreys, after leaving Gurun, stumbled through dense jungle, swamps and rubber plantations with only a vague idea where they were going. With very little food or water, they were incredibly lucky to reach Sungai Petani some 14 miles south of Gurun where they were fortunate to find lorries waiting to take them to Taiping. It was to be a long and slow overnight journey down the main road, the drivers having to constantly weave through vehicles and men as they retreated in complete disarray. With no traffic control of any kind, the competent drivers nonetheless managed to eventually reach King Edward VII School in Taiping late on 17 December.

Regrouping in the school buildings, the remnants of the battalion were unaware that their fate was just about sealed. Back in London, Field Marshal Sir Alan Brooke (1st Viscount Alanbrooke), the most senior officer in the British Army and Churchill's Chief of Staff, was writing in his confidential diary:

'Personally, I do not feel there is much hope of saving Singapore, but feel that we ought to try and make certain of holding Burma.'

The exhausted men of the 2 Surreys were relieved to get a couple of nights rest in the school after their exhausting retreat. This was to be short-lived, however, as two days later they were on the move again, this time towards the town of Ipoh some 75 miles further to the south.

The war-weary battalion eventually arrived at the Saint Michael's Institution in Ipoh at around midnight on 18 December. For the first time in twelve days they were able to have a decent rest and get cleaned up. Hot baths were available in the school dormitories and welcome clean clothes were issued: uniforms were by now in a disgusting state, with trousers and boots that had been caked in mud for several days having to be cut off to get at rotten socks. There was still a shortage of weapons but they had to make the best of what they had. Lewis machine guns were issued to replace Bren guns, but there was only enough for one per section and only four 3in mortars per company. Ten Bren gun carriers were allocated to the carrier platoon.

A lack of sleep and food certainly contributed to the 2 Surreys' defeats at Jitra and Gurun. Captain Gingell's catering crew did their utmost in difficult circumstances to keep their men going, often struggling to reach the men with any food at all. The old adage that 'an army marches on its stomach' proved true in their situation.

After the war, Private Arthur ('Alor') Starr related his account of the retreat from Jitra and Gurun:

'Yes, I remember the monsoon downpours in Jitra, standing in the trenches, knee deep in muddy water and the swarms of hungry mosquitoes at night. Our mosquito repellent was not effective when our rain drenched bodies washed off the chemical. It really was a torture trying to keep them away and there were hundreds of them hungry for your blood.

'I wore the same clothes for more than a week and when I did try to take them off, I could leave my shorts and shirt standing on their own.'

The Director of St Michael's School, Brother Ultan Paul, an Irish priest from the De La Salle Brothers, recalled the arrival of the Surreys and the Leicesters to his institution when he wrote after the war:

'The Surreys came here first – 18 December 1941 – and the Leicesters arrived later that evening. They were put into the classrooms of the ground and first floors and the school hall. They stayed for three days before leaving the school in the early morning of 23 December. We knew that the Japanese were coming, for we heard over the radio that they were already in Kuala Kansar. The Japanese planes were very active over Ipoh daily and were flying very low, machine gunning the Ipoh Railway Station where there were many troop trains arriving from the north.'

Brother Paul looked after the men as best he could in the circumstances. He forged a close bond with the troops, a bond that was so strong that over forty years later he wrote a very moving letter to the 2 Surreys:

'I am happy to know that several of you have survived the war years and all I can say about you is that you fought so bravely and gallantly and unselfishly, thank you ever so much and may God bless you all and your families. May I also grant eternal life to all who sacrificed their lives for us and thank you all again. God bless you.'

At Ipoh, the 2 Surreys were joined by the remnants of the 1 Leicesters, who had also taken a beating during the retreat from Jitra. Both battalions were now well below strength and to turn them into a fighting force again, it was decided that they would be amalgamated into one to be called the 'British Battalion'. This was to be the first and only time in the history of the British Army that two regiments were amalgamated in the field to form a new regiment.

The most senior officers surviving from both regiments were Lieutenant Colonel Morrison and Major Harvey of the 1 Leicesters and Major O'Neil Wallis and Captain Gingell of the 2 Surreys. Morrison assumed command of the newly formed British Battalion, with Harvey as his second in command. O'Neil Wallis became adjutant and Gingell quartermaster.

The British Battalion now had a strength of approximately 790 men and became part of the combined 6/15 Brigade under Brigadier Garrett. A and B companies were made up of Leicesters, with C and D companies Surreys.

At Ipoh, for the first time in many weeks, the men were able to pen letters home to their families. Lance Corporal John Wyatt of D Company wrote a letter to his parents and his fiancée on 21 December, one that his mother kept safely until he returned home:

'Dear Mum & Dad & Elsie,
'Hope this finds you as safe and as well as I am at present. Before I start you will notice that my address is completely changed also that I think it best that you should all just send me an occasional letter as all your letters have not reached me now for over a month and as things are they will take a long time to reach me so one now and again to let me know how you all are. Well mum before I start I would like you all to give thanks to God at church for the mercy he has shown not only to me but to the whole Battalion. 3 times I have just waited for death but with Gods [sic] help I am still here. I have felt all along that with all your prayers God would keep me safe. I will only give you one instance of it. 10 of us were in a trench in a little native village in the jungle, we were told last man last round for we were surrounded by the Japanese, and they were closing in on all sides, some of the chaps were saying good-bye to each other, and I was really frightened at the thought of dying, but as the minutes dragged on I resigned myself to it then all of a sudden 3 aircraft came over, was they ours? Was they be buggered. Down came the bombs all round us all we could do as we crouched there was to wait for one to hit us, but that good old trench saved our lives for it rocked and swayed with the impact. About one minute after they flew off, 4 tanks rumbled up the road, and gave our positions hell. They flung everything at us, grenades, machine guns, but we still crouched in that little trench. We could not return fire for if we showed our heads above the trench the advancing Japs were machine gunning us. All of a sudden, we heard a shout run for it lads, did we run, but the last I saw of the brave officer who said it, I shall never forget him, as we ran past him pistol in hand pointing at the Japs

holding them off while we got away. I haven't seen him since. Anyway, we waded through about a mile of paddy [fields] with bullets whistling past all the time, but we reached the jungle and safety, then on to find the British lines, we tramped 30 miles that day living on jungle fruits. The fight started at 7 in the morning [and] we reached safety at five at night. Then for sleep, food, clean clothes and a shave, for we had been at the front for 8 days without sleep or clean clothes, for we have lost everything, the Japs have got everything, all my personal stuff. Photos, Prayer book everything, but thank God I am still here, most of the Battalion reached safety but a lot of poor chaps are still missing, some of my friends to [*sic*]. We are all together now at a big Catholic school, the brothers here are very kind to us. Excuse pencil as this is the first chance I have had to write in a fortnight, so make do with this.

'Keep smiling Elsie and I hope to see you next year xxxxxxxx.

'Well mum our worries are over. We have just been told that we are moving and our job is looting so all our fighting is finished. Am I glad. We certainly knocked the old Japs about while we were there did we, we are miles better than them and we are sorry we won't be able to get another smack at them. I will have to hurry as the candle is burning out. So I will say goodbye for now, Dorrie xxxx Jimmie, George, Mrs Ward, Church, rest of family and neighbours so please don't worry, God bless you all and keep you safe.

'Your ever loving son

'Johnxxxxxxxxxxxxxxxxxxxxx

'P.S.

'I shall have a lot to tell you when I get home. As usual Jerry is here with the Japs, German pilots and German NCOs. Tell Dorrie that the Corporal who wrote to her is missing but safe I think, and my sergeant who wrote to her got shot in the leg and is a prisoner I believe.'

After five days in the comfortable surroundings of the school, the British Battalion bade farewell to Brother Paul and his staff on the afternoon of 23 December and left Ipoh by train for Kampar. About 20 miles south from Ipoh, Kampar is the fourth largest town in Perak and the centre of the state's tin mining and rubber planting area. Lieutenant General Percival, General

Officer Commanding Malaya, had decided that Kampar now provided the next best location for a defence of southern Malaya. If it could be held for at least a month or more, there would be time to bring in more reinforcements currently on their way from the UK via Singapore.

After a short train journey, the rejuvenated British Battalion marched proudly in formation from Kampar railway station down the road towards the Anglo Chinese School near the town centre. Large crowds of Malays had turned out to watch and many gave the troops the thumbs up and V for victory signs, returned by the men as they marched along.

The Anglo Chinese School was set up in 1903 by the missionary Sir Edmund Horley. It gave Malays the opportunity of an English-speaking private education.

My father told me many years later about his time spent in the Anglo Chinese School in Kampar:

'As we settled into our new surroundings and made ourselves a comfortable as possible, we were all well aware that the next few days would severely test the limits of our endurance and fighting ability as a newly formed regiment.'

Quartermaster Captain Gingell and his men served up a hot and very welcome dinner of chicken and fresh vegetables they had bought in the local market, a veritable feast that was washed down with vast amounts of local beer.

A crag over 4,000ft high overlooking the town was considered to be a major obstacle to any Japanese advance. The battalion was allocated a northerly position near the trunk road a mile out of the town where three parallel ridges run down from the crag. A Company took up a position on Thompson's Ridge, B Company near Green Ridge, C Company just west of Green Ridge and D Company with the Bren gun carriers platoon kept in a reserve position.

On Chrismtas Eve, and with no thought for the festive season, Japanese aircraft constantly strafed their positions as the men sweated and toiled preparing defences on the ridges. Despite the strafing, the Rev. Short conducted an emotional service on Christmas morning, followed by a wonderful Christmas dinner drummed up by Captain Gingell and his men. Turkey with all the trimmings was served, along with some welcome bottles of beer, followed by the singing of carols.

For the next four days, the British Battalion dug in and prepared to meet the expected onslaught. The Japanese continued to push south down the main road towards Kampar and the sound of artillery could be heard up ahead. It was the afternoon of 29 December when Japanese tanks and troops were first spotted approaching the iron bridge over the Kampar River. The British Battalion opened up with every weapon they had at their disposal.

Private Arthur Starr takes up the story of that day in his memoirs:

'On 29 December morning, we were told to check our weapons and ammo and later we marched up the road towards Kuala Dipang where there was heavy fighting and the sound of artillery could be heard. We marched up the road for five miles and our company was split into sections about 100 yards apart. Later, about 500 yards [away] we could see the iron bridge from our forward positions off the road on the slope covering the main road. The Gurkhas were to our right covering the branch road to the loop road towards the 28th Brigade HQ.

'Amidst heavy mortar fire from our side the Japanese artillery was hitting near the bridge and we saw the Jocks [Argyll and Sutherland Highlanders] crossing the bridge and the Gurkhas gave good covering fire. The iron bridge was blown and after the thick smoke had cleared, we could see only the middle span was damaged and it fell into the river.

'Our chaps had their weapons at the ready and our grenades were ready for the enemy. The Jocks passed through our lines and we handed out cigarettes, chocolates, biscuits and water to them. They were calm and were grateful for the snacks passed them and from the looks on their faces we knew that they had fought a hard fight against the enemy.

'It was dark by the time all the Jocks had passed through and they were picked up by the MT [motor transport] waiting for them further down the road from our positions. Our plan was to wait for the Japanese in our ambush and we were to fire a long burst of heavy machine gun fire and all weapons down the road including hand grenades all thrown in to do a good job.

'Sure enough the bloody Japanese came in sections and at the pre-arranged signal our CO gave them hell and in the dark we heard groans and yells of pain. After ten minutes of heavy saturation fire, we held our fire and made our way back towards Kampar. It was fortunate the Japanese did not press after us, thinking that perhaps another ambush was further down the road. We made our way back to our forward positions section by section and we suffered a few minor casualties and arrive safely to a hot and welcome meal prepared by Captain Gingell and his men.'

For the next two days, Japanese planes constantly strafed the British Battalion positions. Propaganda leaflets were dropped, urging them to surrender with the promise that they would be fairly treated if they did. Mortar and artillery fire rained down on the men as they huddled in their trenches.

At the stroke of midnight on New Year's Eve, despite the barrage, the war-weary troops celebrated the passing of the old year in their waterlogged trenches as best they could in the circumstances. They shook hands, wished each other a happy new year and sang Auld Lang Syne with gusto, well aware of course that 1942 was unlikely to be a very happy new year.

The Battle of Kampar started at dawn on New Year's Day when the Japanese opened up with 3in mortars and heavy machine guns. The British Battalion's back-up artillery replied immediately with heavy and accurate fire.

John Wyatt recalled this early onslaught with the usual Surreys' irony: 'Perhaps they thought we would all still have a hangover from the previous evening's festivities.'

For the rest of New Year's Day, the British Battalion took heavy mortar fire, resulting in several casualties, especially in the weapon pits on the forward slopes of Thompson's Ridge. Lieutenant Leage was wounded in the eye and Lieutenant Cave had to be evacuated with shell-shock. As darkness fell that day, the situation was becoming critical as the Japanese had gained a foothold on the eastern edge of Green Ridge and the defences began to creak.

Around 0800 hrs on 2 January, D Company, led by Captain Vickers, was ordered to counter-attack and dislodge the enemy. Vickers, a fearless company commander with revolver in hand, led two rifle platoons up the slope, driving into the Japanese positions. The small group managed to destroy several machine-gun nests before some of the men were cut down by rifle and machine-gun fire. Three 2 Surrey men received awards for bravery that day near Kampar: Captain Vickers himself was awarded the Military Cross, Sergeant Major Craggs the Distinguished Conduct Medal and Private Graves the Military Medal. Sergeant McLean of C Company was also awarded the Military Medal for his bravery in destroying an enemy machine-gun nest whilst under heavy fire, and for rescuing 2nd Lieutenant Randolph when he fell wounded.

Corporal John Wyatt, who was in Vickers' platoon, gave me a blow-by blow account of the incident when I met him at his home in Sydenham:

'At about 0800 hrs Sergeant Craggs kicked me in the ribs to rouse me with the instruction "fix your bayonets lads we've got to dislodge some of the little … Corporal, search that officer." I rolled him over and found a school map with all our positions circled in red ink, which I later handed to Captain Vickers, and also a pocket watch which I kept as a souvenir. It was probably a foolish thing to do as I might have been captured later, and God knows what would have happened, but for some reason we went to great lengths to get souvenirs. It probably gave us some sense of reassurance that we had a future beyond this hellish situation we found ourselves in.

'We eventually managed to dislodge the Japs from their positions on the ridge but by now the situation was at stalemate. We were lying on a bit of an incline and every time I put my arm up, machine-gun bullets would zap over my head. We were well and truly pinned down. I managed to crawl into a trench overlooking the road with some others of my company, including Private Pierce – a real joker who was always singing cockney songs. The trench was too small for all of us and I didn't like listening to him anyway, so I moved to another one a few feet away. Seconds later, Pierce's singing was silenced by a shell from a Jap tank that landed right in the middle of the trench, killing several of the boys and badly wounding Pierce. A few of us tried to help the wounded, but every time we moved towards the trench we were machine-gunned.

'We lay in our trench all day – the heat was unbearable and we had no water for ourselves or the wounded, who were moaning dreadfully. At about 1500 hrs we heard screams and shouts from just up ahead and as I peered over the edge of the trench I saw the chilling sight of hundreds of Sikhs running towards us throwing their weapons away as they ran. They had been ordered to counter-attack but it seems they had decided to run. "Me no fight Jonnie – me had enough," they shouted as they ran past us.

'As the day wore on, the dead bodies in the adjoining trench began to smell. Pierce was still alive but continually groaning, so Private Holloway and I decided we would try to get him out to the field hospital. We found a couple of planks of wood and made a crude stretcher, but every time we tried to get him on it he rolled off, making his wounds worse, and as the machine-gunning around us was so heavy, we eventually gave up. There was a great temptation to run away, but somehow the comradeship of the company held us together and none of us wanted to let our mates down. As darkness fell that evening we could hear the Jap patrols moving around, but somehow they missed us. How I don't know, as the wounded men were crying for help, but we were reluctant to try to move.

'At around 2100 hrs that evening, the Japanese increased their barrage. Every time I tried to move, Jap bullets were spattering the ground all around me and I tried to claw myself into the earth like some sort of insect scrabbling for food. Eventually a runner crawled up to us with orders from Captain Vickers to move out just before midnight and try to get to a safer position. About half an hour before we were due to move out from our positions, a Jap patrol appeared and a quick skirmish ensued. On hearing Captain Vickers shouting, "Down here, lads", I made a beeline towards his voice and he started leading us out in single file one by one. As I lay waiting for my turn, I could hear the shouts of the remainder of our lads who were trapped in the jungle below, but there was nothing we could do to help them.

'As we left the area, Captain Vickers turned towards the jungle of Kampar, saluted and said, "Gentlemen, we've left behind some brave lads in that jungle tonight." I shall never forget his words.'

The whole of 11th Indian Division at Kampar was now coming under intense pressure from Japanese assaults. With the situation becoming critical, once again Captain Vickers and D Company were ordered to try to clear the enemy from the eastern sector of Thompson's Ridge. At around 0830 hrs they charged the Japanese positions, taking many casualties in hand-to-hand fighting before being driven back into the jungle. Lieutenant Cater, hit by a mortar bomb, suffered injuries to his legs and feet and was evacuated to hospital in Singapore.

Private Pardoe found himself isolated after the assault, and on his way back alone came across a machine-gun nest where he killed eight men with grenades and captured two sub machine guns. For his actions, he was awarded the Military Medal. Pardoe was not to collect his medal as lost his life almost three years later by drowning when the *Hofuko Maru*, a ship carrying him and 1,289 other prisoners of war from Manilla in the Philippines to Japan, was sunk by American torpedo-bombers.

Lieutenant General Percival paid tribute to the British Battalion during the Battle of Kampar in his book *The War in Malaya*:

'The [enemy] attacks were made with all the well-known bravery and disregard of danger of the Japanese soldier. There was the dogged resistance, in spite of heavy losses, by the men of the British Battalion and their supporting artillery. The battle of Kampar had proved that our trained troops, whether they were British or Indian, were superior man for man to the Japanese troops.'

The official history of the 11th Indian Division also praised the British Battalion's brave stand at Kampar:

'Throughout the two days of heavy fighting every effort of the enemy to force a passage had been frustrated with heavy loss. The battle had been marked by many deeds of outstanding gallantry. The whole brunt of the enemy's attack had been borne by the British Battalion. In the short time between this Battalion's organisation and its first battle, Lieutenant-Colonel Morrison had permeated it with an esprit de corps second to none. The Battalion's spirit may perhaps be discerned from the answer to a questioner who asks a man whether he belonged to the Leicesters or the Surreys. "Neither," he replied, "I belong to the British Battalion."'

With the Japanese now firmly entrenched in the hills around Kampar, Lieutenant General Lewis Heath, GOC 3 Indian Corps, had no alternative but to order a complete withdrawal. At 2200 hrs on 3 January, under a full moon and clear skies, troops of the British Battalion wearily made their way on foot southwards out of the deserted town. Enemy patrols had already infiltrated the town, and they were very wary of the threat of snipers as they marched along towards a rendezvous with their transport.

It was around midnight when several 15-hundredweight trucks picked up the men and headed out of Kampar on the main road. Due to traffic congestion and almost non-existent traffic control it was chaos as the vehicles, often three abreast, headed south.

After a most uncomfortable journey of around 10 miles, the British Battalion unloaded their gear at the small town of Bukit Pagar and took up a new defensive position in a rubber plantation.

After almost four weeks of constant action, Brigadier Moorhead, commanding officer of 15 Indian Brigade, decided that this 'fought out' battalion, as he called them, should be laid back for much-needed rest and resupply.

Boarding lorries of 2/3 Motor Transport section of the Australian Imperial Force, they headed for the town of Tanjung Malim, some 50 miles north of Kuala Lumpur.

The battalion was to owe a great deal of gratitude to these men of the Australian Motor Transport Company. My father said:

'They always managed to produce a very welcome bottle of whisky which was passed round us as they picked us up. The welcome whisky not only warmed us but also [strengthened our nerves] for the perilous driving ahead as the big lorries seldom travelled at less than 50 miles per hour, swaying about in the most alarming way.'

But with an inevitability that they had now become used to, any rest was once again to be short-lived. They were soon on the move again to engage a possible Japanese landing on the west coast near Kuala Selangor at the mouth of the Sungai Selangor River. After another long night drive of nearly 70 miles in the AIF lorries, they took up a position in the Sungai Rambai Socfin rubber and oil estates near Batang Berjuntai. The constant withdrawal continued and there was no respite for the exhausted men as they kept on moving south onboard the Australian lorries. The leading truck struck a mine laid by British sappers, killing the driver and two others, with ten wounded.

With the risk of mines now very much in evidence, Lieutenant Bingham of the Surreys bravely volunteered to go ahead of the column in a Bren gun carrier to check for further mines. As the column neared Malaya's capital, Kuala Lumpur, Bingham's carrier was blown up, killing one member of the party and badly injuring Bingham himself. With life-threatening injuries, he was immediately evacuated by train to hospital in Singapore.

Bingham's great friend Lieutenant Abbott had also been evacuated by train to Singapore a week or so earlier, with of all things a suspect appendix. On learning of Bingham's injuries, Abbott went to see him in the Alexandra Hospital where Bingham lay in a very bad way. After an emotional reunion the two officers bade farewell to each other for the last time, as Abbot outlines in his book *All My War is Done*:

'As I entered the ward one figure lay still in bed and I knew it was Bing. I was almost hoping to find him asleep but he was awake. "Hello Stephen thanks for coming," he muttered from beneath his heavy bandages. A lump stuck fast in my throat as I had been made aware that he would not live.

'After an emotional fifteen minutes, the ward sister asked me to leave. "My time is up Bing, I'll come again tomorrow," I said, my voice heavy with emotion.

'"Don't worry about me old chap," he replied. Bing knew he couldn't live, yet he wasn't scared of dying: he wasn't even bitter. He had both faith and courage.'

Lieutenant Bingham died of his wounds in Alexandra Hospital Singapore on 8 January 1942 and his memorial stone is in the Taiping War Cemetery.

The battalion's constant withdrawals continued for the next four days as they headed south towards the small town of Batu Pahat, where it was suspected that the Japanese had landed. Upon arrival at the town there was no sign of any Japanese, despite an extensive search, so they laid up under trees for the night. The next morning they moved on again 30 miles inland to the Coronation Estate near Kluang.

Setting up camp amongst the rubber trees proved difficult as they were continually harassed by Japanese aircraft, but the thought of a week's much-needed rest raised their morale. The General Officer Commanding Malaya, Lieutenant General Lewis Heath, visited them at Kluang, offering some news about other theatres of the war: 'The Germans are being held in Europe. The lads are doing well in the Middle East and I expect you lads to do the same. But please do not damage any rubber trees.'

Naturally this caused a great deal of amusement within the ranks, as the preservation of a few trees was the last thing on their minds as they prepared once again to fight for their lives.

With the situation in Malaya now even more critical as Japanese units advanced rapidly down the peninsula, Lieutenant General Percival had no alternative but to order all troops on the mainland to fall back to the island of Singapore.

With no motor transport available, the war weary men of the British Battalion prepared to retreat and move out of their positions at Kluang on foot. Streams and ditches blocked their path with thick clinging mud, making putting one foot in front of the other a huge effort. Some six weeks after they first engaged Japanese forces at Jitra, the priority now was to get as many men back to Singapore as possible.

After a few hours' rest, they set off again for Benut, bypassing the coast road. Progress was slow and Lieutenant Colonel Morrison decided that the battalion should split up into three groups, with each attempting to make their own way south. Marching on through the night, they stumbled through thick mangrove swamps, often knee-deep in muddy streams. Officers encouraged the exhausted men to keep going, with Majors Harvey and O'Neil Wallis making superhuman efforts. All three groups eventually reached a fast-flowing river but, with no obvious way of crossing the swirling waters, they were forced to move westwards towards the coast, reaching a small fishing village at the mouth of the river just before dawn. Here they were joined by many other parties from 15 Indian Brigade, including the Cambridgeshires, the Norfolks, 155 Field regiment, 3rd Field Company, 3rd Cavalry and men of the Malay Regiment. Around 1,500 men were gathered in and around the village. The British Battalion, along with their comrades, were now in effect cut off: the only way to reach Singapore would be by sea.

Fortunately for the trapped men, two Royal Navy gunboats, HMS *Dragonfly* and HMS *Scorpion*, were waiting a mile or so offshore from Kampong Ponggor, five miles further south. The ships had been summoned to assist the retreating troops.

A few hours before dawn on 28 January Lieutenant Victor Clarke RN, a survivor of the sinking of HMS *Repulse*, stepped ashore on the mudflats and greeted Lieutenant Colonel Morrison with the words:

> 'Dr Livingstone I presume. How many of you are there and where do you want the medical supplies and rations I've brought you? One platoon should board the ship immediately, but due to the risk of Japanese air attacks you should lay up the rest of your men ashore for the rest of the day. I'll send in some shore parties from my crew with food and provisions to see you through the day.'

Following Clarke's instructions, the troops laid up in a coconut palm grove only a mile or so from the busy main road to await their turn to board.

It was just before dusk on 30 January when Morrison prepared to evacuate the last of his men onto the *Dragonfly* and *Scorpion*. Moving to the mouth of the river, they waited in mangrove swamps for darkness and the tide to rise. The Navy soon arrived in rubber boats to transport them out to the waiting ships, where they clambered aboard to be greeted by a delicious smell of bacon and eggs.

The two Royal Navy gunboats were well suited for such an evacuation, with their flat bottoms, triple rudders and large upper deck. They had a surface armament of 6in and 4in guns, three anti-aircraft machine guns, along with Asdic (sonar) and depth charges. Both ships only drew 7ft and had a maximum speed of 12 knots.

When all the men had boarded, the gunboats warily made their way out of the estuary and headed south along the Malayan coast towards Singapore. This dangerous operation by the Royal Navy has been dubbed the 'Malayan Dunkirk' and the British Battalion owe a great deal of gratitude to Captain Clarke for his efficient and orderly evacuation of so many men under extremely hazardous conditions.

Corporal John Wyatt outlined to me his company's evacuation from Ponggor during those fateful few days:

'We marched on through the night, stumbling through thick mangrove swamps, often knee-deep in muddy streams but with the great enthusiasm and kind words of encouragement, Majors Harvey and Wallace keeping us going through a very difficult night. Although the Japanese were near, we pressed on and eventually reached the Sungei Bata River. As there was no way across, we then moved westwards towards the coast and reached Ponggor just before dawn on 27 January. It was clear to all of us that we were in effect 'cut off' and the only way to reach Singapore from here would be by sea. Fortunately, the Navy boys were waiting for us a mile or so offshore and one platoon could board HMS *Dragonfly* before daylight arrived. The rest of the battalion were looked after by some Navy shore parties who supplied us with food and provisions for the rest of the day.

'Our positions were in a coconut palm grove only a mile or so from the busy main road where the Japanese Imperial Guards division were travelling south, and we expected an attack at any time. They were so close in fact that we could hear the noise of their vehicles as they made their way down the road. Although we had one or two false alarms, fortunately no Jap patrols came our way.

'By late afternoon on the twenty-eighth, Lieutenant Colonel Morrison prepared to evacuate the rest of the battalion onto the two

Navy ships. Commander Clarke Royal Navy oversaw the operation and he had arranged for as many men as possible to move to the mouth of Sungai Ponggor, where we were to wait for the tide to fall before wading out to a disused junk. The rest of the battalion hid in mangrove swamps nearby.

'As darkness fell and the tide began to rise, the Navy lads arrived in rubber boats and we waded out to meet them. One of the sailors said, "Jump in, soldier," and they rowed us out to the gunboats. As we clambered aboard, a delicious smell of fish and chips and bacon and eggs greeted us, and it was not long before we were tucking into a good old navy breakfast. I managed to get aboard the *Dragonfly* and as soon as we had loaded a full complement of troops aboard we set sail for Singapore. It was a great feeling to get cleaned and fed, and as I was able to relax for the first time in several weeks, it dawned on me how near we had been to total annihilation on that treacherous coastline. We certainly owed our lives to the good old Navy boys.'

Over 1,500 men were successfully evacuated by the two naval ships over three nights, with Commander Clarke of the *Dragonfly* awarded a bar to his DSO for his actions in rescuing so many men.

It was early on the morning of 1 February when the two ships docked in Keppel Harbour, Singapore. After disembarking, the men were taken by trucks to the Bidadari evacuation camp on Senggarang Road near the outskirts of the city, where waiting for them was Quartermaster Gingell and his transport platoon. Gingell had managed to get his group away before the Senggarang to Rengit road was cut by the Japanese, and had driven south through Johore and across the causeway into Singapore. The transport boys, including my father, were delighted to see their colleagues again.

With almost two-thirds of the British Battalion missing, dead or injured, the remnants settled down in Singapore to re-equip and lick their wounds. Ships were still coming and going out of Singapore harbour, albeit with great difficulty due to Japanese air raids, and twenty badly injured 2 Surrey men were evacuated on board the hospital ship *Talamba* on 2 February.

The first task for the weary men after the rigours of the previous six weeks was to reorganize and re-equip with fresh clothes, arms and equipment.

There was no shortage of equipment in Singapore at that time, contrary to what many unit commanders said, as verified by the recently promoted Major Gingell in his report.

'I place on record that there is no shortage of clothing, supplies and equipment. New arms were obtained which consisted of Lewis guns and fair supply of Thompson sub-machine guns. Small arms ammunition was plentiful and those units that complained of a shortage are entirely to blame as their representatives did not make efforts to obtain same. I say this as I heard of some units who were short in fairness to the RAOC and RASC. I consider it entirely the fault of the unit and not the department who was responsible for providing same.'

Shortly after their arrival back in Singapore, Lieutenant Colonel Morrison left the battalion to take over temporary command of 15 Indian Infantry Brigade, leaving Major Harvey of the Leicesters in command.

Chapter 4

The Battle for Singapore

Big guns had been installed on the south coast at Singapore Island to combat any invasion from the sea, but the northern coastline had been neglected. For many years it was thought that these guns could not be turned around to face a threat from the land, but this was a fallacy. They were capable of traversing through 180 degrees to provide considerable firepower against any invasion across the Straits of Johore. Unfortunately, only armour-piercing shells were available, which were totally useless against an invasion from the land as they simply buried deep into the ground before exploding.

On 31 January 1942, the last troops to cross the causeway from Johore onto Singapore Island were the Gordon Highlanders, their pipes and drums beating out a defiant message. Minutes later, the causeway was blown up by the Royal Engineers and Singapore was now isolated.

With so many losses in the Malayan campaign, the 2 Surreys and 1 Leicesters of the British Battalion settled down in the relative security of the Biddadari camp to lick their wounds and reorganize. With the Japanese now threatening the island, rest was again impossible and they took up a defensive position just east of the naval base facing the Straits of Johore. Their first task was to prepare coastal defences, much of which should have been done during the previous weeks, but wasn't. My father told me that, 'We were baffled as to what the tens of thousands of troops stationed in Singapore had been doing whilst my regiment had been laying down lives fighting in Malaya.'

The northern coastline of Singapore was made up of small sections of beach with Kampongs (hamlets or villages), divided by belts of mangrove swamps. Such topography was to make it very difficult to defend.

For several days, the men of the British Battalion laboured, digging trenches, making weapon pits, filling sandbags and laying barbed wire along the beach, whilst naval launches patrolled the straits between Singapore and the mainland.

Lieutenant General Percival was now well aware that the Japanese were massing their forces just across the straits in Johore, but for the moment they confined their efforts to sporadic air attacks on the island's airfields, harbour, city and military installations.

On 29 January, five ships carrying the long-awaited reinforcements of the British Territorial 18th (East Anglian) Division arrived in Keppel Harbour. Led by Major General Merton Beckwith-Smith, the troops of 54 and 55 Brigade landed along with a light tank squadron from India – the only tanks to reach Malaya during the entire campaign – and a number of Hurricane fighters. The newly arrived troops, however, soon proved to be badly trained and had little idea about fighting a war in such a hostile environment.

Private Frank Farmer of the 2 Surreys recalls the arrival of the 18th Division:

'I tell you that the 18th Division boys, fresh out from England, had no idea of the thick jungle and the hot and damp weather and now to put them straightaway from the docks on arrival to face the Japs was suicide. They were in no condition to fight, hardly had any training under the local conditions and were out of battle fitness to meet the fanatical Japs. The civilians, especially the civil servants and the planters and tin miners from up country, were still not aware of the enemy so close to their doorstep and the rounds of drinking parties and the big crowds at Raffles and the other top hotels made me sick inside. These fellows felt that Singapore was an impregnable fortress and that the soldiers could stop the invaders, and they refused to accept the fact that the island was isolated and surrounded and that it would fall. I remember talking to some British rubber planters who told me that the Japs would not be able to land on the island and that they would soon return to their large rubber estates. Only a few knew the truth and saw the gloomy writing on the wall. Here we [were] fighting since 8 December 1941 and yet we [had] chaps who could not care less about the seriousness of the situation.'

Confidence was further dented when they learnt that the Royal Navy base to the west of the sector had been evacuated, with all the staff there sailing for Ceylon. It was heartbreaking for the troops, who had fought so valiantly up country, to see the pathetic scene of an empty naval base, supposedly the pride of the Royal Navy: a base that had cost British taxpayers millions of pounds and was packed with supplies and rations, now waiting for the arrival of the invading forces. At least the British Battalion troops were able to supplement their supplies from the gigantic stores; Captain Gingell, always on the lookout to help the men, took full advantage of this opportunity to top up his food supplies.

On 4 February, the British Battalion was relieved from its defensive positions on the north-east coast by the 5 Norfolks and returned to Bidari Camp for what should have been five days' rest. Once again, such a luxury was short-lived as the five days turned into just two when they were ordered to 'dig in' on top of a hillock in the Bukit Timah area. On reaching their allotted position, they found the top of the hillock was so rocky that it was incredibly difficult to even break the surface.

Corporal John Wyatt recalls:

'It was like trying to dig through lumps of iron but we eventually managed to scrape enough away to create a defensive position. Our task was made even more difficult by enemy planes flying overhead, strafing us on a regular basis. They flew in so low that I could even see the grins on the faces of the pilots as they machine-gunned us completely unhindered. We should have had air cover but the RAF had also completely vanished, leaving us very vulnerable.'

Japanese aircraft were now bombing Singapore's defensive positions daily, causing a great deal of damage. Large parts of the city now lay in ruins and many civilians were killed or injured in the attacks.

On 5 February, a new order came through from General Archibald Wavell, commander-in-chief of British forces in India, once again causing much amusement among the battle-hardened troops of the British Battalion when he said: 'Stand firm men. We are holding the Germans in the Middle East and you have got to stand here and fight and not turn back.' The men wondered what he meant when he said 'not turn back', as they knew if they did turn back now they would all have ended up in the sea.

On Bukit Timah hill, the war-weary troops settled down to face the final enemy onslaught. Most of the island was now covered by a thick haze of black, acrid smoke and grey dust covered everything as the Japanese laid down fierce bombardments.

As darkness fell on 8 February, under a heavy covering barrage from their big guns on Johore, nearly 13,000 troops of the 5th and 18th Imperial Japanese divisions landed on the beaches near to Choa Chu King and Ama Keng villages. By daybreak the following morning, they were attacking Tengah aerodrome and, with another 10,000 troops landing, they were now firmly established on Singapore island.

Now under the command of Major General Gordon Bennett's 8th Australian Division, the British Battalion was tasked with covering the west of the island including the important Bulin-Jurong defence line that ran from the River Kranji to the River Jurong.

As dusk fell on 9 February, the men piled into lorries and set off towards a point near to Singapore racecourse and Bukit Timah village. Due to the choked state of the roads, the short journey took nearly five hours and they did not arrive at the racecourse until nearly midnight. A further march west under heavy mortar fire took them to Jurong Road, where they arrived at their allotted positions around 0400 hrs on 10 February. Their role was to fill a gap that existed between 44 Indian Brigade and the Australian Imperial Force. B Company took up a position on the right of the road, with C Company to the left and D Company held in reserve at Battalion Headquarters near the brickworks. A Company covered the road running to the north.

The situation now became totally confused as the Japanese broke through their first line of defences. Private Hall of D Company recalled his experience of this part of the conflict after the war, writing:

'We were in the trenches near the 11th milestone on the Jurong Road. At around 1100 hrs the Japs broke through and we started to engage them. After a few minutes Sergeant Austin came to our trench and informed us that the battalion was to withdraw as the Japs were surrounding us. Our first attempts to break clear failed, resulting in four of the men being wounded and [us running] out of ammunition.

'Our NCOs decided that we should make another attempt to withdraw and ordered us to fix bayonets. As we charged the Japs began to fire at us and six more men were wounded. We were now surrounded and had little option but to surrender. The Japs took us to a tent and soon after Sergeant Austin was taken out. Half an hour later we heard screaming and on peering out of the tent we saw him being bayonetted by two Japs whilst lying on the ground. We were then ordered out of the tent and told to form a single line, holding our wounded up. With our attention focussed on the Jap officers in front of us we were taken by surprise when several Japs attacked us from behind with fixed bayonets. I shouted run for it and grabbed Private Hunt by the arm and dragged him along, knocking one of the officers to the ground. The Japs opened fire on us but we managed to get away. We could hear the screams of the men lying on the ground whilst the Japs bayonetted them. Private Hunt and I managed to escape the carnage.'

That same day, Winston Churchill sent a terse signal to General Wavell:

'There must be no thought of saving the troops or sparing the population. The battle must be fought to the bitter end at all costs … Commanders and senior officers should die with their troops. The honour of the British Empire and the British Army is at stake. I rely on you to show no mercy or weakness in any form. With the Russians fighting as they are and the Americans so stubborn at Luzon the whole reputation of our country and our race is involved.'

Sitting in his comfortable office back in London, Churchill had no idea what my father and the rest of the dispirited troops in Singapore were going through as the Japanese pushed towards the city.

Wavell passed on Churchill's comments and attempted to lift the spirits of the troops by sending a letter to the senior officers in Singapore, penned in his usual inspirational language:

'It is certain that our troops in Singapore outnumber the Japanese troops who have crossed the Straits. We must destroy them. Our whole fighting reputation is at stake and the honour of the British Empire. The Americans have held out in the Bataan Peninsula against far heavier odds. The Russians are turning back the packed strength of the Germans. The Chinese, with almost complete lack of modern equipment, have held the Japanese for about four and a half years. It will be disgraceful if we cannot hold our much-boasted Fortress of Singapore against inferior forces. There must be no thought of sparing the troops or civil population. No mercy must be shown in any shape or form. Commanders and Senior Officers must lead their troops and, if necessary, die with them. There must be no thought of surrender and every unit must fight to the end and in close contact with the enemy. Please see that the above is brought to the notice of all Senior Officers and through them to all troops. I look to you and your men to fight to the end and prove that the fighting spirit that won our Empire still exists to defend it.'

On the morning of 10 February, the Japanese began to push inland from their landing positions near the causeway. The remnants of the British Battalion were attacked in force as they sheltered near a large hilltop house. After several hours of hand-to-hand fighting, they were able to halt the Japanese advance, albeit temporarily, but more than twenty men were killed in the skirmishes, with many more wounded. Corporal John Wyatt was one of those wounded, and he outlined the situation to me:

'I took a piece of shrapnel in my shoulder, causing me great pain. I also had a badly seeping ulcer on my leg, all of which left me thoroughly miserable and depressed. One of our officers asked for a volunteer to take me out and there was no shortage of offers as I managed to struggle out along a jungle path helped by Private Nicholls. Within a few minutes we stumbled upon a truck carrying Chinese Communist guerrillas who helped me on board, leaving Nicholls to disappear back into the jungle. The truck then set off in the direction of the Queen Alexandra Hospital in the south of the island.

'Struggling to the ground from the back of the truck outside the hospital main entrance, I was appalled at the sight that greeted me. Hundreds of injured civilians and soldiers were lying around on the ground and I found it difficult to weave my way through the mass of moaning humanity. I managed to find a doctor just inside the main entrance who told me to go to an upstairs ward. The fact that I was only slightly wounded and was able to walk up the stairs probably saved my life.'

With the Japanese closing in on the city of Singapore and casualties mounting by the hour, the hospital was under severe pressure. Wyatt was allocated a bed on the first floor and given painkillers, but the medical staff were unable to remove the shrapnel from his shoulder.

Three days later, Japanese mortar bombs began landing just to the rear of the hospital buildings, damaging the chapel and some other outbuildings.

By early afternoon the shelling had increased and the Chief Matron, along with her eight nursing sisters, were driven to the docks, where they were to be evacuated to safety. Unfortunately, many of these brave women died when their ships were sunk shortly after leaving the island. The hospital was bursting at the seams with around 800 patients, mainly British but with some Indians, Malays and Australians. New casualties were arriving by lorry-load every hour: it was total chaos. Patients were crammed into wards, with many left lying on the floor or in camp beds lodged in every nook and cranny of the hospital; even the dining room had been converted into a temporary ward.

One of the biggest problems the hospital faced, along with finding space for the wounded, was the lack of water. Much of the mains supply in Singapore had been damaged by the bombing, and water was being kept in every available container, including buckets, baths and petrol cans. The electricity supply had also been cut off and operations were conducted by torch and candlelight. The situation was becoming desperate for the patients and staff.

Just after 0800 hrs on 14 February, heavy bombs started to land all around the hospital and by lunchtime Japanese soldiers were advancing across the hospital grounds. They entered the hospital and started bayoneting surgeons, nurses and patients, some of them lying in the operating theatres, including five Surrey men. Doctors tried to plead with the Japanese to show some mercy, but their words fell on deaf ears as they went about their awful business. Private Charles Beckness of the 2 Surreys was among those killed during this vicious assault.

Corporal Wyatt was in his bed on one of the upper floors, cowering under his blankets, when two Japanese soldiers came running up the stairs and burst in through the swing doors. He recalled that terrifying moment:

'One was over six feet tall and the other was very short, and for a moment they just stood there motionless looking down the ward. Although I was petrified, it was quite amusing to see that one of them held a squawking and wriggling duck under his right arm. There were five us in that small ward and after a few seconds the taller Jap moved to two heavily bandaged soldiers nearest the door and, after searching their wrists for watches, proceeded to bayonet both to death. My whole body started to go numb and I began to come to terms with fact that I had only a few minutes of my life left. I was certain that they would work their way down the ward, killing all of us.

'Meanwhile, Corporal Sinclair stepped towards them with tea and bread on a tray and tried to pacify them. They were having none of it though, and with cries of "Kurrah, Kurrah" they knocked him unconscious with heavy blows from their rifle butts. They then dragged him out of the ward and that was the last I saw of that brave corporal. At that point, a Jap officer entered the ward and on seeing what had happened screamed and shouted at the two soldiers and shoved them out of the ward. As he turned to leave, he apologised to the three of us left alive and said in English, "I am sorry but my men are tired and hungry – they have been fighting without rest or food for many days."'

What was to happen in the Queen Alexandra Hospital over the next forty-eight hours was one of the worst massacres of the Second World War.

The Japanese troops proceeded to murder in cold blood many of the patients and staff, including five other members of the East Surreys: privates R. Davis, S. Dye, J. Minahane, E. Russell and H. Deakin. Lieutenant Colonel Cravan, Commanding Officer of the hospital, was discussing the gravity of the situation with his officer in charge of radiography, Major Bull, in an upstairs office when a bullet came in through an open window, causing them to throw themselves to the floor. The colonel decided to go downstairs to see for himself what was going on, but before he could leave the room, all hell broke lose below, with explosions, gunfire and screaming echoing through the corridors. He decided to sit tight for a while, but after about half an hour, when things began to quieten down, he went down to the ground floor with his aides to assess the situation. The scene that greeted him was one of utter carnage. More than fifty patients and staff had been shot or bayoneted, with many others taken away by the Japanese soldiers.

Some of the patients lying on the floor in the dining room saw, through the open doors, soldiers of 44 Indian Brigade moving swiftly along the corridor from the medical wards, closely followed by a cluster of Japanese troops. Why the Punjabis were fighting in the hospital no one knows, but some believe that the presence of armed troops in and around the hospital inflamed the situation, causing the Japanese to react as they did.

The Japanese assault on the hospital was undertaken by a company of about 175 men. They were dressed in full combat kit, consisting of green tropical uniforms, steel helmets, rifles, bayonets and machine guns. They were heavily camouflaged with small branches, twigs and leaves stuck all over their bodies, and were dirty and smelly. They also gave the impression to the patients of being either drunk or high on drugs. One group came in from the adjacent railway line and quickly entered the hospital through the main entrance. A second group came in through the rear entrance and the patients' dining room, with a third entering through operating room windows and the surgical wards. Staff in the laboratory saw the first group coming towards the hospital; they tried to escape towards the main building, but were cut down by a burst of machine-gun fire. The officer in charge, Major J.A. Calder RAMC, was killed, along with Sergeant Williams RAMC, but Corporal Saint managed to crawl to the main building with a wounded arm, where he was attended to by Private Sutton.

Two of the second group of Japanese soldiers who had pursued the retreating Punjabi soldiers entered the temporary ward in the dining room, where over 100 patients were lying on makeshift beds. One of the pair started beating the helpless patients with a brush whilst the other humiliated another by urinating on him.

Lieutenant Weston, who oversaw the reception area, decided to take a white sheet and wave it out of the back door of the hospital, but when the first Japanese soldier reached him he simply bayoneted the defenceless officer through the white flag. The blade entered through his upper chest and passed out through his lower back.

The rest of the soldiers in this group stormed into the room and began shooting and bayoneting many of the helpless patients. Among those killed in this early orgy of violence was Padre Smith of the Gordon Highlanders, Staff Sergeant Walker of the Royal Army Dental Corps and Sergeant Sherriff of the Royal Army Medical Corps.

With the hospital in a state of disarray and panic, many people tried to escape from the marauding assassins. Those who tried to escape through the main entrance were simply mown down by rifle and machine-gun fire. Others met their fate in the rear corridor, where they were bayoneted or shot before they had a chance to leave the building. Corporal Collins was bayoneted through the chest, but the blade missed his vital organs and he survived the atrocity. Company Quartermaster Sergeant Hartley was not so fortunate: aged 57, he was the oldest man to die in the massacre.

This group of Japanese soldiers seemed to have completed the worst atrocities. They proceeded to enter the medical wards, bayoneting patients and beating up others. They forced the entire medical staff and wounded who could walk into the corridor, where they left them standing in terror.

Whilst all this was going on, the surgeons proceeded to carry on with the operations, firstly in the theatres, but when this proved too dangerous because of stray bullets, in the corridors, only moving back into the theatres when the firing stopped. Operations were carried out under the most stressful of situations, and the dedication and bravery of the medical staff was of the highest order. The staff became aware that the Japanese were now in the corridors outside the operating theatres, and Captain Doctor Smiley moved over to the doorway and indicated the red cross clearly displayed on his armband. He motioned to the Japanese soldiers to come into the theatre to show them that they were not at any risk, and that it was simply an operating theatre. One of the soldiers fired at him, but the shot missed and hit Private

Lewis in the shoulder. Smiley told the medical team to stand quietly in the centre of the room with their arms in the air, leaving the patient on the operating table. The Japanese ordered the group out into the corridor, and as they moved down the passage they were attacked viciously with bayonets and rifle butts. The captain took a bayonet thrust to his chest, but his metal cigarette case in his pocket deflected the bayonet. Others were not so lucky though: Private Rodgers, Captain Parkinson, Corporal McEwan and Lance Corporal Lewis were repeatedly bayoneted, and all died almost immediately. Captain Smiley was badly wounded in the groin, arm and hand. He stumbled against Private Sutton and they both fell to the ground, pretending to be dead – an act that probably saved both their lives. Smiley was awarded the Military Cross after the war for his actions in the hospital that day.

During this mayhem, the patient on the operating table, Corporal Vetch, was stabbed to death whilst still under the anaesthetic; perhaps in some respects one of the 'lucky' ones as he would have been completely unaware of the terror around him.

Whilst Smiley and Sutton lay motionless on the floor, they became aware of a large group of patients and medical staff running along the corridor with their arms raised. The Japanese were kicking and beating them with rifle butts as they stumbled along. Other soldiers entered several of the surgical wards and began to systematically beat up the helpless patients, many with fractures and in plaster casts. They took great pleasure in twisting and pulling at the slings holding some of the men's broken legs in the air. In the kitchen adjacent to the surgical wards, two of the medical staff, Privates Sayer and Bruce, were hiding a badly wounded soldier, Private Guillim, when another patient burst into the room, bleeding profusely from a bayonet wound. Almost immediately, two Japanese soldiers stormed into the room and shot Bruce three times in the abdomen. Guillim lay motionless on the floor in a state of abject terror whilst this attack was going on, the two Japanese soldiers standing over him. They must have been convinced he was dead because they left the room soon after, leaving him to crawl back to the main ward.

At about the same time this was going on, a grenade went off in the ward office next door, shattering Regimental Sergeant Major Rideout's hand and arm so badly that it later had to be amputated.

Half an hour after the initial assault on the hospital, around fifty staff and patients were dead, with many more lying around in great pain from their wounds. By 1530 hrs, a group of over 200 patients and staff were roped together in groups of eight and forced to walk to a piece of open ground about 100 yards from the main buildings. A second group of around sixty (mainly officers) were taken to a separate piece of land and roped together.

Many of the patients in first group were walking wounded with arms in plaster; most were in bare feet and with only pyjamas on. Those who had difficulty walking were supported by their comrades, and if they fell they were brutally bayoneted.

This large group was then marched alongside the main railway embankment, past the Normanton fuel oil tanks, which were on fire and belching huge clouds of black smoke into the hot and humid air. As they stumbled along, they also had to endure heavy shellfire from their own artillery, causing them to dive for cover in the undergrowth on several occasions. At one point the party were told to stop and rest. They then had all valuables such as rings, watches, pens etc. taken from them, and were again subjected to beatings with rifle butts and fists. One man whose arm was in plaster had it forced behind his back and rebroken – the Japanese brutality knew no bounds. By now their rope bindings had tightened in the heat, causing considerable pain, and some men's hands began to turn blue.

The building into which they were now forced was part of the old hospital's sisters' quarters, a red brick two-storey house raised above the ground on piles, with a block of outbuildings surrounding a small courtyard. The group was forced into three very small rooms, each with double doors opening directly onto the courtyard. They were crammed so tightly into the rooms that it was impossible for everyone to sit down. The doors were secured with wooden poles and the windows nailed closed and shuttered with wood, preventing any daylight entering. There was no ventilation, and within minutes the heat became unbearable for the prisoners. Their hands were still tied but they eventually managed to untie each other, enabling them to raise their hands above their heads to allow a little more space. They had to suffer the indignity of relieving themselves on each other: the smell soon became appalling.

The Japanese made no effort to provide food or drink, and many of the men had not eaten or drunk anything for many hours. The conditions under which they were held were such that many of the men became mentally unstable, shouting and screaming at the tops of their voices appealing for food and drink. Others just slumped on the floor, giving up the will to live.

By now it was late evening, and for the rest of the night they endured the most difficult of situations. One of the officers said that food and water had been promised by 0600 hrs the next morning, but the screaming and shouting went on all night. At one point a voice was heard from outside the rooms speaking in perfect English: 'If you keep quiet I will try and get you back to the hospital tomorrow.'

As dawn broke on 15 February, several of the men had passed away – at least seven in the central room alone. As the morning wore on with no sign of food or water, desperation began to set in amongst the prisoners. At around 1100 hrs, a Japanese officer opened the door of one of the rooms and announced in broken English: 'We are taking you behind the lines – you will get water on the way.' A few minutes later, prisoners were taken out in pairs by the guards. Everyone assumed that they were being taken out for a drink until they heard screams and shouts in English from nearby: 'Oh my god – mother – don't – help me.' It dawned on the remaining prisoners that they were being executed; this was confirmed when a Japanese soldier was seen wiping blood from his bayonet with a large piece of cloth.

As the guards worked their way through the rooms, removing prisoners in twos, the men in the last room became very distressed. Several tried to commit suicide – one by cutting his wrists and another by hanging himself. By mid-afternoon, more than half of the men had been taken from this last room to meet their fate.

As all this was going on, heavy fighting was raging all around the buildings. A shell landing nearby blew open the doors and windows, showering the remaining prisoners with dust and rubble. Several were injured by the flying debris, but those left could make a dash for freedom – some through the broken door and others through the windows. A number managed to get away, but most were killed by a burst of machine-gun fire from close range.

Among those who escaped were Corporal Bryer, Private Hoskins, Private Gurd, Captain De Warrenne Waller and Corporal Johnson. When Bryer escaped through the doorway, he turned left, ran around the rear of the building and along Alexanda Road, where he bumped into Hoskins. Both men ran along together, zig zagging to avoid enemy fire, but Bryer was hit in the back and fell.

'I'm done for – you go on,' he called out to Hoskins, who, realizing that if he hesitated he too would be a goner, ran on towards a hut on the other side of the road. Here he came across an Indian family who gave him some water.

As the Japanese were nearby, he ran on until finally reaching a patrol of the Beds and Herts, who took him to their company headquarters and from there back into Singapore city.

Meanwhile, Bryer found that he was not too badly wounded and was able to get up and try to get away from the area. Unfortunately, he came across a Japanese patrol that stabbed him four times with their bayonets. Trying to get away from them, one of the stabs went into his ribs and another hit him on the side of his head, knocking him into a semi-conscious state. Bryer then lay pretending to be dead and the patrol went away, leaving him in a bloody heap. He lay in his own blood until dusk, and as he was not too far from the hospital, stumbled and crawled back there to seek help.

Private Gurd had also turned left out of the door and run across the road and the railway looking for safety. He saw other figures in pyjamas nearby and, after diving into some waist-high grass, eventually crawled into a drainage ditch where he took a drink of water. (He was so thirsty and desperate by this time that he was oblivious to the possible consequences of such an action.) As he lay in the ditch, he heard someone shouting for help and discovered Captain Brown nearby badly wounded, bleeding profusely from a bullet wound near the base of his spine. Gurd did what he could to plug the wound and stem the bleeding, but without much success.

By now darkness had fallen, and he made the decision to leave Brown to his fate as there was nothing more he could do for him with the Japanese all around them. He managed to stumble and crawl for about a mile and a half along the Alexandria Road towards Mount Eccles, where he eventually reached the Thye Hong biscuit factory. The factory was occupied by Allied troops, who tended his wounds and took him back to safety.

Corporal Johnson, one of the other successful escapees from the room, was hit in the ankle as he ran some 10 yards along the road and dived into a monsoon drain under heavy fire. He stayed in the drain overnight: the next morning, he crawled out onto the road to seek some way of escape. Unfortunately, he stumbled upon three Japanese soldiers who beat him up using rifle butts and boots, even though it was now 16 February and Singapore had already capitulated. Fortunately for him, a Japanese officer came along and gave him a pass to make his way back down the road to the hospital.

Back at the hospital, a clearing-up operation had begun, hampered by large numbers of very determined Japanese looters, resulting in some unpleasant scenes. Many of the patients still in possession of their watches, rings, pens etc. were robbed, and much of the hospital's food was stolen.

Lieutenant Moore, who was in the hospital at the time, recalls a Japanese senior officer entering on 17 February:

'He expressed his regret at what had happened and assured the staff that they had nothing further to fear. He also told the O.C. of the hospital that he was to be regarded as a direct representative of the Emperor and that no higher honour could be paid to the hospital.'

By the time that fateful weekend of 14/15 February was over, around 250 victims of various nationalities – including three of the five East Surrey men, Privates C. Beckness, H. Deakin and J. Minahane – had been murdered. Such an atrocity went against the Japanese Army's thirty-page booklet that was given to all their troops prior to the invasion, which included the following:

'Troops who are really efficient in battle do not plunder and rob, chase after women, or drink and quarrel. Destroy the genuine enemy – but show compassion to those who have no guilt. Bear in mind that the behaviour of one soldier reflects upon the good name of the whole army, and discipline yourself.'

As darkness began to fall on 10 February, the rest of the tired and dispirited men of the British Battalion waited with bated breath on the Jurong Road for the next Japanese attack. Fortunately, no further attacks came that night, but sleep was impossible as the enemy kept up a constant barrage of mortar and gun fire on their positions.

As dawn broke the next day, Japanese infantry attacked the British Battalion positions in force, and by 0800 hrs the situation was becoming critical. They were now in grave danger of being cut off and annihilated if they remained in their current position, so the brigade commander decided they would have to fight their way through to Bukit Timah and then across country to Reformatory Road.

Moving off in three columns, led by Major O'Neil Wallis, they were fired on by mortars and light machine guns, as well as suffering strafing from the air, and were lucky to get through. That day, 11 February, was a disastrous one with over twenty East Surrey men killed.

The situation for Percival's forces on Singapore island was now critical. The Japanese were closing in on the city itself and there was virtually no air support as almost all the aircraft and pilots had been evacuated to Java. The reservoirs and water supplies were also now in Japanese hands.

13 February was quiet and the battalion settled down to try to get some much-needed sleep. Communications had broken down, and no one had any idea of what was happening. The battalion was now too weakened in numbers to be an effective fighting unit, and was put into brigade reserve.

By daybreak on the fourteenth, the remnants of the British Battalion were moved for the final time to Mount Echo on the Tanglin/Alexandra Road, overlooking the golf course. There they wearily dug in once again and waited for the inevitable end. From their final position they had a good view over the doomed city that looked like a volcanic island. Black smoke mushroomed upwards, lit by the glare of many fires.

Sunday 15 February dawned with heavy mortaring and shelling of the battalion positions. They took more casualties when two trenches occupied by the Surreys suffered direct hits. Confusion reigned. Rumours and counter-rumours circulated about a possible ceasefire and at 2040 hrs Lieutenant General Percival issued the final order to his commanders:

'It has been necessary to give up the struggle, but I want the reason explained to all ranks. The forward troops continue to hold their ground but the essentials of war have run short. In a few days, we will have neither petrol nor food. Many types of ammunition are short, and the water supply upon which the vast civilian population and many of the fighting troops are dependent, threaten to fail. This situation has been brought about partly by being driven off our dumps, and partly by hostile air and artillery action. Without the sinews of war, we cannot fight on. I thank all ranks for their efforts throughout the campaign.'

Percival formally signed the surrender document in the Ford Motor factory on 15 February 1942. He was never given a copy of the document as the Japanese only made one copy but after the war he recalled the conditions:

'There must be an unconditional surrender of all military forces in the Singapore area. Hostilities will cease at 20.30 hrs. All troops to remain in positions occupied at the time of cessation of hostilities pending further orders.

'All weapons, military equipment, ships, aeroplanes and secret documents to be handed over to the Japanese Army intact. In order to prevent looting and other disorders in Singapore during the temporary withdrawal of all armed forces, a force of British armed men to be left temporarily in the town area until relieved by the Japanese.'

When the battle for Malaya and Singapore ended, only 265 East Surrey men were accounted for out of the 960 who started the campaign at Jitra seventy days previously.

Back in London, Prime Minister Winston Churchill told Parliament that 30,000 Japanese troops had overwhelmed 120,000 British and Allied soldiers in Malaya and Singapore. Recent evidence, however, suggests that this statement was not true, as some 50,000 Japanese troops had infiltrated Thailand from Indochina between 2-6 December 1941 with the agreement of the Thai government. As the Japanese lost 20,000 men, with 5,000 missing, during the battle for Malaya and Singapore, it is now believed that there might have been an initial force of around 170,000 Japanese soldiers involved in the conflict.

The Annual Register, a long-established British reference work that records and analyses the year's major events, developments and trends throughout the world, recorded the defeat in 1942 rather bleakly:

'The position of Great Britain as an Imperial Power in the Far East has suffered a shattering blow, from which it was doubtful whether it would ever be able to recover.'

How true this blunt statement turned out to be.

Chapter 5

Escape Attempts

The desire for freedom, one of man's innate traits, is something universal to us all. Faced by a choice of imprisonment or liberty, a drive to remain free dominates our thinking. Soldiers are thrown into situations that require courage, dedication and innovation if they are to survive. As prisoners of war, as we shall see later, they had all human rights taken away: their rank, esteem and self-respect, but there was always a glimmer of hope – they could attempt to escape.

From the beginning of the Japanese invasion on 7 December 1941, many men who had been isolated from their units during the chaotic withdrawal down the Malaya peninsula attempted to escape from their clutches. Quite a few of them made it back to Singapore and rejoined their units, but others fell into the hands of the enemy. As they advanced down Malaya, the Japanese put a price on the heads of any prisoners who attempted to escape, and the natives had no compulsion in turning them over for a bounty. Despite this, many men tried to make their own escape plans both before the surrender and during captivity in Changi and the camps along the Thai/Burma railway.

The evacuation from Dunkirk of the British Expeditionary Force in May and June 1940 is well documented. Whilst the numbers evacuated were much greater, the British had command of the sea, often enjoyed parity in the air and the distance to safety across the Channel was a mere 40 miles. At Singapore, the situation was quite different as the enemy had complete command of the air and sea, with safety many miles away.

By the end of January 1942, the Singapore War Council recognized the fact that the island was now highly likely to fall to the Japanese, and a route to safety now became paramount for those wishing to escape. Colonel Alan Warren of the Royal Marines, who worked for the Far East section of the SOE (Special Operations Executive), was given the task of organizing an escape route via Sumatra to Ceylon, India or Australia. The War Council quickly realized that this was the only way to get large numbers of people to freedom, as the Japanese were now in complete control of most of the territory to the east of Singapore. Escape from Singapore to Sumatra would be possible for anyone with resources and the ability to handle small craft. The prevailing wind until the end of March was from the north-east, leading straight to Sumatra through the mass of densely forested islands lying south and west of Singapore.

With the Dutch still in control of Sumatra, Warren identified the town of Padang on the west coast of the island as the best place from which to evacuate escapees to India and Australia. Padang had an excellent port with easy access into the Indian Ocean, but getting escapees there across the island was a problem as the terrain was difficult. Warren eventually settled on a route from Tembilahan, a small rundown town on the east coast, down the Indragiri River and thence overland to Padang, a route that was to be known as the Indragiri River Escape Line. A food dump was set up on Durian Island, with a second at Prigi Rajah at the mouth of the Indragiri River, to feed the anticipated flow of escapees out of Singapore.

From 9 February onwards, a steady stream of small craft began to flow out of Singapore towards Sumatra. By the sixteenth, around 150 people had reached Padang, from where they were shipped off to India. Accurate figures are not available, but it is estimated that over 2,500 troops made it to safety between 9 February and 7 March 1942.

Officially, any military personnel who tried to escape before the surrender was signed were deemed to be deserters, other than those who were ordered to leave. After that, it was the duty of all military men to try to escape.

With Singapore doomed, Sergeant Denis Gavin from Newcastle upon Tyne decided that he was not going to linger on the island and accept his fate as a prisoner of war. As the Surreys waited for orders on Mount Echo during the evening of 15 February, Gavin decided that he was going back into the jungle. He floated the idea of escape with several of his colleagues, but few had the stomach for such a plan, except for Sergeant Major Len Avery, Corporal Joe Hocking and three orderlies who agreed to join him.

The initial idea of an escape attempt through the jungles of Malaya to Burma was fraught with difficulties, due to the distance, so they decided that an escape by sea was the only way. Avery had access to a motorbike, and at around 1830 hrs, with Gavin riding pillion, they made their way towards the docks. Hocking and the three orderlies had agreed to make their own way there and meet them later.

The waterfront was swarming with hundreds of men with the same idea of trying to escape when the two Surreys screeched to a stop. Groups of men had been getting away at regular intervals over the past few days, and as they looked around they realized that finding a suitable vessel was not going to be easy, as most had already been commandeered.

When the three orderlies arrived, the group sat down amongst the chaos at the docks to wait for Hocking and discussed what they would do next. Despite Gavin's confidence that they could make a break for it, Avery and the three orderlies had a change of heart and decided that they were not willing to risk the escape attempt, leaving Gavin on his own on the dockside to wait for Hocking.

A few minutes later he arrived and the two men set about looking for a vessel that might suit their needs. After scouring the docks for several hours, they stumbled upon a sampan that everyone else seemed to have neglected. It was only 9ft long and had no oars, but the duo were undeterred. Gavin went looking for oars, eventually finding six short paddles – not ideal, but, as he said, 'they were better than nothing'.

As the boat was big enough to hold five, the two Surreys enlisted the help of three other men who had been hanging around the quay also looking to escape. All three had been drinking and were a bit the worse for wear, but Gavin and Hocking decided to take a chance and enlist them anyway as they needed the extra manpower for the journey ahead.

Their first priority was to stock up on supplies of food and water, so they split up to scour the docks. An hour or so later, having scrounged and scavenged supplies, they returned to the sampan, but Hocking was missing. After waiting patiently for another hour, and with dawn approaching, the four decided to leave Hocking and make a run for it. It was important they get away from the island before daylight to stand the best chance of escaping undetected.

As the four men paddled out of Singapore, they looked back towards the fiercely burning city with deep sadness. As Gavin recalls, tears came to their eyes as they remembered their comrades left behind at the mercy of the Japanese:

> 'Singapore was dying and there, on that burning island, were so many of my friends. I had also had a thousand comrades of war who now lay stinking and unburied in the jungles of Malaya, or were just corpses left to rot on the route of the retreat as even the scavenging ants abandoned them.'

Their initial plan was to skirt around to the south-east coast of the island and land on mainland Malaya somewhere in Johore, from where they could head north through Malaya into Burma and then on to India. Such a plan of course was fraught with difficulties, not least the fact that the Japanese were in control of Malaya and Thailand, and the Burmese border was 1,500 miles away. They also had no idea as to whether Burma was still in Allied hands.

Gavin had heard rumours in Singapore that an escape route had been set up across the neighbouring island of Sumatra, a mere 100 miles across the Straits of Malacca**. Sumatra was still in Dutch hands, and to the four men this seemed a much better option, even though a 100-mile sea journey in a 9ft sampan was daunting. It was also rumoured that a supply of food and water had been set up on the island of Sinkep, in the Lingga Archipelago, so the small group decided to try to make their way there.

For the next ten days, the four men took turns at paddling their way towards Sinkep, island-hopping as they went. The rumours proved correct, as upon reaching Sinkep (which they christened 'ration island') they were able to stock up on food and water and rest up for a few days. It also allowed time for their blistered hands to heal.

It was the last day of February when the party left Sinkep island and struck out for the east coast of Sumatra. This stage of their journey proved uneventful, with no sightings of Japanese ships or aircraft, and they finally arrived at a small village near the mouth of the Indragiri River. The village was already fully of escapees, and Gavin was surprised and delighted to see

---

** The Indragiri escape line.

Jimmy Jewell and John Freeman, another couple of East Surrey men who had also managed to escape from Singapore. After a great deal of hugging and back slapping, Jewell and Freeman were invited to join Gavin's group for the rest of the trip. It was here that another officer of the Indian Army joined them, taking the party back up to six. Three of the original crew had decided not to go any further and stayed in the village.

The following morning, the three East Surreys, a Scots signaller and two warrant officers of the Indian Army set off again in their trusty sampan down the east coast towards Tembilahan. This town was the main base of the escape organization on the east coast of Sumatra, where a well-oiled structure was in place for taking escapees by road and rail across the island to the port of Padang on the west coast. Upon reaching Tembilahan without mishap, and as they no longer had any need for the sampan, they sold it for twenty dollars.

With so many escapees now arriving into Tembilahan, the town was in chaos. The six men were given food, water and accommodation, but the authorities were not able to give them any indication as to how long they might have to wait for transport across the island. This was frustrating for the group; whilst Gavin was all for waiting, for some reason Jewell, Freeman and the Scots signaller decided to strike out on their own, leaving Gavin's group now a trio. It is not clear what became of them when they left Gavin's group, but it is known that they were subsequently taken prisoner and survived Japanese captivity to return home at the end of the war.

The following day, the remaining three members of the group were allocated a place on a truck out of Tembilahan, eventually arriving into Padang by train on 6 March after an arduous journey. They were relieved to at last reach the port, where ships were leaving for India on a regular basis. Gavin was convinced that his war was over and that he would soon be home with his family in Newcastle.

At Padang, the escape 'organization' ruled with an iron fist. Strict military discipline was enforced. Men were ordered to hand in their weapons and behave in a civilized manner. The officers in charge operated a strict 'first in first out' policy, and as there were around 3,000 escapees already in Padang when Gavin and his party arrived, they were well down the list for evacuation.

It was now 7 March, and due to Japanese naval activity in the Bay of Bengal, no ships had docked in Padang for several days. The escapees were now in grave danger of falling into Japanese hands after all as the Dutch had declared Padang an 'open' town and were preparing to surrender to the Japanese. After a brief discussion, Gavin and his two friends decided that they were not going to wait around for the Japanese to arrive but would make another run for it. They felt that a larger group would have a better chance, so recruited the help of a group of nine like-minded men who were all anxious to get away. A heated discussion ensued about whether they should head for India or Australia, but India won the vote.

A week later at dawn, the group set off south out of Padang on foot, heading along the coast to look for a suitable vessel in one of the many fishing villages. By nightfall they reached a small fishing village, where they began to search for a boat. With what money they had left they managed to buy a 27ft-long vessel. It had a beam of 8ft with a 30ft mast, not ideal for crossing the Indian Ocean, but it was all that was available to them and would have to do.

Their plan was to island-hop up the west coast of Sumatra as far as the Nicobar Islands in the Andaman Sea, from where they would strike out for the final 900 miles across the Bay of Bengal for Ceylon. Food and drink was always going to be a problem, but they hoped to pick up supplies on the island. With only a school atlas, a Chinese map and two basic compasses, navigation was going to be one of their biggest challenges during the voyage, but they were undeterred and determined to succeed.

It was St Patrick's Day, a month after the fall of Singapore, when Sergeant Paddy Gavin and his eleven friends set off from Sungei Pinang on the west coast of Sumatra in a boat they had named the *Venture*.

Their first island target was Siberut, about 90 miles due west of Sungei Pinang. With a stiff breeze blowing, the little boat fairly flew over the white-topped waves, 'India here we come,' shouted Gavin as they all clapped and whooped.

After two days' uneventful sailing, except for a broken boom that was quickly repaired, the small vessel reached Siberut, an island still under Dutch control. More by luck than good judgement, they headed straight through a small entrance into a sheltered bay, where they stumbled across a friendly native village where the locals provided the tired men with copious amounts of food and drink in exchange for some of the dollars they had retained from Singapore.

For over a week they remained in the village. The villagers fed them and helped ready the *Venture* for the next leg of the journey. Gavin recalled:

> 'They caulked the open seams, built a floor over the bilge, erected an attap [thatch] and bamboo roof, put shelves under the eaves, strengthened the outriggers, cut spare outrigger arms, made a new boom, gave us two spare booms, stitched and reinforced the sails, gave us spare oars, supplied bamboo sweeps and when all was shipshape they stocked the boat with provisions for us.'

Whilst they were tempted to linger on Siberut and enjoy the good life, they were aware that the Japanese could land at any time and their escape would be over. With the *Venture* well-stocked with food and drink, they set off again for Ceylon – 1,500 miles across the Indian Ocean.

Shortly after leaving Siberut, the wind dropped and the vessel was becalmed just a few miles off the coast. They became frustrated with their lack of progress, wallowing in the calm sea for three days before an easterly breeze sprang up and they began to make good progress. The boat fairly skipped along as the wind gradually increased in intensity. Within minutes it began to shriek and howl through the rigging. They had to frantically ease the sheets to avoid disaster. Without warning, the wind whipped the mainsail away and the mast split in two, crashing down onto the deck and narrowly missing the soaked men. 'It crashed down like a stricken forest giant taking everything before it and the boat filled with water,' recalls Gavin.

The twelve men struggled to keep the *Venture* afloat and under control as giant waves swept over them and the wind tossed them about like a cork. It was just a matter of survival as they bailed furiously to keep afloat. As suddenly as it had arrived, the wind dropped and the *Venture* settled down once again on an even keel. Gavin continues:

> 'We paused for breath and to look about us. The boat looked gaunt and naked without its towering mast and was indeed a wretched hulk,

barely afloat. The hold was half full of water and every article of food and clothing was floating about in the swishing waters. Underneath, and out of sight in the dark water, all the water containers mixed their freshness with the salt sea, and the tinned foods rattled and clinked. What price India now?'

With the mast broken, they now had no option but to head back and look for land using the oars. After several hours of backbreaking rowing, they eventually reached what seemed like a deserted island, where they beached the stricken boat on a sandy strip of beach. Two of them decided to explore the island on foot, returning an hour or so later with armfuls of freshly cured fish given to them by a couple of native fishermen.

Making themselves as comfortable as possible under the trees, they toiled and sweated for the next ten days to repair the damaged vessel. Fortunately, most of their food supplies had survived the storm and they were able to dry everything out on the sunny beach. There was an abundance of coconut trees in the vicinity that added to their diet, along with a bricked-in well offering a constant supply of sweet, fresh water.

They eventually prepared to set off once again on their journey towards safety. It was agreed that the *Venture* was now in no fit state to attempt the 1,500-mile trip across the open sea to Ceylon, and that Burma would be a better option. A series of island-hops should take them to the northernmost of the Andaman Islands, from where a last 250-mile hop would take them to the south-east coast of Burma. They had no way of knowing if Burma was still in Allied hands, but they had little alternative so decided to take the risk.

For the next two weeks, the intrepid group sailed from island to island until, on 22 April, they passed the last of the Andaman Islands and headed directly for Burma. They had covered more than 1,000 miles since leaving Padang. They calculated that the south-west tip of Burma was about 250 miles from the northernmost of the Andaman Islands, and that it would take them about three weeks.

Their calculations proved correct, and on 13 May they all stumbled excitedly on deck to the sight of what looked like land in the distance. Gavin spotted mountains through the binoculars. 'We have won boys; I think it's Burma and we should be safe. Hopefully in a few days we will be flown to

England,' he called out cheerily. For the rest of the day the mountains came in and out of view numerous times until darkness fell.

The following morning, as they approached land, they spotted the entrance to a river and decided to run aground on a sandbank. After wading ashore, the twelve men found themselves in a native village and discovered they were indeed in Burma. Due to language difficulties, they were unable to ascertain if the area was occupied by the Japanese. They were unsure as to whether the native people were friendly. For some reason they felt secure as the villagers provided them with food and water, including a live goat and two ducks.

The next morning, they decided to push on further, and as they crept up the coast they spotted a large estuary that proved to be the entrance to the Burmese port of Moulmein. A great cheer went up, as they felt sure that Moulmein was still in Allied hands and they were now safe.

Suddenly the *Venture* hit a sandbank. The impact forced the rudder out of its socket, sinking instantly to the bottom. Without a rudder, they were now at the mercy of a strong current that swept them into the harbour, but with safety within reach, they were unconcerned even if the vessel was grounded.

Their cheering was instantly silenced when they spotted a large cargo vessel flying the Japanese flag. They were now helpless as the *Venture* was in the grip of a rip tide that took them towards the harbour. Fortunately, the Japanese on board the ship paid no attention to them as they were swept past into a tree-lined tributary.

It was obvious that Moulmein was now in Japanese hands, and the dispirited men realized that they were still 800 miles from India. Their only option now was to try to escape overland.

Beaching the *Venture* in a quiet creek, the group gathered up what supplies they could carry and headed into the jungle. Soon they came across a small Burmese settlement where the villagers provided them with food and water, suggesting that they lay low until nightfall before making for India as the Japanese were in the area.

Just as they were preparing to leave the village that evening, with the light fading, several dozen heavily armed Japanese soldiers sprang out of the undergrowth, surrounding them. 'Put your hands up,' shouted the Japanese officer in English. 'Walk over this way.' The twelve men looked around for

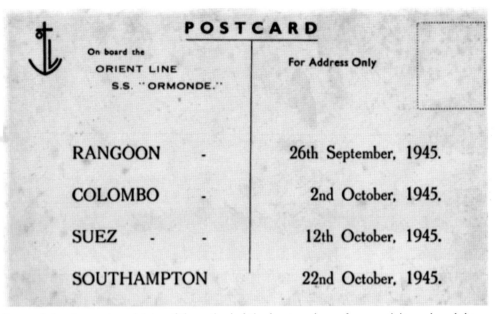

POSTCARD

On board the
ORIENT LINE
S.S. "ORMONDE."

For Address Only

RANGOON	-	26th September, 1945.
COLOMBO	-	2nd October, 1945.
SUEZ	- -	12th October, 1945.
SOUTHAMPTON		22nd October, 1945.

Postcard showing route and dates of the author's father's return home from captivity on board the SS *Ormonde*.

SERGEANT C.G. MARTIN

MITSUSHIMA POW CAMP

JAPAN 1944

WEIGHT 7 STONE 12 POUNDS

Sergeant Cliff Martin of the 2 Surreys.
Photo taken by the Japanese in
Mitsushima PoW camp, 1944.

The SS *Ormonde*.

The 2nd East Surrey Regimental Colours, retrieved from a bank in Singapore in August 1945 but destroyed in a fire at the Regimental Museum, Clandon, in 2015.

Captain Con O'Neil Wallis MC, one of the most outstanding officers in the regiment during the Second World War.

A home-made banner of the 2nd East Surrey Regiment in Shanghai from 1939.

Prisoners in Aomi Camp, Japan, in 1945, including Lieutenant Stephen Abbot and sixteen other 2 Surrey men.

Lieutenant Stephen Abbott, the heroic young commander of Aomi Camp, Japan, from May 1943–August 1945.

The Japanese record card of the author's father. These cards were kept by the Japanese for all prisoners, recording their movements during captivity.

Lieutenant Colonel G.E. Swinton MC, Commanding Officer of the 2 Surreys, 1939–1945.

Captain (later Major) W.G. Gingell MM, Quartermaster of the 2 Surreys, 1938–1945. Gingell was one of the few 2 Surreys to escape the clutches of the Japanese.

Headstone of Private H.G.T. Wilson of the
2 Surreys, Kanchanaburi War Cemetery.

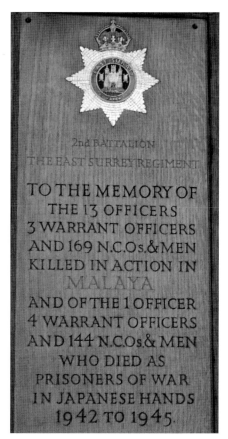

2nd BATTALION
THE EAST SURREY REGIMENT

TO THE MEMORY OF
THE 13 OFFICERS
3 WARRANT OFFICERS
AND 169 N.C.Os.& MEN
KILLED IN ACTION IN
MALAYA
AND OF THE 1 OFFICER
4 WARRANT OFFICERS
AND 144 N.C.Os & MEN
WHO DIED AS
PRISONERS OF WAR
IN JAPANESE HANDS
1942 TO 1945.

Plaque erected in All Saints' Church, Kingston
upon Thames, by Lieutenant Colonel Swinton
MC to commemorate the 2 Surreys men lost in
the Malaya campaign.

The *Kachidoki Maru*, a Japanese prison transport sunk by US submarines on 13 September 1944:
800 Allied prisoners died, including five 2 Surrey men.

The 2 East Surrey regiment arriving in Shanghai in November 1938.

The author with Corporal John Wyatt of the 2 Surreys at the launch of their book *No Mercy From the Japanese*, November 2008.

The 2 East Surreys cross-country team at Colchester in 1938, just prior to embarking for Shanghai.

The 2 East Surreys cross-country team in Shanghai, 1938.

some way of escape, but Gavin quickly realized the game was up. Their escape attempt was over after four months at sea.

The Japanese decided that their prisoners should be fed, and they were given chicken and rice. Despite their predicament, the men decided to eat their fill as they had no means of knowing if or when their next meal was going to come. 'All we needed was a crate of beer,' recalls Gavin. After eating the food, they were pulled to their feet and marched across the fields towards a river, where a motor boat was waiting to take them to Moulmein Jail. There the men were shoved unceremoniously into an isolation block, cut off from the rest of the prison, and given little indication as to what was likely to become of them.

For the next six months, Paddy Gavin and his colleagues languished in Moulmein Jail. They were now prisoners of war.

Just a few days before Christmas 1942, Gavin's group was driven down to Moulmein port, crammed into the hold of a dirty tramp steamer and taken to Rangoon, the capital of Burma. They were then locked up in Rangoon Jail, where they were to be imprisoned for the next two years.

Towards the end of 1943, daily Allied air raids on Rangoon became commonplace as they stepped up the pressure on the Japanese. The whole city was on constant alert, and when the sirens went off everyone, including the prisoners, ran to the shelters. Whilst they were in danger themselves from the bombings, such raids raised the morale of the incarcerated men as they felt that freedom was close. This rise in morale was shattered when they learnt that they were to be moved south into Thailand, much further away from the approaching Allied forces. The whole camp was angry and thoughts of escape once again sprang into all the prisoners' minds.

On 24 April 1944, the prisoners were marshalled, given Japanese uniforms and ordered to march through the city that had been devastated by Allied bombs, just as Singapore has been by the Japanese more than two years earlier. Gavin had decided that he would take the risk of trying to escape from the column of men as they marched east out of Rangoon towards Pegu some 40 miles away. Allied aircraft strafed the column, thinking that they were Japanese soldiers, and they had to dive for cover into the roadside on several occasions. During one such raid, Gavin and two friends made a run for it whilst the Japanese guards were hiding in the ditches, heading across open paddy fields towards the jungle a couple of hundred yards away. His second escape attempt from the clutches of the Japanese had begun.

Before leaving the prison, the three men had managed to secrete some supplies of food and water, but this was unlikely to last long as they could only manage to cover about 7 miles a day, with the nearest main road around 50 miles away.

Stumbling across a Burmese village near Pegu, they had no alternative but to ask for food and shelter. They were concerned that they would be turned over to Japanese as had happened at Moulmein in 1942, but fortunately, the villagers were Karens, a tribe who were fiercely loyal to the British. The Karens had been waging a guerrilla war against the Japanese since Burma was invaded almost three years previously. The villagers welcomed the men with open arms, and they enjoyed a much-needed meal of savoury chicken and rice.

Paddy Gavin and his friends lived in a hut in the village for nearly a week. It was deemed by the Karens to be too dangerous for them to attempt to move on due to Japanese activity in the area. The villagers were able to keep them abreast of news of the Allied advance into Burma from India.

On 30 April, Pegu was reoccupied by the Allies and the Karens now deemed it safe for them to try to make contact with the British troops. They escorted the men back to the main road, where they crouched in the undergrowth waiting to see if the trucks and tanks passing by were Allied.

When the Union Jack was spotted flying from the lead vehicle, Gavin and his friends strode into the middle of the road and held up their hands. He recalls:

'When a vehicle pulled up, and I explained who we were, the driver took us to see an intelligence officer. On approaching him, I marched forward and tried to click my bare feet. "Sergeant Gavin sir, second battalion East Surrey Regiment," I said, as forcefully as I was able.'

The intelligence officer was astounded when Gavin told him about their audacious escape attempts, and welcomed them back to the British Army with open arms. After more than three years and two escape attempts, Sergeant Denis Gavin was safe at last.

Whilst Gavin made one of the many unofficial escape attempts from Singapore, by 12 February 1942 Lieutenant General Percival, knowing that the island was doomed, decided that as many men as possible should be officially evacuated to India. Colonel Coates was given the task of commanding a group of around 1,800 troops chosen to try to get away.

By then the Japanese were heavily shelling most of Singapore city, including the docks, making embarkation on the few ships left very difficult. Captain Gingell, the Quartermaster of the East Surreys, had been charged by Coates to choose fourteen men from the 2 Surreys to make up a party and get away as soon as possible. Gingell chose the following men: Colour Sergeant T. Cahill, Sergeant J. Vaughan, Sergeant T. Baldwin, Corporal V. Clothier, Lance Corporal J. Bray and Privates R. Ambler, W. Carpenter, R. Holmes, D. Jenkins, A. Leatherland, P. Noad, M. Ray, R. Robinson and S. Stallwood.

He gave them a last-minute choice whether to stay or go: 'This is a voluntary show and it won't be a [Thomas] Cooks tour. If you don't want to come, then hop it now.' Not one of the fourteen men decided to stay.

They were instructed to make their way on foot to Colliers Quay after dark on 13 February, where the *Dragonfly* would be waiting for them. Ironically it was the ship that had evacuated many of the British Battalion from Batu Pahat earlier in the campaign.

Making their way towards the docks, the group had to shelter in sewage drains as bombs rained down. In the chaos, they got split up and were unable to locate the *Dragonfly*, but fortunately they stumbled upon one of the ship's Asdics ratings, Able Seaman Taff Long. Long had been sent out to look for the group by Captain Sprott, who was anxious to depart the docks as soon as possible due to the heavy bombing. Long guided the party to the vessel and wrote after the war:

'We made our way along the jetty, hugging the warehouse sides for cover. Confusion reigned supreme and I remember thinking, this is what hell must be like. We ran towards the ship with mortar bombs exploding around us, scattering shrapnel in all directions. On arriving alongside everyone in the party threw their weapons over the guard rail and clambered aboard with a few well-chosen words. The captain shouted ["]we can't wait any longer["] and we were away.'

When the Surrey men eventually boarded, there were already more than 200 people on the *Dragonfly*, three times her normal capacity. These included civilians, army nurses, women and children, along with several Japanese prisoners of war. Captain Sprott edged the vessel out of Keppel Harbour at 0100 hrs on 14 February along with her sister ship, the *Grasshopper*, with Colonel Coates and his party on board. The two gunboats were followed in close formation by a fully loaded dockyard tugboat and two pleasure steamers, all heading south-west towards Sumatra.

As the small convoy reached the Singapore Straits, tension on board the ships was running high. The captains were fully aware that other vessels leaving the stricken city earlier had been sunk.

As the men settled into their cramped accommodation, they could hear the howl of Japanese dive bombers as they swept in over the city, dropping bombs on the densely packed buildings. The final demise of British Singapore was evident to all on board the *Dragonfly*.

The following morning dawned cloudless with a calm sea, as the small and vulnerable flotilla made it through the Riau Archipelago and into the Riouw Straits, a mere 50 miles from the east coast of Sumatra.

At around 0900 hrs, a lookout spotted a Japanese Kawasaki H8 four-engine flying boat heading straight towards them. Almost immediately, the ship's tannoy burst into life and 'action stations, action stations, don life belts' boomed out across the crowded decks. With a top speed of 465 miles per hour, the flying boat quickly closed in on the ship as the *Dragonfly*'s gunners opened up. Two bombs were released but missed the ship, to the relief of the passengers as they crouched under tables below decks. The aircraft then turned away, but the course and position of the small ships would have been logged by the Japanese and a further attack was likely. Captain Sprott decided that it would be safer if the convoy proceeded to the nearest land to lay up for the day.

Before they were able to find an island, however, they heard the drone of aircraft approaching. This time it was not a lone plane, but over 100 twin-engine Mitsubishi Ki-21 heavy bombers heading straight for them. As the leading aircraft swooped in low over the vessel, the *Dragonfly* opened up with all its guns as Captain Sprott twisted and turned to try to avoid the attack. The first salvo of bombs missed the ship, but the second salvo struck it amidships, hitting the ammunition store just to the rear of the bridge and causing considerable damage. Several of the civilian passengers who were near the impact were killed instantly and the ship's rear section was torn apart. Within a matter of minutes, the vessel began to sink stern first.

The tannoy once again crackled into life: 'abandon ship, abandon ship, man the lifeboats' came the urgent announcement. The crew managed to lower only one of the lifeboats, into which the wounded were placed, along with several Carley survival rafts, but the rest of the survivors, including Gingell and his men, had to take to the sea. Gingell takes up the story at this point in his report:

> 'The ship was abandoned and sunk in seven minutes. Everyone had to take to the water. Unfortunately, I was only clad in shorts and stockings and got badly sunburnt over the following seven hours in the water.'

Along with Colour Sergeant Cahill, Lance Corporal Bray and Corporal Clothier, Gingell managed to find an upturned lifeboat and they clung to its keel, hoping they would be not seen from the air. Bray was in a very bad state, having drunk a considerable amount of sea water, and died soon after. As they drifted with the currents, Sergeant Vaughan, who was adrift in the sea, decided to swim towards an island that they could see in the distance and was never seen again.

The Japanese pilots, not satisfied with sinking the ship, proceeded to machine-gun the unfortunate men in the water, causing many casualties, including Gingell, who was hit in the leg, and Cahill, who was hit in several places. The one lifeboat that had been launched now held twenty-five people instead of the normal fourteen and was taking in water.

The survivors breathed a sigh of relief when the bombers eventually pulled away and headed on a course back towards Singapore.

Taff Long, the Welsh stoker who had guided Gingell and his men to the ship back in Singapore, vividly remembered the attack:

> 'Suddenly there was a shout of "Aircraft off port beam". Heading for us at low level were nine twin-engined Japanese bombers. The

multiple 0.5 machine guns and twin guns opened fire. The bombers dived down and all hell was let loose. There was a terrific explosion – the ship shuddered and stopped as if it had hit a concrete wall. I looked aft from the wheelhouse and saw flames and smoke from amidships and potatoes rolling all over the place. The force of the explosion had burst open the "spud" locker. I heard the quartermaster report to the bridge "steering wheel jammed. Telegraph US". The *Dragonfly* was already down by the stern as the captain shouted abandon ship. I ran down the ladder to the upper deck and looked into the boiler room to see more flames and smoke. There was a hiss of escaping steam and two or three stokers there with the skin hanging off them (engine room staff in the tropics wore nothing but shorts and slippers and therefore they had no protection whatsoever from the scalding boiling steam). The whaler was being lowered and was level with the upper deck. I helped some of them into the whaler and saw a stoker. He had been hit in the throat and blood was coming from his mouth and [I] helped him to the whaler. By now the whaler was full and I ran to the other side of the ship and jumped in. After a few minutes swimming, I turned to look at the *Dragonfly*. She was down by the stern with about 15 feet of bow sticking out of the water. As I looked the ship sank gradually lower and with a final shudder and a hissing of steam – a maelstrom of bubbles on turbulent water – she slid below the sea.'

Their respite from attack was not to last long, however, as a fresh wave of Japanese aircraft flew in from the east at low level a few minutes later. The first group attacked the remaining crowded lifeboat, whilst the second randomly sprayed the survivors clinging to life rafts and to each other in the open sea, leaving many dead and others badly injured. It was absolute carnage as they struggled for survival.

Gingell, Cahill and Clothier, despite their injuries, managed to swim to the fully loaded lifeboat and hang on to the side as it drifted through shark-infested waters for about seven hours. They eventually managed to crawl ashore on a small uninhabited island where the survivors in the lifeboat – including Lieutenant Stallard, the only remaining naval officer – had already landed. Stallard, who had been very badly wounded in the attack, died during the night.

Meanwhile, about half a mile away, the captain of the *Grasshopper*, Commander Hoffman, aghast at the fate of the *Dragonfly*, immediately ordered full speed ahead towards the spot where the stricken vessel had sunk. Realizing that there was not much he could do, and under attack himself, Hoffman headed for the nearest island, thinking that if his ship was also hit he wanted to be as close to land as possible.

The Japanese aircraft were not about to leave before finishing their task, however, and the *Grasshopper* was soon under attack. A bomb hit the rear mess-deck, followed by one close to the ship's magazine store, but fortunately not close enough to ignite the ammunition. Hoffman knew his ship was also doomed and ordered full speed towards the nearby island. It was a relief that no more serious damage was caused when Hoffman ran the *Grasshopper* onto the deserted Posik island.

Meanwhile on the adjacent island, Gingell and the survivors from the *Dragonfly* managed to relaunch the damaged lifeboat and head for Posik to join up with Hoffman, Colonel Coates and the survivors from the *Grasshopper*.

With the ship close to the shore, they had managed to salvage food, water and medical supplies to help the wounded. All the survivors could do now was to make themselves as comfortable as possible and hope that the 'mayday' the ships had sent out would attract the attention of the Dutch on Sumatra.

Whilst they had managed to get a reasonable amount of supplies from the wreck of the *Grasshopper* ashore, water was their main priority. Fortunately, the ship's mascot, a pointer dog called Judy, managed to find a spring by digging into the sand, thereby providing a supply of fresh water for the survivors. Judy was to be awarded the canine VC after the war for her heroic efforts, not only on the island, but subsequently in Japanese PoW camps in Thailand. There were two heavily pregnant ladies on board the *Grasshopper* and both were to give birth to boys on the beach. Petty Officer George Leonard White had the honour of delivering the two boys, duly named George and Leonard.

For five days, the survivors from both vessels waited on the island for rescue. With food supplies running low, Colonel Coates was increasingly concerned. They had to find a way off the island if they were not to die of starvation. Fortunately, on the sixth day, a wooden sailing ship appeared, heading directly towards the island. To their delight it was a Dutch tongkang ship based on the nearby island of Sinkep, where the local administrator had ordered them to scour the islands looking for escapees.

The survivors from the two ships were taken in the tongkang to Sinkep, where there was a good hospital, and from there on to Tembilahan at the mouth of the Indragiri River. Tembilahan was the starting point for the escape route across Sumatra outlined earlier when Paddy Gavin arrived at the town two weeks later. From there, Gingell, Cahill and Clothier were moved on by boat up the river, arriving at Rengat on 24 February and thence across Sumatra by road and rail to Padang, the main port on the west coast. The journey took almost a week before they arrived early on the morning of 2 March.

By this time, Padang was in a state of confusion and disarray. There was an element of distrust from the Dutch towards the escaping troops, as they blamed the British for the loss of Singapore and the likely fall of Sumatra to the Japanese. Ships were still arriving into the port despite heavy Japanese activity in the Bay of Bengal, and the three 2 Surrey men managed to get on board the SS *Weert* on the evening of their arrival. The *Weert* left Padang late that same evening – one of the last ships to get out before Sumatra fell to the Japanese. The 2 Surrey men arrived safely in Colombo on 9 March, where they spent seven weeks before boarding a ship for the UK, reaching Liverpool on 9 May. Gingell, Bray and Clothier had escaped the clutches of the Japanese. When Sumatra finally fell to the Japanese on 28 March 1942, a considerable number of men, including several groups of 2 Surreys, were not so lucky and were taken prisoner. Most were imprisoned in Palembang PoW camp before eventually being transferred by ship to Burma to work on the Thai/Burma railway.

Of the fifty or so ships that managed to get away from Singapore just prior to the surrender, nearly all were either sunk, captured or ran aground on the various islands in the Lingga Archipelago. It was a maritime disaster of extreme horror, described so eloquently by Oswald Gilmour in his book *Singapore to Freedom*:

'As St Valentine's Day 1942 was nearing its close, a state of affairs which defies description prevailed in this section of the Malay Archipelago. Perhaps never before in the long period of recorded history was there anything to compare with it. Men, women and children in ones and twos, in dozens, in scores and in hundreds were cast upon these tropical islands within an area of say 400 square miles. Men and women of many races, of all professions, engineers, doctors, lawyers, businessmen, sisters, nurses, housewives, sailors, soldiers and airmen, all shipwrecked. Between the islands on the phosphorescent sea floated boats and rafts laden with people, and here and there, the lone swimmer was striving to make land. All around the rafts and swimmers were dismembered limbs, dead fish and wreckage, drifting with the currents; below, in all probability, were sharks; and above, at intervals, the winged machines of death ... It was a ghastly tragedy, a catastrophe beyond measure.'

Chapter 6

Changi and the Thai/Burma Railway

A mighty Island Fortress, the guardian of the East
An up to date Gibraltar, a thousand planes at least
It simply can't be taken twill stand a siege for years
We can hold the place forever, and bring our foe to tears
Our men are there in million. The defences are unique
But the Japs did not believe you, so they took it in a week.

(written by an anonymous British soldier,
see www.themargins.net/anth/1940/anon)

For the remaining men of the 2 East Surreys, their war was over. A deathly quiet hung over Singapore and the smell of defeat and utter desolation was everywhere. The sight of a Japanese flag flying over Fort Canning was demoralizing for the defeated troops. For weeks, my father and his colleagues had lived with the deafening crash of gunfire, along with the sight and sounds of a battle for their lives, but now they were prisoners of war.

The streets of Singapore city were thronged with troops. Most were still fully armed, whilst others had almost no possessions other than the clothes they stood up in. The roads were choked with vehicles of all types: hundreds of private cars abandoned by their owners lined the roadsides, many broken beyond repair from the Japanese bombardment. Bombed-out buildings were still on fire, whilst the Singapore Fire Brigade stood helplessly by. The water supply had been cut and they had no water for their hoses.

General Yamashita ordered his troops to keep out of the city, fearful that they would run amok, but many of his men chose to disobey this order and began to seize the spoils of victory. Tired and hungry, they entered houses and grabbed food, clothes and souvenirs. Some paid for what they took, but others simply took what they wanted. The Japanese severely punished the local population for looting, but in most cases turned a blind eye to the looting of their own troops. Drunk on victory, many of the Japanese soldiers took any women they could find.

Low and Cheng wrote in 1946 in *This Singapore: Our City of Dreadful Night*:

'The raping varied in intensity. Some localities suffered more some less. As was natural, it varied also according to the characters of individual soldiers. Some did it sadistically and brutally, booted and belted as they were, the Knights of Japan, without fear and without reproach; some did it indifferently as men answering mere calls of nature; some shame-facedly, mindful perhaps of the mothers who had borne them and the wives who were suckling their young in Japan. Their victims steeled themselves to accept the inevitable in as seemly a manner as their philosophy and good sense dictated. It would have been foolish to shout their disgrace from the house tops.'

Lieutenant Colonel Morrison addressed the remnants of the British Battalion in sober tones as they waited on Mount Echo for final instructions:

'No matter what the degradation the Japs may inflict on you while we remain prisoners, remember that this day, in being compelled to lay down your arms, you have suffered the greatest humiliation possible for a British soldier. I can only hazard a guess as to how the Japs will treat us, but that there will be many unpleasant incidents is inevitable. Already there have been some in Singapore, officers and men have been compelled to kneel in the streets and perform other acts of humiliation. Naturally you will want to react in the normal manner should any Jap soldier molest you. Take my advice and do not retaliate. I realise that may be difficult for you, but retaliation will only make our unhappy situation worse.'

After he had finished speaking, the men sat smoking their cigarettes in silent contemplation on what was to befall them in the coming days, weeks and months.

The officers had taken over a house near the golf course, whilst the men made themselves as comfortable as possible in the various deserted buildings in the area as they waited for final instructions. Their wait did not last long, as two days later, on 18 February, they were ordered by the Japanese to march to Changi, some 22 miles away in the north-east corner of the island. Two lorries, loaded with food and water, under the command of Captain Barnard, were to accompany the men on the march. Barnard was assisted by his loyal and trusty batman Lance Corporal F. Blake, who was to drown two-and-a-half years later when the *Hofuko Maru* carrying him to Japan was sunk in the South China Sea.

The mentally and physically exhausted men of the 2 Surreys set off in sweltering heat, fully loaded, carrying as much kit as they were able. Moving off in good order at 1700 hrs to what many thought would be the end of their lives, they passed scenes of utter destruction and chaos. Wrecked houses and burnt-out buildings lined the streets, and dead bodies lay everywhere. Shops and cafés were boarded up, black smoke from the oil installation drifted overhead and Singapore was completely devastated. Japanese soldiers drove around wildly in stolen cars, grinning at the troops; some even demanded watches from the weary Allied soldiers. Japanese flags flew from many of the buildings as the local population tried to ingratiate themselves with their new masters. All watches and clocks in Singapore had to be put forward by one-and-a-half hours to tie in with Tokyo time, and the island was renamed Synonan.

The Chinese and Malay population lined the roads to watch the defeated troops pass by in silence. Mile after mile, the weary column of troops stretched along the roads towards Changi, each man immersed in his own thoughts about the future.

Corporal John Wyatt recalled the march to Changi:

'Refusal to hand over your possessions almost certainly meant a stab from a bayonet or a blow from a rifle butt. It seemed to be the end of the line for the British military in the Far East.'

Captain Barnard also recalls his drive into imprisonment in Changi:

'As we drove into the magnificent strip of country known as Changi, bounded on two sides by the sea, we saw the devastation that the Japanese bombers had caused. Many of the palatial barracks and officers' messes scattered all over this large area had been hit, and many buildings were in ruins.'

Lieutenant Stephen Abbott was still very angry about the surrender. He wrote:

'As the long columns of prisoners marched by, we were greeted only by pitiful looks and silence. Here and there a Chinese would raise his thumbs with a faint smile and an understanding wink; but suffering, and the fear of greater suffering were too deep in the hearts of these people to allow them a show of friendliness or loyalty. Who could blame them? Who had assured them of their safety within this "fortress"[?] Like most of my [fellow] prisoners I felt a terrible weight of personal guilt. The disgrace of the Malayan campaign could never be exonerated or forgiven.'

As darkness descended on the eighteenth, the 2 Surreys spent the night sleeping by the roadside; at dawn the next morning they continued their demoralizing journey. Along the way they managed to round up twenty stray goats, the Japanese guards looking on in amusement as the men drove the goats into Changi. The goats were to prove useful in supplementing their rations over the following few weeks. On arrival, the 2 Surrey contingent was quartered in 'coolie' lines, their baggage arriving with Captain Barnard's motor transport later that day.

Changi prisoner of war camp should not be confused with Changi jail, where many of Singapore's expatriate civilian population were held by the Japanese. The military prisoner of war camp, covering a large area of over 6 square miles at the eastern tip of Singapore island, was to be home for around 53,000 men in barracks designed to house only 4,000.

For the past ten weeks, my father and his colleagues had been trying to kill the Japanese, whilst trying to stay alive themselves. Now they had to come to terms with the fact that this 'live or die' situation was out of their hands; their fate lay with the conquerors. They had no way of knowing how long it would be before they would see their families again, and could not even let them know that they were alive. Rumours and counter-rumours spread around Changi. Many thought that they would be prisoners for quite some time, whilst others were convinced that with the Americans now in the war, it would only be a matter of months before the Japanese were overrun.

The 2 Surrey men had no clear idea why they had been posted to Malaya in the first place: thousands of miles away from a war in Europe that was already more than two years old, away from their families under threat of a German invasion and where night after night their homes were being bombed. The sense of impotence and frustration in Changi camp was palpable. The Japanese had produced a pamphlet for their men, explaining the reasons for their invasion of Malaya and Singapore, but no-one had thought of providing a similar one for the Allied troops.

The 2 Surreys were billeted in Tamil huts facing the main road. Despite the overcrowding and a shortage of food, conditions in the camp were reasonably good. Changi was a haven of peace to the exhausted prisoners and as initially there were no Japanese guards, the men being left to look after themselves. As my father said:

> 'In many ways, it didn't feel like a prison camp at all as we could move around freely within the perimeter. Our officers ran the camp in an organized military way and tried to make our lives as comfortable as possible.'

Accepting their imprisonment with stoicism, the 2 Surreys set about making their camp as comfortable as possible. Boreholes were dug for water and sanitation, and the men made the best of it during those early weeks of captivity. Anyone not knowing the truth might have mistaken Changi for a holiday camp, as the men frolicked in the sea from dawn to dusk. Army discipline was still very much in evidence, however. Officers were saluted at all times, and anyone breaking the rules was given extra duties or a day or two in solitary confinement – in effect being doubly locked up.

Lieutenant General Percival advised all prisoners in Changi that it was their duty to try to escape, but warned them that they must prepare thoroughly before any attempt, to ensure that they had a reasonable chance.

Most of them were aware that their chances of escape were slim, and that recapture was likely to mean heavy punishment or death.

During the first few weeks of the Japanese occupation, wounded men who had been in the Singapore hospitals were transferred to the ex-military hospital in Changi. Many had been very badly wounded and quite a few died during those early weeks of captivity, mainly due to a lack of medical equipment and supplies. The Japanese left the military medical staff to look after the injured men with little or no resources and the doctors did everything in their power to save the lives of the badly wounded and ill men. Had the Japanese provided even some of the basic equipment and drugs that were still available in the various hospitals in Singapore, many of those who died might well have survived. During the first three months of captivity in Changi, five 2 Surrey men died from their wounds or illness.

The victors were surprised at the vast number of Allied prisoners they now had on their hands. On Singapore island alone there were around 28,000 British, 18,000 Australian, 67,000 Indian and 14,000 local volunteers. Never in any previous conflict had so many British and Commonwealth soldiers surrendered to invading forces. It is not known exactly how many were taken prisoner, but it is estimated that the number was likely to have been near 200,000.

Colonel Swinton did his best to keep the surviving East Surreys together. The Japanese had other ideas, however, as they deliberately began to break up regiments and separate the men from their officers. They worked on the theory that by breaking up regiments, prisoners were less likely to become an organized threat.

Whilst quite content to let the officers run the camp with minimal interference, they made it clear that any man trying to escape would be shot. Of course, this was totally against the Geneva Convention of 1929, which the Japanese had signed but did not ratify. They had agreed to abide by its terms, but this promise was never carried out.

After 15 February, escape from Singapore proved difficult in the extreme as the Japanese Navy ruled the surrounding seas, their air force was in control of the skies and the nearest friendly peoples were more than 1,500 miles away. Such difficulties, however, did not deter some of the 2 Surreys, and one of the first to try was Bandsman Arnold from Dagenham. Arnold managed to get into Singapore city, where he stayed with a Thai girl that he knew before meeting up with Andrew Moir of the Gordons and Sergeant Doran of the Royal Army Medical Corps. The trio then met up with a Chinese man who said that he could get them a passage on a junk to one of the many small islands. They hired a taxi to take them to the harbour, but on the way were stopped by a Japanese patrol in plain clothes. The four men were taken to an interrogation centre, where they were kept in solitary confinement for fourteen days. There they were beaten up regularly but not executed, and eventually permitted to return to Changi.

After spending seven months in Changi, Private Harold Waters of the East Surreys, along with Victor Gale and Corporal Brevington of the AIF and Private Eric Fletcher of the RASC, attempted to escape. They were quickly recaptured and locked up in solitary confinement in Changi prison.

By the end of August 1942, the Japanese were becoming so concerned about the number of PoWs who were attempting to escape that Lieutenant General Fukuei Shimpei, the new commander of prisoners, demanded that the men should sign a document undertaking not to escape. It read:

'I the undersigned do hereby declare that on my honour I will not, under any circumstances, attempt to escape.'

Almost everyone in Changi refused to sign. On 2 September Shimpei ordered all the prisoners to march to Selerang Barracks in Singapore city. Built to house 800 men and the home of the Gordon Highlanders before the hostilities, the barracks were now crammed with over 17,000 men. The Japanese reduced the water supply, leaving only one tap for drinking water and none at all for the toilets. Dysentery soon broke out and living conditions were dreadful, but the men still refused to sign the document.

Captain Barnard wrote about the conditions in Selerang at the time:

'By the evening, life began to become very uncomfortable indeed. The small building was packed, including the roof, and it was practically impossible to move. The parade ground outside was black with men who could find nowhere to lie down. The doctors had ordered latrines to be dug, and in view of the small area available these were placed right across the parade ground. The question of cooking meals for these thousands of men with one tiny cookhouse appeared to be unanswerable. To make matters worse we had dysentery cases with us, and, of course no hospital. By the morning it really was a shambles. No one quite knew how it would end, except that we were in for a first-class epidemic if it continued for any length of time.'

Doctor Frank Pantridge of the Gordon Highlanders writes about conditions in Selerang in his book *An Unquiet Life*:

'Each block had 1,800 men. Troops jammed like sardines on every floor, on the flat roof of every block and on the stairs and verandahs. It was not possible to lie down. The Japs turned off the water supply to the blocks. Round the whole area was a barbed wire fence manned by sentries.

'Makeshift latrines were dug in the tarmac square, but these could not be reached by those incarcerated in the blocks. Dysentery was rife and the place stank. Diphtheria and septic skin diseases were common.'

With the prisoners still refusing to sign the non-escape clause, Shimpei decided that an example should be set, and Waters of the 2 Surreys, Gale, Brevington and Fletcher, still languishing in Changi jail, were sentenced to death.

Major Francis Magee, Deputy Assistant Adjutant General in the camp, was handed a note by an Indian driver with the names of the four men on it. Colonel E.B. Holmes, commanding British and Australian troops at Changi, protested vehemently and, along with Magee, drew up a plea for leniency, which read as follows:

'I have the honour to submit this earnest appeal for your reconsideration of the infliction of the supreme penalty of four prisoners of war who have been apprehended attempting to escape from this camp. I am aware that it has been made perfectly clear by you that any such attempt will incur the penalty of death and furthermore, there is no mis-apprehension on the part of the prisoners themselves that this is so. I will however take immediate steps again to impress on all ranks in this camp the inevitable outcome of any attempt to escape and would be that in the present instance you will exercise your clemency by the infliction of a less severe punishment than that of execution.'

The plea was delivered by Captain Jones of 122 Field Regiment, Royal Artillery, whose account of handing over the document is as follows:

'I arrived at the gaol soon after 12 noon and the first person I saw was a Japanese interpreter. I explained my mission and stressed the fact that the plea for clemency was to be handed to the General. He wanted to take the papers – I refused to hand them over. Then [he] brought a Japanese officer whose rank I could not make out as he had no insignia. I handed the paper to him. He appeared to know English. He read the plea for clemency, became very angry, tore it up in pieces and threw them in my face. He then picked them up and stuffed them in my waist band. I then returned to camp and reported to Major Magee.'

At midday on 2 September, the four men were driven in a truck to Changi beach. Waters, still in his pyjamas, was in such a bad state from severe beatings that he could not walk or stand upright. Brevington was so weak from starvation and beri-beri that he had to walk with a stick.

Four graves had been dug and the firing party, made up of Sikh soldiers who had defected to the Japanese, lined up facing them. British and Australian officers pleaded for the men to be spared, but Shimpei was adamant they were to be shot. A padre said prayers for the condemned men, and each was given a cigarette before being lined up in front of the graves about ten paces from the execution squad. The officers saluted the men, who bravely returned it before being offered blindfolds: all four refused. By now it was around 1600 hrs, and Lieutenant Okusaki, in charge of the execution, ordered the squad to open fire. The four men were still alive after the first volley of shots, screaming out in agony, before they were finally finished off with a second volley. Private Waters, from Birmingham, was the first 2 Surrey man to die as a prisoner of war. He is buried in Kranji war cemetery, Singapore.

Okusaki turned to the Allied officers witnessing the execution and said via his interpreter:

'You have witnessed four men put to death [two Australian and two British]. They tried to escape against Japanese orders. It is impossible for anyone to escape as the great Nipponese are in all countries to the south and anyone escaping from here must be caught. They will be brought back here and put to death. You officers are responsible for the men under your command and you will again tell them not to go outside the wire. If they do, they will be put to death as you have just seen. We do not like to put them to death.'

Bugler Arthur Lane of the Manchester Regiment, who had been the official bugler in Changi since the capitulation, was called upon to play the 'Last Post' at the execution of the four men. I had the good fortune to visit Arthur regularly at his home near me in Stockport, before his death in 2017. He could still vividly recall that fateful day when the group were executed on Changi beach:

'When we arrived at the scene a large group of Japanese soldiers were already waiting for the carnival to commence. A truck arrived from Changi prison. The back was dropped down and the prisoners were ordered to get down. One of the prisoners [Waters] was wearing his pyjamas, having been brought from the hospital. He could not walk or even stand on his own, so he was assisted by the Padre and one of the officers. The prisoners' names and army details were read out parrot fashion.

'The three able men were taken to a position where five pieces of wood were protruding from the ground. Each one was placed in position in front of each pole and secured by rope. The fourth man (Waters) was carried to sit upright. There was a preamble in Japanese read out loud, which I believe was the sentence of death issued by the Japanese court, this followed by two Japanese officers performing some form of salute using swords. There was a great deal of muttering coming from the English-speaking witnesses, with Colonel Wild stating that the men had not received a fair trial. Whilst this was going on, ten Japanese soldiers [the defecting Sikhs] were marched in line facing the prisoners. A Japanese officer shouted orders at which the ten soldiers lifted their rifles to the firing position. On the order to fire they opened up and all three men slumped forward to meet their maker. Our own officers started shouting and swearing at the Japanese, who at gunpoint then ordered them to fall back. The Padre started to pray for the men and I was ordered to sound the 'Last Post'. I could not do it justice as I was so upset from what I had seen. I was trying not to show my tears and after a feeble attempt at the 'Last Post' the colonel ordered me to follow him. After the war, Lieutenant Okusaki, the officer in charge of the execution, was captured by a group of Australian soldiers who took him back to Changi beach and, without trial, executed him in retribution.'

This was only one of many times that Arthur Lane was to perform the 'Last Post' during his three-and-a-half years of captivity, and the first execution of a 2 Surrey man.

Captain John Barnard of the 2 Surreys also remembers this incident with Private Waters, and relates it in his book *The Endless Years*:

'We had a private soldier who tried to escape the other week which caused a lot of bother. The nips had us out for a roll call in the middle of the night, and generally caused a great deal of trouble. He was recaptured a few days later and badly beaten up and finally shot.'

Back at Selerang, the officers were by now only too aware of the consequences of a very serious epidemic breaking out and the implications for the 17,000 men cooped up like battery hens. Colonel Holmes, the highest-ranking officer there, had no option but to order the men to sign the non-escape document. He told the men:

'I am fully convinced that his Majesty's Government only expect prisoners of war not to give their parole when such parole is to be given voluntarily. This factor can in no circumstances be regarded as applicable to our present conditions; the responsibility for this decision rests with me, and me alone, and I fully accept it in ordering you to sign.'

On 5 September, the prisoners, to their great relief, were released from Selerang and allowed to return to their camps around Singapore.

Lieutenant General Fukuei Shimpei was tried by the War Crimes Commission at the end of the war, found guilty and sentenced to ten years' imprisonment.

Many men of the Indian Army, mainly Sikhs who had defected, were used by the Japanese to guard the prisoners in Changi. Over 67,000 Indian troops were taken prisoner, and quite a number were persuaded to defect by an Indian national leader called Subhas Chandra Bose, who had been campaigning for an India free from British rule for some years. Some who defected had hoped that they would be posted north to Burma, from where they might have a chance to cross over to the Allies again, whilst others believed that the Japanese would win the war and free India from British rule.

With Singapore now in ruins, the Japanese quickly realized that they had a ready-made and well-disciplined workforce available to clean up the city. Within weeks, prisoners were taken in groups to clear and rebuild the bombed-out buildings, clear minefields, carry out bomb disposals, dispose of bodies and even help to build a Japanese victory shrine.

Many groups of 2 Surrey men were sent into the city on such working parties. Whilst the work was hard, these parties proved popular as they warded off boredom and allowed them the opportunity to loot food from the various godowns (warehouses) around the docks.

Some men on these early working parties had the misfortune to witness some of the worst atrocities carried out by the Japanese invading forces. They observed first-hand some of the dreadful massacres of the Chinese population by Japanese soldiers who seemed to have only one thing on their minds in Singapore, to exterminate the entire Chinese population. Reliable estimates put the final number of Chinese killed by the Japanese at between 9,000 and 12,000.

After being rounded up and interrogated by the Kempeitai (the dreaded Japanese military police), the Chinese were obliged to hand over all their personal possessions – rings, watches, jewellery, money etc. – before being forced on to captured British lorries and driven to the Tanjong Pagar Wharf or Changi beach. There they were beheaded, bayoneted or machine-gunned. Others were roped together and taken on barges out to sea, where they were thrown overboard. The slaughter continued for twelve days.

As March turned into April and the weeks dragged on, food in Changi became even more scarce for the prisoners. The mainly rice diet began to take its toll, with many spending a good few 'unhappy hours' in the latrines with diarrhoea, constipation or dysentery. Vitamin deficiency was also to become a major problem, causing many to become ill. Gardens were dug, but with a shortage of water and so many mouths to feed, the meagre vegetables that did survive did not go far. My father told me:

> 'We were now living on a rice diet and very little else. Everyone was beginning to feel the lack of vitamins and I was losing weight rapidly.'

(My father weighed only 6 stones when he was released in August 1945.)

Many of the men in Changi soon began to die from tropical diseases or malnutrition. More than 400 died during the first seven months of captivity, some from their wounds suffered during the fighting and others from diseases like dysentery, beri-beri and diphtheria. The medical officers did their utmost to keep the men alive, but with a scarcity of medicines they were fighting an uphill battle. To try to combat the lack of vitamins in their diets, they came up with the idea of making a vitamin B drink where coarse ground rice, sugar, salt, ground peanuts and yeast were mixed together in large beer bottles and left to ferment. Such a concoction probably saved the lives of many of the men.

The prisoners quickly realized that their captors strictly enforced a regime of corporal punishment. In the Japanese military hierarchy, corporal punishment was handed down through the ranks, and of course the prisoners suffered as they were deemed to be the lowest of the low. An Allied officer was likely to be physically assaulted by even the lowest private in the Japanese Army.

A favourite spot for some of the men was a hill overlooking Singapore harbour. It was a place where they could get away from camp life and be alone with their thoughts. Corporal John Wyatt remembers sitting on that hill in April 1942, a month into his captivity:

'I watched the Japanese Fleet putting to sea. Battleships, cruisers, destroyers, aircraft carriers and supply ships cruised out of the anchorage whilst hundreds of aircraft flew overhead. They looked invincible as they went endlessly past. It was rumoured that we were losing the war in Europe, London was still being heavily bombed, most of the Far East had fallen, and the situation was looking bleak for the British Empire. I felt desperately lonely and yearned to see my parents again. But I was overwhelmed with this dreadful feeling that I would never get back to them or to my beloved Sydenham. London seemed like a million miles away. To make matters worse I had dysentery and my ankles were beginning to swell from the effects of beri-beri.'

One of the few advantages of Changi was that it was right next to the sea where the men could go swimming every day to get some relief from the heat and to wash their sweaty bodies. It was a hammer blow when, in late 1942, the Japanese put the beaches out of bounds. Despite vigorous protests from the officers, anyone caught swimming was severely punished. No reason was given for such an order, but it was assumed that they did not like prisoners of war having fun.

To alleviate the boredom, other activities were quickly arranged, including a variety of sports and entertainment. Changi already had an open-air cinema, which was soon turned into a theatre. A group of men with experience of the stage back in the United Kingdom put on many excellent productions in the Changi 'Palladium'. Private Wally Lord of the 2 Surreys, a sign writer and scenery painter by trade, got together a concert party called the 'Southern Area Concert Party'. The SACP concerts proved very popular before they had to close when men were sent to work up on the Thai/Burma railway.

Religious services held by the various padres were always well attended as many men held strong religious beliefs. Holy Communion was regularly conducted, with fermented wine made from berries collected from trees, or 'chateau Changi' as it was labelled by the men.

Changi village had a well-stocked library, where a ready supply of books were available. The school and garage was also used by Captain Barnard, the Battalion Motor Transport officer, who organized lectures and discussions on motor vehicle maintenance.

Along with the rest of the surviving 2 Surreys, my father sat around in Changi for eight months, with only boredom and lack of food as his companions. 'We were permanently hungry and always scrounging for food,' he told me. They were so hungry that some men even took the risk of going out through the wire that surrounded the camp to look for extra food.

Corporal John Wyatt takes up the story of the search for food:

'Regimental Sergeant Major Camp managed to keep most of the Surreys together and I was billeted in a small hut with Spike Shaw and Tommy Marshall. We were permanently hungry and always scrounging for food. One evening Spike and Tom decided to go outside the wire and try to get something to eat.

"Are you coming John?" said Spike.

"I don't think I'll bother, Spike, I don't feel too well," I said.

'Tom and Spike left the hut and I settled down on my bed space to try and get some rest. No sooner had I closed my eyes than I heard a loud bang and moments later Tom came running in shaking like a leaf and crying.

"What happened Tom?" I said.

"The Sikh guards have shot Spike and I think he's dead," he spluttered.

'It would have been dangerous for us to go back to check on him as we would have been associated with an escape attempt, so we settled down for the night. I got very little sleep that night knowing my mate was probably dead.'

Shaw was indeed shot by the guards that night and is buried in Krangi war cemetery.

Rumours began circulating around Changi from as early as April 1942 that the Japanese were planning to send the prisoners to Thailand to help build a railway. Radios had been banned after the surrender, but with several clandestine sets operating in Changi the men were aware that the Japanese had now taken Rangoon, the capital of Burma, and were pushing towards India. With such a swift advance, they were looking at other ways of resupplying their troops on the Burma front rather than the dangerous journey by sea to Rangoon via the Straits of Malacca. The US Navy was posing a huge threat to Japanese shipping in the seas around Singapore and a new overland supply route was imperative.

The only safe and logical route for the Japanese to supply their Burma front line was overland from Bangkok to Rangoon. The road network between the two cities was poor, with the only existing rail link a 40-mile stretch of track running from Bangkok to a small town in Thailand called Bam Pong. Their only option was to build a railway that would link Bam Pong with the Burmese town of Thanbyuzayat some 250 miles to the north-west.

It has been reported that such a rail link had been considered by the British many years earlier, but was deemed just about impossible due to the difficulty of the terrain. Low-lying plains to the south, high mountains up to 5,000ft high and miles of dense tropical jungle made its construction very difficult. The foremost authority on the Thai/Burma Railway, Rod Beattie, Director of the Death Railway Centre in Kanchanaburi, is sceptical about such claims, asserting:

'Years of research by a number of people have failed to locate any evidence of British plans for a railway along the River Kwai and through the Three Pagoda Pass into Burma.'

With all of Malaya now in their hands and a puppet Thai government under their control, the Japanese decided to push ahead with this project, regardless of the potential for human tragedy. By March 1942 they had 137,000 'disposable' labourers on their hands, and from as early as April, groups of Allied PoWs began to leave Changi on a regular basis for Thailand as the Japanese started to build this 'impossible' railway.

Work was planned to start in June of that year, with a scheduled completion date of October 1943. This date was brought forward to May when the

Japanese Navy was defeated at the Battle of Midway when four of their aircraft carriers were sunk. This left them no longer able to defend their merchant shipping effectively in the seas linking Japan with her conquered territories.

Although the Japanese had signed the Geneva Convention in 1929, they had never ratified it. Its terms stated that prisoners of war were not to be used on dangerous tasks or on those helping the captors' war efforts. The Japanese, however, rode roughshod over the Convention, under the premise that any soldier surrendering had forfeited all his rights, using them on any tasks that might help their war effort.

It was six months into their captivity before the men were allowed to send postcards home informing their loved ones that they were still alive. Once again, the Japanese simply ignored the Geneva Convention that clearly set out rules for the sending of information back to their native country. Captain Barnard wrote:

'We had a pleasant surprise today when the Nips issued us with a printed postcard to send home to England. This really was a surprise, and although the postcard was of the usual army type, "I am ill or I am not ill", it would at least allow our people in England to know we are still alive.'

What he did not know at the time was that many of these postcards took at least a year to reach their destination.

When it was first announced to the men in Changi that they were to be transported to Thailand to work on the construction of the railway, many were excited by the prospect. The Japanese, through their interpreters, had painted a rosy picture of excellent living and working conditions in Thailand, with plentiful supplies of food, excellent medical facilities and all the prisoners being well cared for. They promised:

'The climate of the new location would be similar to that of Singapore, the men would be distributed around seven camps, all would be in pleasant and healthy surroundings, sufficient medical personnel to staff a 300 bed hospital could be sent, as many blankets and mosquito nets as possible were to be taken, a band could accompany each group of 1,000 men, canteens would be established within three weeks of arrival, no restriction would be placed on the amount of personal gear taken, tools and cooking gear were to be taken and transport would be available to take heavy goods and there would be no long marches.'

Many of the prisoners believed these false promises and were happy to get away from the boredom of the crowded Changi camp.

The first batch of 2 Surrey men left Singapore by train in April 1942. The journey through Malaya for this first group was pleasant, the guards were friendly and they found the conditions and food better in Thailand than at Changi. A second group of around forty-three 2 Surreys, with Captain Vickers and 2nd Lieutenant League as the senior officers, left Singapore two months later on 22 June. They were in a party of 3,000 prisoners whose main task was to prepare for the arrival of the main body of men due in October when the monsoon season ended. It was these 3,000 men who first experienced the terrible conditions both on the trains and in the camps for the thousands of men who were to follow.

As Abbott's group packed up their meagre belongings and set off in lorries for Singapore railway station, the harsh reality of the move began to dawn on them. Any thoughts of a pleasant journey through Malaya by train were quickly dispelled by the sight that greeted them as they jumped down at the station.

The trains that were to transport them 1,100 miles were made up of a series of metal cattle trucks around 20ft long, 7ft wide and 8ft in height. There was only one entrance to each truck, a central sliding door about 6ft wide. Thirty men, along with their kit, were crammed into each truck, leaving each one only about 5 square feet. It took some time to get organized, and the only way they could make themselves comfortable was by sitting on top of their kit. Lying down was almost impossible. Stops were only made when the trains needed fuel and water, and the men had to use the nearest piece of ground to relieve themselves, often in full view of the local people. They had to make a quick dash for the water towers along the line to fill their water bottles and try to wash away the ingrained dirt on their bodies.

The only food they had to eat were the cooked rice balls given to them at Singapore station.

After crossing into Thailand, the trains eventually arrived at Ban Pong station. It was a journey of 1,100 miles lasting over forty hours in a train that was described by the men as 'simply hell on earth'.

At Ban Pong, the groups of prisoners were loaded into trucks and driven a short distance to a large open space, where they were ordered to form up for inspection. A Japanese general inspected the ranks of tired, hungry and thirsty men before they were dismissed to their huts.

Ban Pong camp was aptly named as it was a hell hole. It stank to high heaven, especially during the monsoon season when the rains fell in torrents. Rain clouds hung low in the jungle, and it felt to the men that they could reach up and touch them. The whole camp was a huge morass of mud. Bugs and insects of all shapes and sizes crawled over their bed spaces, making conditions almost intolerable.

Parties arriving outside the monsoon season found the temperatures soaring and the ground baked solid by a sun that beat down relentlessly.

Recalling his journey from Singapore, John Wyatt, who travelled there the following year in June 1943, said:

'Dysentery cases weren't allowed off often enough, there was excrement everywhere and men simply wallowed in their own and other people's shit and piss for four days and nights. It was baking hot during the day and bitterly cold by night and dysentery had by now got a grip on many of the men.'

The huts at Ban Pong were built of bamboo, with attap roofs, where the men would bed down for the night on flattened bamboo slats. The floors were often just a sea of mud and maggots or simply hard baked earth, depending on the season. Cockroaches, ants and spiders crawled out from the cesspits that were used as latrines. Large bluebottles hummed and buzzed everywhere – a fertile breeding ground for diseases of all kinds.

Camps were built along the proposed route of the railway at regular intervals, with the distance between them varying depending on the difficulty of the work. On the flat plains the camps were about 4 miles apart, whilst in the mountains they were much closer together and in many cases were built along the river bank to allow supplies to be delivered by barges.

On the night of 11 July 1942, three men, including 2 Surrey Corporal E. Armstrong, attempted to escape from Ban Pong camp. They had managed to steal some canned food and still had a compass that Corporal Smart of the Leicesters had managed to secrete away along with several maps. They also had almost 2,000 Malayan dollars given to Smart by a wealthy Chinese businessman he had befriended in Penang during the retreat to Singapore. He had managed to conceal the cash from the Japanese for four months.

For several nights before their escape attempt, the three men watched the guards' movements. On the chosen night, they placed boards up against the wire, climbed over and made their way through the railway sidings into the jungle. Corporal Smart said in his statement after the war:

'We travelled almost continuously for a year, during which time we lived almost entirely on what we could catch – snakes, jungle rats etc. We were able to get a little help at native settlements, but we usually tried to avoid them as it was difficult to assess their trustworthiness. During the march, the three of us kept reasonably fit except for Armstrong who had one or two bouts of malaria. Fortunately, we had a good supply of quinine. Armstrong spoke Chinese fluently and was able to use it to good effect on several occasions. From Ban Pong, we travelled to Chiang Kong about 450 miles north of Bangkok as the crow flies. We had just left one morning when looking down the trail, I saw a native whom I recognised as having been in the settlement some 20 miles away through which we had passed. I decided that he was following us so we set off more quickly in an attempt to shake him off. This went on for about 24 hours and finally believing that we had done this, we settled down for a rest and some food. On finishing this and standing up we were suddenly surrounded by a crowd of armed natives who detained us and sent for the Japanese. We were then moved to Bangkok by river and then back to Singapore where we were interrogated. The treatment meted out from the time of being captured to the moment of landing in gaol was a continual round of beatings and torture. After a formal trial, we were sentenced to 5 years solitary confinement in Outram Road Gaol Singapore.'

There is some doubt about Smart's account of this escape, as other reports state that the three men were only on the run for a few days. Had they been on the run for a year, they would undoubtedly have been executed. They would then have been captured after the signing of the non-escape document in September 1942 as outlined earlier. All three men survived their captivity and returned home.

Between 9-15 October 1942, another thirty 2 Surrey men – including Captain John Barnard, Major R. Chidson and my father – were transported to the railway from Singapore. Before leaving Changi, they were given only a few tins of food, a pair of boots and a hat from a Red Cross parcel that had been delivered the previous day.

According to my father, the journey into Thailand was a nightmare:

'At Kuala Lumpur we stopped for an hour or so and were given a meal of weak stew and rice and very little water and I dreaded getting back into that steel box. The main problem was not food but water and I was constantly thirsty.'

After Kuala Lumpur, the trains made their next stop at Prai, where the hungry and thirsty men were allowed to stretch their legs. Three small balls of rice and weak stew were provided before the train set off again through Alor Star and on into Thailand.

'It was a strange feeling to be travelling through the point in Malaya near Alor Star where we had all started almost a year earlier,' said my father.

These groups were relieved to arrive at Ban Pong station, but after a short march were dismayed to find their first camp almost completely under water. After travelling on a train for four days in dreadful conditions, the prisoners would now have to sleep and eat knee-deep in water. It was only a transit camp, they were told, and they would be leaving again in a couple of days.

Three days later, Chidson, Barnard, my father and the other 2 Surreys lined up with the rest of the 500 men in their party and set off marching towards the railway. They carried with them everything they could, including shorts, shirt, water bottle, side satchel, full pack, roll of bedding, mosquito net and all their cooking gear. As the day wore on, the men began to throw away what they considered unnecessary items of kit as the debilitating conditions took their toll. They had no idea how far they marched that first day, but Barnard estimated that it was around 15 miles. It was just after dark when the bedraggled group of men eventually reached their first transit camp. There they collapsed into the first available hut, which was little better than at Ban Pong, but at least they were able to wash themselves down from a hosepipe. 'One of the best showers I've ever had,' said Captain Barnard.

The next morning, many of the men were unable to get their boots on their swollen feet. The doctors complained to the Japanese that if they were made to march another 15 miles in the sweltering heat, many would not survive. The only concession the Japanese officer in charge made was to transport the men's packs on lorries. The group set off again not long after sunrise, but after just a few hours, and with the sun blazing down, several men passed out and had to be left by the roadside, despite the kicking and swearing of the Japanese guards. By lunchtime, the column had straggled out to over 3 miles. It was 1900 hrs before they eventually staggered into Kanchanaburi camp after marching for around 12 hours. Out of the 500 men who had started the march, one died and seven were taken straight into hospital seriously ill. Over 200 had feet so swollen and blistered that further walking was impossible. They had covered around 35 miles over two days in sweltering temperatures, with little food or water. After frantic appeals by the British officers, the Japanese reluctantly agreed that they could have one day's rest in Kanchanaburi before the next stage of the march north.

Whilst the day's rest was most welcome, many of the men were still suffering when they formed up again just after dawn and marched out of the camp along a metalled road. Soon the metalled roads ended and they began to cross rice fields into almost virgin jungle, where muddy paths made progress difficult.

For the next five days, the party slogged on for more than 60 miles along the proposed route of the railway before eventually reaching a camp called Kinsaiyok. Fortunately, the last section into the camp was made by boat up the river, allowing them a short rest on the decks. Being so far away from civilization, the prisoners' main concern now was whether the Japanese had made provision to get supplies to them. It seemed that advance planning was non-existent and little provision had been made for food drops; it was usually a case of someone going on ahead and dropping off a few bags of rice and dried vegetables.

As the construction of the railway got under way conditions varied from camp to camp, but food was still scarce and men were dying of malnutrition on a daily basis. The Japanese would never admit to this though, always insisting that the cause of death written on death certificates was malaria or cholera.

From 22-25 October, the main body of almost 190 2 Surreys left Singapore as part of a group of 17,600 prisoners, bound for the railway. Sixteen officers were in this group, headed by Majors O'Neil Wallis and Orme, and crucially included battalion padre Captain Babb. Two weeks later, on 6 November, a small group of twelve 2 Surrey men left Changi, including their commanding officer, Lieutenant Colonel Swinton, the last group of prisoners to leave in 1942.

By March 1943, over 260 men had died, and with work considerably behind schedule, the Japanese now called for greater effort from the malnourished prisoners. More than 5,000 more men were transported up to join those already there, including 154 more 2 Surrey men. By April 1943, the Japanese had instigated what was called the 'speedo' phase, to try to ensure that the railway was finished on schedule. Work was expanded into the overnight period, with the prisoners working in two shifts; even sick men were dragged out of their beds to work, many of them dying during this time. The real tragedy of the railway now began to unfold.

In Tha Sao camp on 9 April 1943, Private J. Hunt of 2 Surrey died of dysentery and blackwater fever (a complication of malaria). Captain John Barnard discovered the young man one night after dark as he was walking across the camp, and wrote:

'I thought I saw a dark object by the side of the path. I bent down and found that it was a youngster who had been ill for some time, lying face downwards in the mud. He was only just over five feet high, and even in pre-war days was very slight, but now after weeks of sickness he was more like a little boy.

'I picked him up and carried him to the tents, and sent for Doc, but there was little we could do. Repeated attacks of dysentery and innumerable bouts of malaria had now been followed by blackwater fever, and although he had fought his way through a series of illnesses that would have knocked out many a stronger body than his, there is a limit to what the human frame can stand, and he died yesterday evening. His death threw a gloom over everyone in the camp as he was very popular. We buried him the same evening by the light of a bonfire, with Major Chidson reading a short service by the light of a flickering candle.'

At the end of April 1943, a group of 7,000 men, known as F force, arrived at Ban Pong, a group that was to suffer more than any other sent to work on the railway.

The railway had now been completed as far as Wang Yai and there was no reason why this group should not have been transported by train to there, but they were not. They were made to walk to their camps near the Burmese border, a trek of around 200 miles that took seventeen days. Fortunately, the journey was done at night when it was cooler than the average 38°C during the day. Many of the men were not able to complete the march, dropping out at camps along the way, whilst others died and were left behind on the jungle tracks.

Almost 400 of the surviving 2 Surreys were now in Thailand slaving for their Japanese captors on a railway that would soon be known as the 'death railway'.

The most important facility in each camp was the latrine. In the larger camps it was necessary to site them close to the huts so that the men suffering from dysentery and other digestive illnesses could reach them easily. This was often counter-productive, however, as they attracted flies, bluebottles and other insects close to the living quarters. The latrines were usually simple: a trench with bamboo poles laid across it for the men to squat on. As most of the camps were situated near the river, during the monsoon season the water levels would rise, often polluting the whole area. The other big problem the prisoners encountered was the disposal of waste. In one camp, the men came up with the idea of burying their waste in some caves nearby, but when the rains came it was washed back down into the river, contaminating it.

Several 2 Surrey men wrote about their time labouring for the Japanese in the debilitating conditions of the railway. Corporal John Wyatt wrote in his book *No Mercy from the Japanese*:

'A few weeks later we were marched the seventeen miles or so to a camp called Tha Makhan. The monsoon season was now well under way and the water poured down from the high ground above the camp, flooding our tents. It brought with it all the dead cats, rats and rotting garbage thrown into the river upstream by the natives. This made the camp a fertile environment for the propagation of the disease we all feared: 'cholera'. The guards were terrified of catching this fatal disease and left us alone, staying at least half a mile away. They wore masks on their faces and left us to bury our own dead comrades. We had no medicines and the only thing that Dr Roy had to treat the disease was his 'saline solution'. He constantly stressed the importance of good hygiene:

'"Before you eat, you must dip your spoons into the saline solution, and don't forget – your lives depend on it."

'I saw one Medical orderly wipe a cholera victim down, forget to wash his hands and smoke a cigarette – he was dead within forty-eight hours.

'Cholera spread through the Camp like wildfire. Someone in the bed next to you would be alive when you went out on a 'Speedo' work detail in the morning and by the end of the shift, his bed space would be empty. At this camp, my comrades were dying at the rate of ten a day and the Japanese instructed us to dig deep pits to bury the bodies. One morning Doctor Roy asked for four volunteers to bury some bodies, so Mick and I, along with two others, put up our hands. We walked about half a mile to a deep pit where five bodies lay wrapped in rice sacks with ropes tied around their ankles, stomachs and necks. We hurriedly lowered the first four bodies on ropes into the pit and as we began to lower the last one in, the sacking came off his face. I instantly recognised him as a young sergeant from the Norfolks. His face was wizened, wrinkled and yellow and his teeth had gone the same colour. It was a very sad moment for me as I remembered him from earlier days on the railway doing an impression of Harry Chapman (an old music hall star). Behind the guards backs he would sing: "Any old iron, any old iron." Then do a little shuffle and sing, "Boiled beef and carrots." As I lowered him into the stinking pit a tear fell from my eye.

'A bit later the Japanese decided that it was better to burn the bodies rather than bury them and I was relieved not to be detailed any more to that horrible task. We could clearly see the flames and smoke from the fires at night and smell the burning flesh.'

Captain John Barnard wrote in his book *The Endless Years*:

'I dread these morning parades, as every day there is a "beat up" for someone over the number of men available for work. The tropical ulcers are getting a real curse. I have heard about them in the past, but now I know what they are like from actual contact. Within two days a nasty sore develops the size of a sixpence. In a few days, it's twice that size and becoming a deep wound and within a few weeks the flesh is so eaten away that often the bone is visible. There is little to be done except amputate the limb.

'Our treatment is getting worse every day. We have incident after incident. Nearly every day men come and complain to me about Japanese brutality. There is no purpose in my saying anything because this just results in getting beaten up.

'What a life this is. Every day is the same as the one before. Deadly monotony with no respite to look forward to.'

Private Fred Cox wrote in his book *Faith, Hope and Rice*:

'No more than slaves. Towards the end of May 1943, when we had been at Kanburi for about six weeks, our lives were made even more difficult by the arrival of the monsoon season. No doubt because of being so exhausted at the end of each day's work, we had adjusted to sleeping on hard bamboo to the extent that we did at least get a few hours' sleep despite the best efforts of the bed bugs and mosquitoes. However torrential rain meant that that we now had to contend with water leaking through the roof of the hut as we tried to sleep. Moving about the camp meant squelching our way along slippery paths, and the rain just kept coming. Dysentery was rife and there were always several chaps who had gone down with it at any one time. This obviously affected our ability to function as a workforce, but rather than trying to restore our health so that we could work more efficiently for them, it became clear that they saw us as expendable; there were plenty more prisoners to take our place.'

On the Thai/Burma railway and in other prisoner of war camps in the Far East, the Japanese did not play according to any international rules regarding the treatment of prisoners of war, making up their own as they went along. Japanese and Korean guards were considered second- or third-rate military personnel, and consequently were bitter towards the prisoners. There was also little contact between the Allied officers and any higher Japanese authority, meaning that they had to deal with lower-ranking guards.

During their captivity, the prisoners did their very best to sabotage the Japanese efforts to build the railway. They understood that anything they could do to slow down the Japanese advance into Burma would be beneficial to the Allies. My father said in his release questionnaire: 'We often left nuts loose on equipment so that wheels would drop off.'

Although conditions were difficult, there were always lighter moments at many camps along the railway. In one camp, the Japanese commander was so concerned about men dying that he decided to get the prisoners to write wills. This amused the men, as most had very few belongings to leave. One man wrote in his will: 'I leave to my mother and father Woolworths, Marks and Spencer, Freeman Hardy and Willis and the Ritz hotel.' This caused great amusement in the huts that night. Many years later, when this man was making a proper will back in England, he was asked by the solicitor if he had made a former will. 'Indeed I have,' he said, 'in a prisoner of war camp on the Thai/Burma railway.' The solicitor found this hilarious and added an amendment to the bottom of his will to the effect, 'I hereby revoke all former wills and dispositions heretofore made by me.'

The prisoners in most of the camps on the railway got one day off work every two weeks – Yasume day, as the Japanese called it. It was an opportunity for them to at least rest, wash their scant clothing and get some much-needed sleep. John Wyatt recalls one Yasume day when a Japanese engineer came into their quarters and asked if anyone was a strong swimmer:

'He told us that they were going to take a boat out on the river to catch fish and they wanted a prisoner to swim around collecting the stunned fish for them after they had dropped some dynamite into the river.

'As my mate Mick Shiels was a strong swimmer he volunteered for the job.

'"Why did you tell them you were a strong swimmer, Mick? You'll just be wasting part of your valuable rest day," I said.

'"Just wait and see Johnny," he replied with a wink.

'Shiels set off with the Japanese down to the river, where they spent some time dynamiting the fish. When the water settled, he swam around collecting the dead fish and throwing them into boat until the Japanese decided that they had enough, whereupon they rowed off leaving him to collect any dead fish left behind.

'A little later Shiels marched triumphantly back into the camp waving three large fish in front of him.

'"These are for you and me, Johnny," he said. "Not to be shared with anyone. I have had to swim hard to get them."'

The two Surrey men cooked the fish over an open fire that evening and ate the lot from head to tail. According to Wyatt it was the best meal he had for nearly two years, although he felt guilty about eating the fish in front of starving men. Shiels reminded him that they all had the chance to volunteer for the job.

Even upon the railway, escape was still on many men's minds, despite the difficulties in getting away from such a hostile environment. In March 1943, four Surrey Privates John Croker, Ernest Cleaver, Norman Dorval and Charles Richardson attempted to escape during a march from Ban Pong to Chunkai. They were quickly recaptured and subsequently executed. Bugler Arthur Lane again had the misfortune to play the 'Last Post' at the execution of these unfortunate men, and recalled:

'They managed to slip away from the main body of men with the intention of stealing a boat or swimming across the river. They were betrayed by Thai villagers and handed over to the Kempeitai for the bounty money on offer. They were duly tried and sentenced to death. The news would have been catastrophic to those who were working on the railway so the matter was kept secret. In agreement, I kept the knowledge to myself at the time, only recording their names on the list of funerals I attended to sound the 'Last Post'. It was intended that the four Surreys should be executed in front of the other prisoners as an example, but due to pressure from senior officers headed by Lieutenant Colonel Philip Toosey at Kanchanaburi their execution took place on 4 February 1943 in semi secrecy just behind what was later to become Chunkai cemetery. The four are buried in Kanchanaburi cemetery.'

Private Carleton from Wexford was in the camp at the time, and described camp commander Lieutenant Colonel Toosey as follows:

'A brave officer and good camp commander, who was often slapped in the face and made to stand to attention for hours outside the guardroom when he tried to save a man from getting flogged.'

Lieutenant Colonel Toosey, at great risk to himself, had helped the four men to try to escape. Each man had a bag of rice and some tinned food saved from their Red Cross parcels, along with a compass and a diary. According to Carleton:

'The leader of the group, Private Dorval, told me that they planned to meet the two officers at a place somewhere he would not tell. Every Sunday all prisoners crowded out of the gate of the camp to the nearby jungle to gather firewood. The weather was cold and the prisoners wore their blankets around their shoulders to keep warm. The four men wore blankets as usual this time to cover the supplies they carried. When they got into the jungle we said goodbye and good luck. Colonel Toosey, at great personal risk, concealed their absence at roll calls for three days before the men were eventually captured and executed.'

Lieutenant Colonel Toosey of 135 Field Regiment Royal Artillery was the British officer on whom David Lean chose to base his main character, Colonel Nicholson in his film *The Bridge on the River Kwai*. In the film, Nicholson is portrayed as a camp commander who helped the Japanese in the building of the railway, but this is far from the truth. Toosey did everything in his power to help his men and hinder the Japanese. He quickly realized that if his men did not make an effort to build the bridge, then they were likely to be punished by the Japanese, with rations withheld and the subsequent loss of many lives. Toosey cleverly walked a fine line between helping the Japanese build their railway whilst ensuring that his men were looked after and fed. Not all the men subscribed to Toosey's ideas and many described him as 'Jap Happy', but he was indeed a great leader and saved many men's lives. I was fortunate to meet Lieutenant Colonel Toosey's son, Patrick, some years ago, and we have since become good friends.

Joe Holland of the 2 Surreys also attempted an audacious escape from a camp on the railway in late 1944. Holland was part of a work group that was transporting goods on small bogies down to the river for loading onto barges. He had befriended some Chinese boatmen on the river and planned to make an escape attempt one day on his way back to camp. He enlisted the help of his friend, Bandsman 'Bunny' Austin, to cover for him when he made his attempt, and on the chosen day the two men managed to drop behind the rest of the group on the way back to camp. Holland shook Austin's hand and disappeared into the jungle.

When the group arrived back in camp, the Japanese quickly realized that one man was missing and Austin, as agreed, had to try to cover for him. Austin told the guards: 'Joe went into the jungle to relieve himself. He had a bad case of dysentery and that was the last I saw of him. Perhaps he collapsed out in the jungle.' Austin was then sent out, accompanied by a guard, to try to find Holland, but of course he was by now well away from the camp and they were unable to find any trace of him.

Three weeks later, when Austin returned to the camp after work, he spotted Holland standing to attention outside the Japanese guardroom, looking in a terrible way, with long matted hair and a huge beard. He was made to stand outside the guard room for several days, with Japanese guards beating him every time they passed. Austin feared for his life. Holland was eventually put into a small hut, where he remained for several weeks before his release back into the camp. He told the rest of the men his story:

> 'After leaving Bunny, I contacted the Chinese who had a boat ready and proceeded up the river. I was taken to join a group of Chinese guerrillas who were making raids on Japanese camps along the railway. I decided that I must move on and on trying to jump aboard a train I was spotted by a guard, recaptured and brought back to camp.'

Private Holland survived his captivity and returned home to Bow in London after the war.

The Thai/Burma railway was finally completed on 17 October 1943 when track-laying parties from both the Thailand and Burmese ends met at Konkoita. Over 150 million cubic feet of earth had been moved and 9 miles of bridges built during the previous sixteen months.

A Japanese general hammered a golden spike into the track, or at least that is what the men were told at the time; the spike was actually made of copper, not gold. It is now in the Death Railway Museum at Kanchanaburi. A C56 locomotive was driven ceremoniously along the section of line, whilst the prisoners were lined up to witness the achievement.

In honour of their efforts, each man was given 2oz of soap, ten Thai cigarettes and some fruit to celebrate; items that had probably come from Red Cross parcels anyway. Wreaths were laid by the Japanese in honour of the Allied prisoners who died on the railway, and an officer made a speech to the men:

> 'Thank you very much for realising the importance of the railway to Nippon. We are sorry some of your friends have died but it is the duty of the soldier to die when necessary. Soon you will be going back to Kanchanaburi and Non Pladuk. Continue to be good soldiers. Take care of your health so that when peace comes you may return to your own country, to your dear wives and children and to all your dear friends.'

To celebrate the occasion, the Japanese decided that a football match should be arranged, with the prisoners playing against the guards. For the emaciated men, this would be a difficult task, but as football was Britain's national sport, the men were delighted to take on their captors regardless of their condition. Colour Sergeant Beach of the 2 Surreys witnessed the match and records with relish in his diary: 'A British football team defeats the Japanese.'

This was not the first time that such a match had been played, as Captain Barnard also mentions a farcical football match in his book:

'Today we had a propaganda inspection by a party of Nips, who arrived and took photographs of the camp. We had not been prepared for this and were surprised when, at about ten o'clock this morning, all work stopped, and we were told to stage a football match at once. We were further ordered to attend it, and told that were all to be dressed in new clothes and that everyone was to "look happy" to avoid punishment. The two teams were issued with new coloured cotton shorts and the game started. The Nips arrived with cameras and took snaps of the game and of the well-dressed spectators. The Japanese staged a further farce by placing a table near the game with several empty beer bottles on it and a few of the men sitting around. After this we all removed our new shorts and went back to work. I suppose now the world will see a photograph showing happy and contented Japanese PoWs playing football amidst the magnificent scenery of their jungle cameos. What a life.'

Many of the surviving prisoners, who by now were in a state of physical and mental decay, were evacuated by train down the line to Kanchanaburi and Non Pladuk. For others the completion of the railway came too late.

With the railway now fully operational, trains loaded with troops and supplies creaked and groaned their way north towards Burma past the camps where so many men died. The Japanese train crews would not have been aware of the cost in human lives as they picked their way over the skeletons of the dead along the line. They would not see the ghosts of the ninety-five 2 Surrey men that crept silently in and out of the jungle and across the line. The Japanese had achieved their objective in building a railway only by a display of callous cruelty and complete disregard for human life.

Most of the surviving 2 Surreys still on the railway, including my father, were in a pitiful state by now, with many suffering from malaria, beri-beri, tropical ulcers and extreme malnutrition. The very sick men were immediately admitted to a hospital in Kanchanaburi, but even it had grossly inadequate facilities to deal with the hundreds coming down from the camps. Official statistics held in the Death Railway Centre and the Surrey History Centre show that 108 2 Surrey men died or were executed on the railway during the period from May 1942 until August 1945, 10 per cent of the men who faced the Japanese at Jitra three-and-a-half years previously.

By the latter months of 1944, the Allies were pressing the Japanese forces in Burma. They quickly realized that if they could destroy this newly built railway, the Japanese would be unable to resupply their troops. Bombing raids commenced, with the supply base at Non Pladuk a prime target along with the many bridges. With the PoW camp adjacent to the railway marshalling yards at Non Pladuk, 100 prisoners were killed and many more wounded in one bombing raid.

Allied air attacks continued on the railway, and by the beginning of 1945 many parts of it had been destroyed, severely restricting the Japanese ability to transport troops and supplies into Burma.

One of the saddest stories to come out of the 2 Surreys' time in captivity comes from Captain John Barnard. His batman throughout the Malaya campaign and in the camps on the railway was Corporal Fred Blake. Blake was a tower of strength for his boss, always managing to scrounge food and to look after him when he fell ill, as did Barnard when Blake fell ill. The two had an incredible bond.

Barnard relates an amusing story when Blake's hair began to fall out in one of the camps:

'He tried everything he can to stop it, but yesterday was forced to have his hair shaved off and a comical sight he is. He has not taken his hat off since.'

Captain Barnard became quite influential with the Japanese during his time on the railway. One of the Japanese doctors, whom Barnard had befriended, recommended that a more temperate climate would suit many of those who were suffering in the tropical climate. As Blake was one of those suffering badly, Barnard reluctantly put him forward to be transferred back to Singapore and then on to Japan.

Barnard wrote:

'Many drafts have now left for Japan via Singapore, and I regret to record that Blake has left with them. I miss him a great deal, and I can only trust that in letting him go I did the right thing.'

Tragically, Corporal Blake drowned when the *Hofuko Maru* was sunk enroute to Japan later that year. One can only imagine Barnard's feelings when he discovered Blake's fate after the war.

Not all Allied prisoners were transported from Changi to work on the railway. Many were left back in Singapore to work on clearing up the ruined city or to simply stagnate. The remaining 2 Surreys left in Singapore spent their days alternating between boredom and starvation.

Tony Cox of the 2 Surreys recalled his first Christmas in captivity in one of the working camps in Singapore city:

'We realised that if we were to get any enjoyment at all out of Christmas we would need to eat something other than rice. The challenge was acquiring it but we managed to secure four chickens, one duck, five fish, a hundredweight of mixed vegetables and some fruit. Those tasked with the preparation and cooking of this lot did us proud and to us it seemed a feast.'

Cox also tells of boxing tournaments in Changi, usually between conscripts and regulars, when he ended up with two black eyes.

Early in his captivity in Changi, twenty-one-year-old Corporal Terry Reynolds of the 2 Surreys met a Chinese girl whom he called Little Flower. Reynolds fell deeply in love with her and was devastated when he was transferred to the Burma railway in October 1942. For the next year, the youngster managed to survive the hardships in the camps, with her memory always in his thoughts. Reynolds passed away the day before the railway was completed and was not able to see the love of his life again.

During their three-and-a-half years as captives of the Japanese, 2 Surrey men were scattered all over South-East Asia, with varying degrees of comfort and treatment, as Hugh Clarke outlined succinctly after the war:

'Being a PoW of the Japanese was to become an involuntary subscriber to an extraordinary lottery. You could remain hungry and bored in Changi Singapore but relatively undisturbed by the Japanese captors; you could work on the wharves and food dumps and grow fat, if prepared to risk the inevitable bashings or worse if caught scrounging; you could journey to Japan in the early years of the war and live in conditions not much worse than a Japanese miner or factory worker; or you could crack the bad-luck jackpot and end up on the Burma-Siam railway.'

Whilst conditions in Changi were difficult during the years of Japanese occupation, they were not as bad as the camps on the railway. Men returning to Changi during 1944 found it a great luxury to be able to sit again at tables on real chairs for their meals, and to have a shower. At one farewell concert on the railway, one group of men sang a song about Changi as they prepared to return:

'Changi is an Island at the south end of Malay;
'We used to think it Hell on earth and prayed to get away;
'But since we've been to Burma, we have grown a bit more wise;
'Now Singapore's the promised land, Changi Paradise.'

Back on the Thai/Burma railway when 1945 dawned, the Japanese grouped most of the remaining senior officers, including Lieutenant Colonel Swinton of the 2 Surreys, in Kanchanaburi. Eric Moss of the Argyles recalls an incident concerning Swinton and Private J. Lewis of the Surreys in Kanchanaburi at that time:

'All the colonels and majors were put together in one big hut called the Imperial War Museum. We had a colonel of the Surreys there.

And there was this chap called Lewis also of the Surreys. We had been confined to huts for some reason and you weren't allowed to smoke, but this chap Lewis who always had a pipe in his hand was walking between the two huts. He may have had the pipe in his mouth but he wasn't smoking. He was hauled in by the Japs and put in front of the guardroom. He stood in front of it for a whole week – Jap military practice. When they let him go he was all black by the sun, he was parched with thirst and dying of hunger. He was staggering back to his hut when this fool of a colonel came out. "How are you feeling old boy? Of course, it was your own fault, wasn't it?" I'd have flattened him.'

In 1957, fifteen years after the first group of prisoners, including my father, set off for the railway, the film *The Bridge on the River Kwai* was screened in cinemas. Directed by David Lean and starring Alec Guinness, it proved to be a blockbuster of its time. It depicted images of brutal and incompetent Japanese soldiers relying on a group of willing British prisoners of war to help them build a wooden bridge over the River Kwai. The film was based on a novel written in 1952 by Frenchman Pierre Boule, portraying Colonel Nicholson, the British camp commander, as a willing partner, driving his men to help the Japanese.

The film was a complete work of fiction, as my father was happy to point out when he took me to see it as a 9-year-old in 1959. His comment to me as we were leaving was, 'What a load of rubbish, but I enjoyed it.' I was a bit too young to realize that he had actually worked on the same bridge and the effect it had on him. Many of his colleagues took exception to the portrayal of them as willing workers helping the stupid Japanese to build the railway. They knew the real story of the well-organized and efficient engineers, totally committed to brutality, and of the Allied officers who did everything in their power to look after the welfare of their men. Ironically, there is no bridge over the River Kwai: there is not even a River Kwai. At Kanchanaburi, where the famous tourist bridge is located, the river that it straddles is called the Maeklaung. It's here that a tributary called the Maenam Kwai Noi joins the Maeklaung, the River Kwai that is mentioned in the book and film. The railway followed the eastern bank of the Kwai Noi as it made its way towards the Burmese border. Near the border with

Burma, the railway crosses a tributary called the Song Khalia River close to Songkurai camp, where 1,200 Allied PoWs died; this is the camp and bridge that Pierre Boule wrote about in his book.

If you have watched the film, you will be aware that it follows a group of commandos struggling through hundreds of miles of jungle to blow up one of the 688 bridges with explosives. This again is pure fiction, as the bridge was bombed by 9 and 493 squadrons of the US Air Force, with B24 Liberators making thirteen-hour round trips from their bases in India. The first air raid on the bridges took place on 29 November 1944, killing or wounding a large number of prisoners.

The release of the film, however, did spark an interest in the war in the Far East and the 'forgotten army' who were taken prisoner by the Japanese. People started to visit Thailand to see the bridge for themselves. With such a surge of interest, the Thai government changed the name of the river from the Maeklaung to the Kwai to make it appear more authentic. That means there are now two River Kwais. The tourist bridge at Kanchanaburi today spans the Kwai Yai, whilst the remaining operating section of railway runs along the eastern bank of the Kwai Noi.

Chapter 7

The Hellships

J ust a matter of weeks after the fall of Singapore, the Japanese began
to move many of the PoWs to various locations around the Far East,
including Japan itself. With most of their able-bodied men away fighting
in the outlying parts of their new empire, they had a severe shortage of
manpower on their home islands. Their prisoners of war were a disposable
supply of cheap labour and were quickly used to plug that gap. From as early
as August 1942, prisoners were loaded onto Japanese merchant ships to be
transported all over their conquered territories.

If the prisoners returning to Changi from the Burma railway at the end of
1943 thought that for them the worst was over, they were to be disappointed
as many of them were also to be shipped overseas. At the base camps on the
railway they were assessed as to their health and ability to continue working.
Those who were deemed fit were chosen. For some reason, red-headed and
blue-eyed prisoners were chosen first.

On 12 August 1942, the first group of six 2 Surrey men were loaded,
along with 400 other prisoners, onto the *England Maru*, bound for Formosa.
According to Gunner John McEwan of the 155th Lanarkshire Yeomanry, the
ship was 'a battered old rust bucket – a stinking, rat infested, disreputable
hulk, seems like this was to be our potential mass coffin'.

The men were forced down into holds that had not been cleaned from
their previous guests – cattle. Excrement still fouled the holds, rats ran riot
chasing cockroaches, whilst bluebottles buzzed about above their heads.
This hellish journey lasted two weeks, during which three men died, their
bodies simply thrown overboard by the Japanese crew. The *England Maru*
arrived at Keelung Formosa on 29 September, where most of the men were
sent to work in the copper mines at Kinkaseki.

On the same day, another five 2 Surrey men, along with 1,200 other
prisoners, were loaded onto the *Fukkai Maru*, an ancient 3,829-ton cargo

ship built in England in 1898. Upon boarding, the men were undressed, disinfected and powdered for lice before being crammed into the forward and aft holds. There was not enough room to stand or even kneel, so they were compelled to lie, sit or crawl on the straw matting provided.

The prisoners sat in the holds for five days whilst a convoy was formed, before leaving Keppel Harbour on 16 August. During the voyage, the prisoners were fed a diet of rice twice a day, with a thin soup made of flour and water. One prisoner recalled, 'Sardines had more room in a can than we had in that ship, the holds stunk, the heat was dreadful and the food was disgusting.'

The *Fukkai*'s convoy stopped briefly at Cape St Jacques outside Saigon before moving on to Formosa, before eventually arriving on 29 August at Takao. There the prisoners were set to work on the docks as stevedores unloading bauxite, coal and rice. They laboured at Takao for two weeks before moving on again in the same ship to Pusan in Korea, arriving there on 22 September. After leaving the ship, the men were again sprayed with disinfectant, photographed and robbed of their personal possessions, including watches, wedding rings and photographs. They were then marched through the streets under a hot sun, led by a Japanese soldier on horseback, to the railway station. Korean children jeered and spat at them as they marched along in columns of four. At the station, they were given a small box containing cold rice, a bit of dried fish and some cucumber, the first food they had been given all day. Before boarding the train for the capital Seoul, the prisoners were given a similar box for the next leg of the journey that lasted twenty-four hours. Upon arrival at Seoul, they were once again marched around like prize chickens before entering the camp where they were to spend the next three years working for the Japanese war effort.

The next group of fourteen 2 Surreys left Singapore on 10 October. Almost 2,000 men were crammed on board an unnamed ex-British freighter bound for Kutching, Borneo. It was another big, dirty, rusting cargo ship and conditions on board were once again poor, with little drinking water provided and none for bathing. The food was reasonable on this ship, with the occasional piece of meat provided during the three-day journey to Kuching. At Kuching, however, the food was so poor that they had to use some of their precious Red Cross parcels as they watched hundreds of bags of tapioca and sugar being loaded on board. The mood among the men lightened when some of the bags burst and they were able to scoop up handfuls and secrete them away. The next day the ship moved on up the coast and the water shortage became so serious that the men's tongues began to swell up. Some crept up to the steam winches, where they were able to open the taps and release a small amount of water to quench their thirst.

The possibility of revolting and taking over the ship was discussed as it neared the coast of Borneo, where they might escape and join guerrillas who were still fighting against the Japanese. This plan was shelved due to the uncertainty as to whether the Borneo people were pro-Japanese or not. Had they known how strong the anti-Japanese feelings were amongst the local population, they might have gone through with it.

The ship eventually reached Miri on the north coast of Borneo on the sixteenth. There they were taken ashore and set to work on the docks for just one day. Some of the men described Miri as 'the last place that God made'. Their work included unloading cargo such as paint, batteries, engineering equipment and hundreds of tyres. The following day, the ship moved on again under conditions that became even worse. Dysentery was rife and the smell was unbearable as the ship moved on up the coast. One of the prisoners jumped overboard as he could no longer stand the strain.

On 19 October, the ship finally docked at Jesselton, near the northern tip of Borneo. There the prisoners were taken to a camp, where they spent the rest of the war lodged in atap huts and working for the Japanese.

It was to be another five months before the next group of seven 2 Surrey men, along with 1,000 others, left Singapore on 28 March 1943 on board the *De Klerk*, a captured Dutch freighter of 1,000 tons, again bound for Borneo. The British prisoners were under the command of Lieutenant Colonel Whimster, with the Australians led by Major Fairley. Conditions were as bad as any of the previous ships, but some of the prisoners managed to break into a storage area and steal a large quantity of beans, sugar and cigarettes. After an uneventful voyage of four days, the *De Klerk* docked at Kutching on 1 April and the men were put to work on the wharves. There they managed to sabotage some of the cargo by 'accidentally' dropping goods into the water or allowing cargo nets to smash into the wharf. Five out of the seven 2 Surrey men on the *De Klerk* were to die in Kutching.

A month later, on 26 April 1943, sixteen more 2 Surreys joined 1,500 men on board another disgusting vessel, the 6,783-ton cargo ship *Kyokko Maru*. They had no idea where they were heading and the journey proved to be another nightmare. Crammed into filthy, evil-smelling, airless holds, each prisoner had a space of only 2ft by 5ft to lie down in, with not enough height to stand or sit up. The Japanese provided very little food or water, and rats roamed the holds at will. The ship had no medical officers on board; a handful of medical orderlies struggled to cope with the number of dysentery cases that broke out. They had no medical supplies for a trip that was to last twenty-five days.

According to Lieutenant Abbott of the 2 Surreys, who was the senior British officer on board:

'Except for two hours each day on deck, the whole time was spent battened down in a filthy evil smelling hold. I had to sit on the edge of the lower platform which two hundred of us shared as a bed, my head bent to prevent it hitting the bunk above. Rats, dysentery, total absence of doctors or medical supplies, little food or water, and brutal guards. It was a terrible journey.'

The *Kyokko Maru* arrived at the port of Takao in Formosa on 3 May, but they were not allowed out of the holds for some much-needed fresh air. It was to be another eighteen hellish days before the *Kyokko* eventually docked at Moji on Japan's south island of Kyushu, where much to their relief they were allowed to disembark. After picking up their paltry possessions, they were unceremoniously pushed and shoved like cattle into the station yard, before being marched down cobbled streets into Aomi prison camp.

On 16 May 1943, another sixteen 2 Surrey men, along with 917 other prisoners, were herded aboard the *Wales Maru*, a 6,586-ton cargo ship owned by the Kawasaki Kisen Company, again bound for Japan. This group was fortunate to have three doctors in the party. On leaving Changi each man was given a cup of peanuts, half a loaf of rice bread and a bottle of cold tea. Whilst not much, these were to prove to be a life-saver during the journey.

It was dusk when the prisoners were shoved down into the dark dank hold of the ship. The hold so cramped that that they had to interlock arms and legs just to lie down. They were not given any food and, as the ship progressed over the South China Sea, the peanuts and rice bread they had been given was to be a life-saver. Four days after leaving Singapore, the *Wales Maru* stopped at Cape St Jaques near Saigon, mooring some 400 yards from the shore. Some of the men contemplated jumping overboard to try to swim to land, but the sight of several sharks put an end to that idea.

Approaching Takao Taiwan, the prisoners were ordered below. It was rumoured that the Japanese did not want them to see the harbour defences, but they were hardly in any position to pass information to the Allies even if they did see them. The ship remained at Takao for four days with the men locked down in the stifling holds, before setting sail again at daybreak on 4 June for the final leg of their torturous journey to Japan.

The following morning, whilst some of the men were on deck getting some fresh air, the crew began to shout and scream, pushing them back down into the holds. The Japanese were terrified as they had heard that that a United States submarine was in the vicinity. One man, who managed to hide on deck, reported seeing two torpedo tracks heading for the ship, both of which missed by only a few yards.

The *Wales Maru* eventually made it unscathed to Moji on 7 June after twenty-two days at sea. Fortunately, there were no deaths on board despite the conditions and it was a huge relief for the men to be eventually taken up on deck. Before disembarking, they were lined up and subjected to a humiliating public glass rod treatment, where Japanese medical officers shoved a glass rod up almost 1,000 backsides. After this, they were taken by train to Hokkaido camp, where they worked for the rest of the war.

On 5 June, eight 2 Surreys joined 500 other prisoners on board the *Teia Maria*, a 17,537-ton former French ship originally called the *Aramis* that had been captured in Saigon in April 1942. Conditions on board were again poor, but at least the men got two mugs of sticky rice per day and occasional watery soup on a voyage that lasted fourteen days, arriving at Moji on 19 June. There were no deaths on the journey, and upon arrival the men were taken to Funatsu-Nagoya 3B camp, where they laboured in lead and zinc mines until the end of the war.

On 4 July 1944, a convoy of ships with almost 5,000 Allied prisoners on board, including fifty-nine 2 Surrey men, left Singapore. The ships were the *Asaka Maru, Hakushika Maru, Sekiho Maru, Rashin Maru* and *Hofuku Maru*. After boarding, they were handed a badly written leaflet outlining the rules and regulations to be observed during the journey. This initially caused a great deal of merriment, but the prisoners were later to discover that the Japanese carried out these rules to the letter:

Regulations For Prisoners on board ships

The prisoners disobeying the following orders will be punished with immediate death.

Those disobeying orders and instructions.

Those showing a motive of antagonism and raising a sign of opposition.

Those disobeying the regulations by individualism, egoism, thinking only about yourself, rushing for your goods.

Those talking without permission and raising loud voices.

Those walking and moving without order.

Those carrying unnecessary baggage in embarking.

Those resisting mutually.

Those touching the boats materials, wires, electric lights, tools, switches etc.

Those climbing ladder without order.

Those showing action of running away from the room or boat.

Those trying to take more meal than given to them.

Those using more than two blankets.

Since the boats are not well equipped and insides being narrow, food being scarce and poor you'll feel uncomfortable during the short time on the boats. Those loosing [*sic*] patience and disordering the regulation will be heavily punished for the reason of not being able to escort.

Be sure to finish your 'Nature's call' evacuate the bowels and urine before embarking.

Meal will be given twice a day. One plate only to one prisoner. The prisoners called by the guard will give out the meal quick as possible and honestly. The remaining prisoners will stay in their places quietly and wait for your plate. Those moving from their places reaching for your plate without order will be heavily punished. Same orders will be applied in handling plates after meal.

Toilets will be fixed at the four corners of the room. The buckets and cans will be placed. When filled up a guard will appoint a prisoner. The prisoner called will take the buckets to the centre of the room. The buckets will be pulled up by the derrick and be thrown away. Toilet papers will be given. Everyone must co-operate to make the rooms sanitary. Those being careless will be punished.

Navy of the Great Japanese Empire will not try to punish you all with death. Those obeying all the rules and regulations and believing the action purposes of the Japanese navy, co-operating with Japan in constructing the 'New order of the Great Asia' which lead to the world's peace will be well treated.

The End

The Japanese seemed particularly interested in men who had trades that might be beneficial to their war effort. Corporal John Wyatt of the 2 Surreys recalled to me the comical interviews they had with a Japanese officer in Changi prior to boarding the *Asaka Maru*:

'He asked each one of us if we had a trade in England. The first bloke was a carpenter and he was immediately pushed to a spot for skilled men. "You Japan," grunted the officer.

'Word quickly spread down the line that if you did not admit to having a trade then you just might get out of being sent to Japan. At that point, everyone started telling him that they were a window cleaner.

'When it came to Mick's turn he again said, "Me window cleaner – me clean Crystal Palace." Of course, we all burst out into fits of laughter but the officer began to get very agitated and shouted. "All British solders pukking winda cleaners, no pukking Crystal Palace." In the end, it didn't matter anyway because if you were able to stand you were chosen and we were told, "Now you go to the land of the Cherry Blossom."

'"Maybe we'll be working in a shoe polish factory," I whispered to Mick.'

Those who were selected to go to Japan were addressed by a Japanese colonel before setting off for the docks:

'You are to be transferred from the jurisdiction of PoW camp, Thailand, to that of Japan where you are to resume labour duties. Since the opening of the Thailand PoW camps you were diligently carrying out imposed labour duty for more than 20 months. Especially you were employed in railway construction in which your discharge of duty attained aimed objective as scheduled, for which we appreciate warmly.

'On completion of above mentioned, you will be transferred to the Holy Land of the Rising Sun, where scenery is simply superb.

'The Emperor of Great Japan, proper appellation Bis-Y-Yasima Dai Nippon Takoken, is populace [*sic*] with nationals of up-righteousness, acts of morality, brave yet courteous, humanious [*sic*], but strictly severe on vices. The proverb most common in use thereof, 'Even hunter himself will not slay a strayed bird seek refuge on her lap', will properly explain the attitude of Japanese sentiments.

'The land has four distinct seasons; Spring – with abundance of various blossoms, where birds chirp peaceful everywhere; evergreen Summer – with cool breezes easing the universe; transparent Autumn sky with clement moon; and with Winter, in which snow whitewashes the whole country, purifying the inhabitants.

'These are nothing but the image and reflection of His august Majesty's greater virtues, to which all nationals are bound to follow in loyalty towards the Imperial family and filial piety towards parents, creation of benevolence, etc., etc. to eternal efforts.

'Therefore, I tell you, officers and men, go to Japan with ease of mind and do your imposed duty to perfection. Then I verily tell you that our billion nationals will be welcoming you to share the imperial favour with you.

'On the other hand, should any one of you still retain conscience of any eniminal [*sic*] nationals, and project or proceed things up against to the interest of Japan, consequential results must be borne on his own shoulders, however regrettable to all concerned.

'I reiterate, believe in Japanese chivalry and go forward in the right way not straying on proper and mature consideration.

'In conclusion, I should like to call your attention to take good care of your health for the sudden change in climatical conditions and wish you the happy future.

'With my blessing for your "Bon Voyage".'

It's not difficult to picture the reaction of the hundreds of men who had been subjected to Japanese brutality as they lined up to listen to this address.

Wyatt recalls his voyage on the *Asaka Maru* in his book *No Mercy from the Japanese*:

'It was 4 July 1944 when this whole comical convoy of ten wrecks loaded with over 5,000 allied prisoners of war, set off for the land of the rising sun. As Singapore fell away behind us, we passed the tropical islands of Pulaw Batau and Palau Bintan before leaving the last point of Malaya Tanjong Penyosoh and heading on towards Labuan.

'Conditions on board were by this time almost unbearable and every one of us was in a state of great physical and mental distress. The latrine was a large wooden box lashed to the side of the ship with an opening in the middle and a ledge on either side for your feet. With dysentery still rife there was always a constant queue to use this primitive contraption, with some men going up to fifteen times a day. Matters were made even worse as the inside of the box was slippery from the blood excreted by the dysentery sufferers. My bare feet would often slip as I squatted down and I was terrified of being washed into the sea when a big wave broke or the ship rolled. You had to hang on with all your strength. I saw one man tragically get washed away as he was so weak that he was unable to hang on. When we reported this to the Japanese guards they just shrugged their shoulders and turned away, completely oblivious to our distress and suffering. To them another

PoW's death was probably one less living prisoner to deal with. We had no toilet paper and had to use what we could find or scrounge including pages from the few books left in our possession.

'Malaria broke out again with a vengeance on board and as we had almost no quinine, we had to suffer the dreadful effects of this awful disease. Beri-beri was also on the increase. Many of my comrades were to die on this fateful voyage and we wrapped them in rice sacks and tipped them into the sea. Not even a prayer was said as they were consigned to a grave somewhere in the depths of the sea.'

After two days at sea, the convoy reached the coast of Borneo, eventually docking on 8 July at Miri, where the *Hofuku Maru* remained for several days whilst its engines were repaired. It eventually left Miri four days later, arriving at Manila, the capital of the Philippines, on 20 July. The unfortunate prisoners sat in the holds of the ship at Manila for two months, many suffering from disease, hunger and thirst. Around fifty men died on board this ship during this terrible period. Despite the lack of proper medical equipment and drugs, the men tried their best to treat the sick. Hollow spokes from wheels were used as needles to inject condensed steam from the engine room pipes. A group of seventy-one very sick men were eventually taken ashore and taken to an American camp at Bilibid. A doctor in the camp, Paul Ashton, recalled their arrival:

'Our overtaxed medical facilities in the prison were not equipped to deal with them and they were dropped like orphans on our doorstep. The Japanese suspected that they had cholera and would transport them no further. I suppose the name "cholera" frightened them off. I treated cases of dry beriberi, edema, scurvy, optic nerve degeneration, pulmonary congestion, enlarged hearts, vocal cord paralysis and a virulent form of dysentery. They were collectively the sorriest seventy-one men – absolutely frightening. To this day I cannot think of a reason why the Japanese had not thrown them all overboard, such was their fear of contagion.'

Nine of the men died during their time in the Bilibid prison.

For the next two weeks, the rest of the prisoners sat either in the oppressive heat of the hold or on the deck, covered in coal dust and soaked by the torrential downpours, whilst coal was loaded and a new convoy was made ready to sail. One of the Surreys who was offloaded at Manila was Sergeant John Beach, who outlined his experiences during those dreadful days in his diary:

'18th June 44: Farewell address from Japanese Colonel on our leaving Thailand for Japan. Marched to the docks where we remained until midday before embarking on a single funnel type steamer. Men marched down into the hold at aft part of the ship. Twenty-seven men in a space estimated to be 12ft wide, 13ft deep and under 3ft high. Only able to sit with knees up, impossible to lie down or stand up. Several men fainted and we were all suffering from heat exhaustion. Total on board 750 British prisoners of war. That evening pulled out of the harbour and anchored.

'General note: three meals a day, rice very small and thin coloured soup at 8am. Fish water and rice at 11am and watery stew and rice at 4pm.

'25th June: Parade of all men with life belts. Wooden rafts on ship's deck very old and worm eaten.

'26th June: Rained during the night, no shelter for men on deck, everything soaked. Korean driver deliberately aggravating conditions by making men keep away from cars and tipping water from pools on tarpaulins over men's kit.

'3rd July: Still anchored off Singapore. Seventeen very sick men taken off and sent to Changi.

'4th July: Ship sailed at 0900 hrs.

'8th July: Pack from ice boxes thrown over the side. Anchored in open harbour. Many oil derricks on shore. Several small Japanese tankers in harbour. Place believed to be Miri, Borneo.

'10th July: Ship sailed in convoy of fifteen or sixteen ships.

'11th July: Passes two islands in a large bay and anchored at 2000 hrs. Believed to be Kamabulu.

'16th July: Pass Corregidor and anchor at 2100 hrs.

'19th July: Went into harbour and tied up alongside wharves. British Officers request for men to exercise on dock but refused by Japanese.

'20th July: Very little supplies on board. No meat, no fish, few vegetables, mainly wilted. Many sick on board now, malaria, beri-beri and dysentery.

'30th July: One death.

'8th August: Myself and twenty other men evacuated by barge to American prison camp, Bilibid, Manila. Camp beds, mattresses, blankets and stone buildings. First time in two and a half years.

'9th August: Twelve dead bodies of British prisoners of war brought ashore and buried, from other ships still in the harbour.

'25th August: Thirty one bad cases came in from the ships. Terrible condition, mainly dysentery and beri-beri. Doctors work all night giving blood etc.

'31st August: Eight of this last party of thirty-one have died. Allowed to send postcard home. Red Cross parcels distributed. Conditions now much better for all the men.'

Sergeant Beach was to spend the remaining year of the war in Bilibid prisoner of war camp.

On 20 September, the *Hofuku Maru* and ten other ships eventually formed convoy MATA-27 and sailed out of Manila heading for Japan. The following morning, the convoy was attacked 80 miles north of Corregidor by more than 100 American torpedo bombers and the *Hofuko Maru* was sunk, with the other ten ships also badly hit. One survivor of the *Hofuko* wrote the following account of the sinking:

'Sunk by US torpedo bombers on 21.9.44 about 140 miles from Manilla Bay and four miles from land. Engine room was blown up. The living accommodation was packed and was divided by a shelf half way up allowing two rows of men sleeping. Ship had plenty of lifebelts. When the ship sank nearly everyone was trapped below and also the fact that nearly 75% were absolutely helpless with beri-beri, dysentery, lack of vision and mental deficiencies. After the sinking, one ship stopped and picked up some of the Jap crew and then sailed on. The boats which later picked up others searched for about three hours but no sign of anyone living left. Many men were so weak when they came to the surface that they could not keep their heads above water. We were left to sink or swim as the Jap rescue ship proceeded on course. Twelve fishing boats converted for coastal patrol arrived and twenty men were taken back to Manilla.'

Of the prisoners on board the *Hofuku Maru*, 1,047 out of 1,289 died, including thirteen of the 2 Surrey men, in what was one of the worst disasters from friendly fire during the entire war.

The rest of the original convoy that arrived at Miri on 6 July had now been reorganized and left Miri two days before the *Hofuku Maru*. This convoy moved on up the coast before eventually entering Manila Bay in the Philippines. The men on board the *Asaka Maru*, including John Wyatt and his mate Mick Sheils, prayed that they would be put ashore off this disgusting ship for the first time in a month. This was not to be, however, as the Japanese were anxious that it should continue its journey to the land of the rising sun.

It was 8 August when another convoy, MATA-26, including the *Asaka Maru*, set off out of Manila towards the northern tip of Luzon and Formosa. With American submarines operating in the area, the Japanese crew were particularly jumpy. According to Wyatt:

'The crew began to get even more agitated and some of them started to prepare rice balls. They donned two suits of clothes and hats and sat on life rafts with all their personal possessions. Not a very reassuring sight but quite an amusing one. Apparently, they were preparing themselves for the 'after life' where they would need the extra suits of clothing.'

On 13 August, about 100 miles out from Luzon, a terrific gale blew up and the ships began to roll and toss violently. The *Asaka* began to take in water through a damaged hatch and the hull was starting to crack in several places, flooding the holds.

The storm raged throughout the night, and as dawn broke things were starting to get desperate. The pumps could not keep up with the ingress of water and the ship began to list more and more to starboard. At dusk the next day, the men heard an almighty bang followed by a great crunching noise. The ship had struck rocks and began to list heavily to starboard. The men locked down in the holds were by now terrified, but the Japanese still would not allow them out. As dawn broke the following morning, the stricken ship had settled on the rocks and the starving prisoners were issued with some dried fish and seaweed and told to wait for a rescue ship to come. For two days, they sat in the holds of the stricken ship, firmly wedged on the rocks, waiting for help that never seemed to come. Several men who had been ill passed away and their bodies were simply tipped over the side wrapped in rice sacks. On the third day, two Japanese destroyers approached and launched several lifeboats, eventually evacuating the crew and some of the prisoners from the *Asaka*.

The following day, the destroyers docked at Keelung on North Formosa. There the prisoners were herded into barges and ferried out to another large ship called the *Hakusan Maru* sitting at anchor in the bay. The *Hakusan* began life as a USS federal freighter that had been acquired by the US Navy during the First World War as a military transport ship. After the war it was sold to the British before being captured in 1941 by the Japanese.

The holds of the *Hakusan* were even worse than the *Asaka Maru*. There was no air, it was overcrowded and the heat was unbearable. John Wyatt recalls:

'We lay naked on wooden shelves, sweating profusely, and it was an effort to even move. To try and get some sort of air movement, again we resorted to stringing our G strings and bits of clothing on a line across the hold and took it in turn to swing it back and forwards all day and all night. The hold was in almost complete darkness except for one small low-powered bulb swaying in the corridor which threw a small shaft of light over us. We sat in the gloom, sweating profusely, with nothing to do except talk to each other for hours on end and watch that light swinging to and fro. Every night at least two of the lads passed away from disease and/or starvation and I was just about at breaking point on many occasions.'

The *Hakusan* left Keelung on 22 August heading for the port of Moji in Kyushu, the most southerly of the Japanese islands – around 1,000 miles away – arriving safely on 28 August. From Moji, the surviving PoWs made the short sea crossing to Simoneseki on Honshu Island and then travelled by train to Osaka – a distance of around 300 miles – and then on to Amagasaki, where they were set to work in a factory.

On 6 September 1944, a further eleven 2 Surrey men boarded the 10,509-ton *Kachidoki Maru* in Singapore as part of a contingent of 900 prisoners. Originally an American ship called the *President Harrison*, the *Kachidoki Maru* had been captured by the Japanese near Shanghai on 8 December 1941 and was now being used as a transport ship. As well as the 900 prisoners, it also carried 6,000 tons of bauxite, the ashes of 582 Japanese soldiers who had died in battle, Japanese wounded and a group of women nurses. As usual, the Japanese did not mark the ship to distinguish it as carrying PoWs.

The 900 men were crammed into a space designed for 180 passengers, with only six small wooden toilets to serve them all. Sergeant Johnny Sherwood of the Royal Artillery, a former professional footballer, was one of the men who boarded the ship. He recalled:

'We were herded onto this forbidding grey ship. Herding was the word – treated no better than neglected animals. We were just cattle to our guards. Nine hundred British PoWs were pushed and shoved along the deck to two hatches, where we were forced down into the dark and dirty holds, shoulder to shoulder. The heat enveloped us like a steaming wet blanket and there was nothing down there but a rudimentary scattering of straw, reinforcing our animal status as far as the Japanese were concerned.'

The prisoners languished in the hot, airless holds for thirty-six hours before the ship eventually sailed out of Singapore, along with the *Rakuyo Maru* with 1,300 men on board, and twenty-five other ships as part of convoy HI-72. By noon the following day, they were about 150 miles east of Kota Bahru on the east coast of Malaya, and by 11 September around 100 miles north-east of the Paracel Islands and 200 miles off the east coast of Vietnam. The Japanese were well aware that American submarines were active in the area, and tensions began to rise amongst the crew and prisoners. One Japanese crew member was overheard to say, 'this is the day we sink'.

Conditions in the holds of both ships were dreadful, as Gordon Highlander Alistair Urquhart recalled:

> 'The noise was constant and deafening, an awful cacophony of throbbing engines, moaning, coughing and occasional panic-stricken screaming the background music for this latest torture. The chilling screams of the mad and insane would stop abruptly. I didn't know how they were dealt with but I could imagine. The smell inside the hold was indescribable, a repugnant stench. An overpowering mixture of excrement, urine, vomit, sweaty bodies, weeping ulcers and rotting flesh clogged the atmosphere. People died down in the holds from suffocation or heart attacks. The men who died were not taken away. Their bodies lay among us.'

By this time in the war, with the Japanese codes cracked, the US Navy's Fleet Radio Unit in the Pacific was listening in to Japanese radio messages and was aware of the course of the convoy. Three US submarines, the *Growler*, *Sealion II* and *Pampanito*, were dispatched to intercept it. The three submarines had spent the previous weeks attacking Japanese shipping in an area that the Americans had nicknamed 'Convoy College'.

On the morning of 12 September, the *Sealion* attacked the convoy, sinking a destroyer and the *Rakuyo Maru*, leaving over 1,314 PoWs floundering in the sea. Out of these unfortunate men, only 135 survived. The *Kachidoki* escaped this attack unscathed, but the following evening just off the coast of Hainan Island, the convoy was again attacked by the *Growler*. The *Kachidoki* was not hit, but in trying to avoid the *Growler*'s torpedoes, it struck another vessel in the convoy, scraping along it from bow to stern, causing severe damage. The prisoners, locked down in the holds, began to panic and hysteria set in as they shouted and screamed to be let out. Fortunately, the ship slowly came back on an even keel, to the great relief of the men. Their relief was not to last, however, as minutes later several other ships in the convoy were torpedoed. The few men who had managed to get on deck stood looking in shocked awe at the carnage that was going on around them, but again the *Kachidoki Maru* escaped unscathed.

For the next twenty-four hours, the surviving ships sailed on towards Taiwan. At around 2300 hrs on 13 September, the third US submarine, the *Pampanito*, fired torpedoes towards the *Kachidoki*. All hell broke loose in the holds when two hit the ship amidships and within minutes the ship started to sink. Some of the men had managed to climb out of the holds and jumped into the sea but many others were trapped below. As the *Kachidoki* slipped below the waves, the Japanese began shooting their own wounded and sick men in a series of mercy killings when they realized that they would have little chance of survival in the oily sea. Around 800 young British prisoners of war were entombed in the watery holds of the ship that night, including five of the eleven 2 Surrey men on board.

As the war entered its final phase in early 1945, the final group of twenty-three 2 Surrey men joined 2,500 prisoners on board the *Haruyasa Maru*, a 3,000-ton cargo ship, in Keppel Harbour, Singapore, on 31 January. The men sat around in the hot and humid holds for four days before setting off for Saigon on a journey that was to end in disaster. The first two days at sea were uneventful, but on the morning of 6 February the convoy was attacked by the US submarines *Pampanito* and *Guavina*. Two of the ships were hit by torpedoes and sank quickly, but the *Haruyasa* was lucky and managed to escape when the submarines decided to pursue the two escort vessels. The *Haruyasa* reached Cape St Jaques on 8 February, where the prisoners were disembarked and put into camps. There they spent the remaining 7 months of the war.

When the war against Japan ended in August 1945, the British public were led to believe that all prisoners of war in the Far East worked on the Thai/Burma railway. This misconception was reinforced by the film *Bridge on the River Kwai* in 1957. The tragic story of the hellships was neglected. Estimates of the number of deaths on these ships vary, as the Japanese destroyed the records, but around 21,000 Allied PoWs died at sea out of around 126,000 carried on the ships. The Japanese for some reason never marked these ships, meaning that submarine commanders had no way of knowing that they contained prisoners of war.

Accounts also vary as to the treatment of prisoners on the transportation ships, but conditions were undoubtedly bad. On some ships, men were forced to drink their own urine, whilst sick prisoners were trampled to death or suffocated. Cannibalism was also reported. On the *Oryoku Maru*, some men were killed by their fellow prisoners for their blood, with only 403 men surviving out of the 1,621 who had set off from Manila in December 1944. Even the Japanese were stunned by the conditions they found on board when ships docked.

Most of the men who had worked on the death railway thought that nothing could ever match the hardships they endured there, but they quickly found out that being in the hold of a hellship was much worse. At least on the railway they had fresh air and could move about, but on the hellships they were deprived of exercise, food and light. Prisoners who had the misfortune to endure the hellships claim that they were the worst days of their lives.

After the war, many of the captains and crew of the hellships were brought to war crimes trials for their treatment of the Allied PoWs and sentenced to various terms of imprisonment. Captain Odake Bunji, in charge of the *Asaka Maru* (Wyatt's ship), and Lieutenant Ino Takeo were charged with ill-treatment of prisoners due to gross overcrowding, improper sanitation, lack of food, drinking water and medical supplies on board. They were also charged with a lack of safety precautions for attacks, given that there was no indication that the ship was carrying prisoners. Both defendants were found guilty and sentenced to terms of imprisonment.

One hundred and sixty-five 2 Surrey men were transported overseas during the three-and-a-half years of the Japanese occupation of Singapore, with forty-nine of them losing their lives on board these terrible vessels.

Chapter 8

Overseas Camps

The first group of five 2 Surrey prisoners to be sent overseas from Singapore arrived at Takao Formosa with 1,500 other prisoners on the *Fukkai Maru* on 29 August 1942. They were immediately set to work on the docks as stevedores. They laboured for two weeks in Takao unloading bauxite, coal and rice, before moving on again to Pusan in Korea. Upon leaving the ship in Pusan, they were lined up in fours and marched through the streets to the railway station and then on by train to their camp in Seoul. The five men spent the next three years labouring for the Koreans before returning home at the end of the war.

On 20 October, another two 2 Surrey men were transported from Singapore to Formosa. Arriving at Keelung, they were set to work in the Kinkasaki copper mine, located in the village of Jinguashi. The mine, around a mile from the camp, produced the highest amount of copper in the Japanese Empire. It was a long march up a hill and down the other side each day for the prisoners. At the start of their shift, after an exhausting walk, they had again to walk several hundred yards inside the mine to get to the face, a huge effort considering their poor physical shape. The Kinkasaki mine had no lighting and conditions were hazardous, resulting in numerous accidents. The only light was from carbide lamps and just getting to the face was an extremely hazardous task, putting a severe physical and mental strain on the prisoners. With no ventilation system in the mine many of the men passed out while digging due to heat, lack of oxygen and lack of vitamins.

Bill Notley of 155 Field Regiment recalls his time spent at Kinkasaki:

'Once I remember that I was working down the mine and I saw a break in the chain in part of the mining machinery. I decided to hit it in the hope that it would break and we could have a rest. When the chain came round again, I hit it. It made a loud noise but didn't break. I hoped that if I did it again it might break. I waited for the point to come round again and hit it – it made a loud noise and the guards came. Although they didn't realise it was one of the men who had broken it, we received no break. Instead they made us fix it and wouldn't allow us to leave the mine until we had reached our quota. We had to work for an extra hour to fill the quota.

'I was worried about being buried in the mine and killed, so I decided to try and break my foot. I lifted a large lump of coal above my foot and dropped it. My foot was crushed, and I told the guard that the wall of the mine had collapsed onto it. He said to carry on working. At the end of the day two men carried me out of the mine, I was given [a] few days off from the mine.'

The Kinkasaki mine was closed in early March 1945 as Japanese were losing control of the Philippine sea and were unable to transport the copper from the mine back to the home islands. Some of the prisoners were then moved to Kukutsu camp in the mountains south of Taihoku Taipei, whilst others were sent to Kyushu in Japan, where they were again sent to work down the mines.

On 1 April 1943, fourteen 2 Surreys were transported to Kuching, where they were put to work on the docks. Out of the fourteen, Lance Corporal Donaldson was to die of beri-beri and malaria, and Corporal Brown was also to die a month later.

On 21 May, seventeen 2 Surrey men were part of a large group of prisoners who landed at Moji. The men were unceremoniously pushed and shoved like cattle into the station yard before being marched down cobbled streets into the Aomi prison camp, where the gates were slammed shut behind them.

Lieutenant Stephen Abbot of the 2 Surreys was the senior British officer in the camp, which was a frightening prospect for him, as he wrote:

'I realised what a frightening responsibility lay ahead of me. Because I was a mere three weeks' seniority over my two other brother officers, I as a 23-year-old Subaltern of the East Surreys – was now senior officer of this camp. I felt an upsurge of panic which I fought to control.'

Upon arrival, Abbot was unable to take any part in the management of the camp as he was struck down with dysentery and malaria, and at one point thought he may die. He continued:

'For the first two months, I had been desperately ill and no amount of mental effort could have got me out of bed. Dysentery, coupled with malaria and starvation, is a terrible enemy to fight. I was one amongst many in the camp who doubted his ability to survive.'

But survive he did, and to his credit he assumed command of the 300 British prisoners in the camp, assisted by his batman, Private Charlie Vause. Previously a cook, Vause was assigned the task of preparing meals for the Japanese guards, a job that gave him the opportunity to steal extra food from their rations.

The prisoners at Aomi laboured in a quarry, a cement factory and in open-hearth furnaces, chipping out carbon ingots. The work was hard and tedious; even those with malaria, dysentery and beri-beri were forced to work. Sick parades were held twice a day, and even men who were very sick were kicked out of bed regardless of their conditions.

As winter 1943 set in, conditions in the camp became almost unbearable. By Christmas, 8ft of snow buried the huts; with no heating, the men shivered under their thin blankets and greatcoats. Their biggest fantasy during those long winter evenings was of sitting by bright log fires in English country pubs sipping a hot whisky. Abbott summed up the situation during that long Japanese winter:

'The room was dark and cheerless, colourless save for the green of wet overalls hung, dripping, from each bunk: groups of men sitting, cramped, huddled together for warmth – their faces old and lined with the strain of chronic disease, anxiety, and months of back-breaking toil on starvation rations. Other men – too weak to sit up – lay on their straw mats staring at the ceiling, lost in thought.'

With Christmas looming, Abbott knew that at least they would have a day without work. He pondered how they could create any sort of Christmas spirit in this hell hole of a camp. He needn't have worried, as when the day arrived, the men embraced it with fervour and turned it into a day to remember. After a moving religious service, they were given the contents of Red Cross parcels, one split between twenty men. For the rest of the day they were able to relax and listen to 1920s records on an old-fashioned gramophone.

Christmas dinner, consisting of fish and potato soup, sweet beans and bread, was served in the evening, followed by an impromptu concert. It was a Christmas Day that prisoners in Aomi camp would never forget for the rest of their lives.

For the next seventeen months, Abbott and his men slaved away in the factories and the quarry with hope in their hearts that freedom would soon come their way. At the beginning of August 1945, with the end of the war only a matter of weeks away, the men in Aomi found that their relationship with the local population was, according to Abbott, 'remarkable'. For more than two years, the sixteen men of the 2 Surreys and their comrades had endured conditions in a camp that to any civilized person would not even be fit for animals. They had every reason to hate the Japanese, but for some reason not one single man attempted to exact revenge for what he had gone through when their freedom eventually came.

Initially, only organized parties were allowed to leave the camp, and they had to be accompanied by an officer, an NCO and at least one member of the military police. Many of the prisoners were invited into the homes of the Japanese people alongside whom they had worked for over two years. Abbott wrote:

'I made no attempt to stop this fraternisation. Indeed, I welcomed and encouraged it. I felt that the past was past and that if men who had suffered so much were ready to forgive, it was a good omen for the future.'

After the Japanese surrendered on 15 August 1945, it took three weeks before the men in Aomi were finally to start their journey home. Abbott took a telephone call from an American officer on 2 September informing him that a special train would arrive at 1830 hrs on the fifth, and that the men were to be packed ready to leave. Abbott insisted that during those three days, the men should clean up the camp, remove every piece of litter and leave it spotless. This clean-up operation turned into a competition between the British and Americans to see who could leave their quarters the cleanest. During the last few days before they left for home, many of the men paid a visit to the houses of the Japanese people who had been friendly towards them. They gave them gifts from the Red Cross parcels they had received.

Lining up the men for the final parade, Abbott had a lump in his throat as he walked down the rows of emaciated but proud and upright men:

> 'At that moment, I realised that I had gained far more than I had lost through this experience. I had served a practical apprenticeship in human relations. In the confines of that camp, the Brave New World had become more than an idealist's dream: it had approached the borders of reality. As we left those few yards of Japanese soil we loathed with all our hearts – but on which a volume of human tragedy and learning had been recorded.'

The men off the ill-fated *Asaka Maru* and subsequently the *Hakusan Maru*, including John Wyatt and Mick Sheils, arrived at Osaka on 28 August 1944. From there they were transported by train to Amagasaki and set to work in a factory.

Amagasaki camp had high fencing all around, was heavily guarded around the perimeter, and had two armed guards manning the entrance. The men were at a loss to understand why, as if they did escape from the camp, they would have been quickly recaptured and heavily punished. When the 2 Surreys arrived, there were already some 200 British PoWs in residence, most of whom had been transferred from Hong Kong in January 1943. They had been in the camp for over eighteen months. The prisoners were each given a number and a green uniform with a peaked hat, uniforms that had been taken from the Dutch when the Japanese invaded Java. Designed for wear in the tropics, the clothing was totally unsuitable for a Japanese winter.

Amagasaki camp was made up of a series of wooden huts, each housing around 300 prisoners. Each hut had two tiers of bunks, and men who were allocated a top-tier bunk had to climb a ladder and fight for bed space. There they lay side by side, head to toe, squashed like ants and surrounded by their bits of sacking and mess tins.

Upon arrival, Wyatt said to Shiels, 'I think this is going to be hell when the weather gets bad.' 'Don't worry Johnny, we have survived up to now and we are not giving up now,' Shiels replied.

After just one day to settle in, the prisoners were marched to work in a factory that made metal fabrications for the Japanese Navy. Their main task was to load pig iron into large trucks that were taken away and tipped into barges moored on the canal which ran alongside the factory. Conditions during the first couple of months at Amagasaki camp were reasonable, as it was autumn when they arrived and the weather was fine and warm. It was about a fifteen-minute walk from the camp to the factory. Each morning they had to stand in line along with the civilian workers to be counted, then all had to salute the factory official in charge of the tenko (roll call), turn to the east, face the rising sun and clap their hands.

When winter set in, the temperature in Amagasaki dropped dramatically, particularly during the night, and the men found it impossible to stay warm. Both ends of the factory were open, with little shelter from the incessant wind and rain. The lack of food, and the fact that their bodies had become accustomed to the tropical temperatures of Thailand and Malaya, made things even worse. One freezing morning, Shiels said to Wyatt, 'So this is the land of the f.....g rising sun, John.'

At the beginning of June 1945, the prisoners were ordered to pack up their paltry belongings and be ready to move out of Amagasaki. A few days later, they were transferred to Nagoya No. 9, a camp that had only been opened a few weeks previously. For the next two months they worked for the Tsuun Company, unloading ships that were bringing in cement, coal, timber and beans.

During the third week in August, when the Nagaoya prisoners were trudging wearily to work one morning, they found out that the war was over. Passing a group of Americans, the Yanks shouted cheerily over to them, 'Put those shovels down Limeys, it's these bastards' turn now. You're free.'

Eight 2 Surrey men were shipped from Singapore to Mitsushima PoW camp in Japan, arriving on 28 November 1942. The senior British officer in the camp at the time was Lieutenant Rhys of the Royal Air Force.

The camp consisted of thirteen wooden huts, covered with shingles or tree bark, and was surrounded by a 10ft-high wooden fence with nails protruding from the top boards. The prisoners were allowed an area of just 30in by 73in each as their living quarters, and as the floor was just dirt and sand, when it rained it was a quagmire.

When the 2 Surrey men arrived, winter had already set in. Ice would form under their sleeping mats and on the inside of the windows, making living conditions very difficult. Fleas were also a constant problem. A small amount of disinfectant was provided by the Japanese, but not in sufficient quantities to rid the camp of the hordes of bugs. During the summer months, the prisoners would organize 'fly campaigns' in which they would spend their rest hours killing flies and other insects to try to ease the terrible conditions. Rats were another major problem and the men did everything to try and eliminate them, without much success.

Water was pumped into the camp from a well near the Tenryu River, but it was so polluted and unfit for human consumption that it had to be boiled before drinking or cooking. During the extreme winter months, the well would freeze and the water had to be carried by buckets from the river. Only one bathtub was provided for the whole camp. There were no tables or chairs provided, the men having to either sit on their bunks or on the dirt floor to eat their meals, which were usually only a mixture of barley and rice. Meat and fish were seldom provided, but the prisoners would occasionally get the intestines and bones of cattle.

The Japanese did not provide any medical help in Mitsushima camp. It was left to Royal Navy doctor Richard Whitfield to attend to the sick as best he could. With little medicine available, Whitfield had to give the most severe cases special consideration, using the scant supplies furnished.

Although there was an ample supply of Red Cross clothing available in the camp for everyone, it was never issued in quantity, and the men were compelled to work in straw shoes or go barefoot. In early 1945, the Japanese supplied scrap cloth for repairing clothing and an issue of rubber-soled shoes. Continuous heckling by the guards caused unimaginable hardships for the prisoners. The guards would often, for no reason, call a prisoner out of the barracks and beat him severely, using any made-up excuse. The men worked from dawn to dusk, carrying cement for the building of a dam, under extremely difficult conditions. Forty-three men died in this camp, recognized as one of the most brutal camps in Japan. After the war, nine Mitsushima guards were convicted of war crimes and executed in 1946.

Another sixteen 2 Surrey men arrived at Fukuoka 17 in August 1944. This camp was located on the bay about 17 miles north-west of Kumamoto on Kyushu, Japan's most southerly island.

Formerly the labourers' quarters for the Mitsui Coal Mining Company, the prisoners were set to work down the coal mines. Conditions in the mines were dangerous, but an experienced coal miner gave the men safety talks, pointing out some of the dangers they might encounter.

Quite a few men were injured in this camp, but only three were killed during the twenty-two months it was open.

Living conditions in Fukuoka 17 were reasonable, but the prisoners were always cold due to malnutrition and lack of suitable clothing. Food usually consisted of steamed rice and vegetable soup made from anything that could be obtained. Those working down the mines were given 700 grams of rice, whilst others had to make do with 450 grams. This daily allowance was described by one doctor as 'insufficient to support life in a bed patient never mind a man required to do manual work'.

As was usual in Japanese PoW camps, men were beaten without cause with fists, clubs and even sandals. Failure to salute or bow to the Japanese resulted in a prisoner being compelled to stand to attention in front of the guard house for several hours at a time. Some men were beaten daily, whilst others were harassed by the guards while trying to sleep during rest time. All sixteen of the 2 Surrey men who were in Fukuoka 17 camp managed to survive and return home after the war.

On 20 September 1944, six 2 Surrey men arrived with 242 other prisoners at Sendai 9b camp at Sakata on the west coast of Honshu. Most of these men were survivors of the *Kachidoki Maru*, whose sinking was described in an earlier chapter. The men were used as stevedores at the train yards and the docks, loading and unloading all forms of materials, including military equipment and ammunition. The medical officer at Sendai was Doctor Jim Roulston, a fellow countryman of my father, also a survivor of the ill-fated *Kachidoki Maru*. Despite Roulston's best efforts and without the help of medicines, the winter of 1944, Japan's coldest for seventy years, took its toll on the prisoners. Many died of pneumonia alongside the more familiar tropical diseases they had endured since their capture two-and-a-half years previously.

One of the guards at Sendai 9b said to an investigator after the Japanese surrender that 'When the prisoners were imprisoned at this camp they averaged 57 kilograms in weight and when they were released they weighed 66.25 kilograms.' This was obviously an attempt to prevent him being charged with war crimes.

On 30 September 1944, a group of 289 prisoners, including three 2 Surrey men, again survivors of the sinking of the *Kachidoki Maru*, arrived at the newly opened Fukuoka 25 camp on the southern tip of Japan near Nagasaki. There they were set to work in a carbide factory or a nearby coal mine. The senior officer in the camp was Captain Wilkie and the medical officer was Captain Kenneth Mathieson of the Gordon Highlanders.

Conditions in Fukuoka 25 were good compared to many other camps in Japan. The accommodation was a large group of two-storey wooden buildings, each with a series of rooms housing about five men. The bathrooms had washbasins and proper toilets, the first that the prisoners had seen for nearly three years. Bedrooms had proper beds with rubber mattresses.

When they arrived, they couldn't believe their luck after the dreadful condition of the railway. The Japanese issued the men with two sets of new clothes, one set was work clothes and the other for casual wear. The food was basic, but still the best they had received for quite some time. Fukuoka 25 was probably the best camp in Japan.

With the war turning badly against them in early 1945, the Japanese embarked on the construction of an airfield at Ubon in north-east Thailand. Ubon is some 372 miles from Bangkok and close to the Indochina border (Laos and Cambodia today).

Ubon already had an airstrip, built by the Thais in 1921 to provide medical supplies to the outlying areas, but a second runway would enable the Japanese to operate in greater secrecy and to defend their positions in the region. Around 3,000 British, Dutch, Australian and American PoWs were transferred to Ubon, mainly from camps on the Thai/Burma railway, with over fifty 2 Surrey men among them. No officers were allowed to join the party, so Lieutenant Colonel Toosey chose RSM Sandy McTavish of the Argyle and Sutherland Highlanders, a well-respected NCO at Non Pladuk, to lead the group. McTavish had been Toosey's senior NCO at Non Pladuk and he had great faith in him. Although a strict disciplinarian, McTavish was fair and well liked by the men.

The first group arrived by train from Bangkok in early February 1945, sleeping on the station platform on their first night. The following morning, they crossed the River Mun in boats before marching 8 miles to Ban Nong Phai. Unfortunately, despite surviving the Thai/Burma railway, Lance Corporal J. Heath died of cholera during the journey, the only 2 Surrey man in the Ubon group to die.

For the next six months, the men toiled to complete a runway that was 1,500 yards long and 40 yards wide, digging ballast for the foundations and levelling the ground in preparation for the final surfacing. Discipline was strict but not too harsh, and they were fortunate that the camp had good underground water supplies. With twenty-five medical officers in the party, medical treatment was better than in most of their previous camps. A canteen was set up, along with a hospital, and many of the men testified that Ubon was an improvement from the camps they had been in on the Thai/Burma railway.

As the war progressed, the men at Ubon felt much safer as it was some distance away from the Allied bombings in the west of Thailand. They were allowed to build a theatre and a chapel, and to level land to make a football pitch. The local population were sympathetic towards the prisoners. Often, at great risk to themselves, they passed food, clothing and medicine into the camp. Some even set up food stalls outside the camp. In charge of the camp was Major Chida. Chida was a weak commander but he could be harsh, as the men found out when two prisoners attempting to escape were caught and executed.

Work ceased on the Ubon airstrip at the beginning of July when the Japanese, under intense pressure from the Allies all over South-East Asia, realized that they were heading towards defeat. Major Chida ordered the prisoners to dig trenches across the landing strip, supposedly to stop the landing of Allied aircraft, but evidence emerged after the war that they intended to shoot the prisoners and bury them in the trenches should Japan be invaded. Tension in the camp increased and the men prepared themselves as best they could to meet any sort of Japanese onslaught.

When the Americans dropped the atomic bombs on Hiroshima and Nagasaki, Major Chida announced the surrender to the prisoners on 18 August. The following day, British, Dutch, Australian and American flags were raised over the camp, replacing the rising sun. A week later, Lieutenant Colonel Toosey arrived at Ubon by train from Bangkok to meet up again with the men that he had said goodbye to seven months earlier. Toosey was concerned that they should be in good health and wanted to personally arrange their repatriation. The men gave him a huge cheer when he marched into the camp.

When Chida called for RSM McTavish to tell him the war was over, he offered him his sword. The Australians started to sing and dance around the camp, and the camp gates were torn apart. The following day, McTavish got a local Thai to come into the camp and put on a film show for the men. The first officer to arrive at Ubon camp after the Japanese surrender was David Smiley of SOE force 136, who wrote later:

'The camp seemed clean and efficient. The inmates had improvised bamboo pumps to draw water out of the ground. Most of this was thanks to McTavish, a remarkable man who managed to keep up a surprisingly high morale among the prisoners.'

The 2 Surreys in Ubon camp were also full of praise for McTavish.

It took several weeks for the men to be repatriated, but these were spent socializing with the local population who had taken them to their hearts. Sports, film shows and horse racing events were quickly organized to celebrate their new-found freedom. RAF Dakotas regularly dropped supplies of food, medicine and clothing. One of the more well-known prisoners to have been in Ubon was magician Fergus Ankorn, who shot to fame at the age of 98 when he appeared on Britain's Got Talent with Army officer Richard Jones on 28 May 2016.

The work carried out by the prisoners in Japan varied greatly. Some worked in shipyards and steel works, but those who worked in open cast mines had the most difficult and dangerous time. For those arriving off the hellships, a few had managed to keep their own clothes whilst others relied on the Japanese to provide uniforms, which in many cases were too small, particularly boots. Food in the camps was often of poor quality and usually consisted of rice with millet and sweet potatoes, with water the only drink. Drugs and medicines were almost non-existent. In one camp five aspirin tablets, one bandage and ten vitamin tablets were issued daily to serve 450 men.

Around 3,500 men died in camps on the Japanese home islands alone, with most of the deaths resulting from disease, malnutrition, overwork and poor sanitary conditions. Many of the deaths happened immediately after the prisoners arrived in Japan from South-East Asia, as they were already in a weak condition prior to embarkation.

At the end of the war in August 1945, there were around 130 camps on the Japanese home islands, with over 36,000 men detained in them. For many who survived, their experiences during those terrible years shaped their thinking, their philosophies and their attitudes for the rest of their lives.

Chapter 9

Japan Surrenders – Homeward Bound

When the news of the Japanese surrender on 15 August 1945 spread throughout the prisoner of war camps in the Far East, the prisoners reacted in many different ways. Some were euphoric and celebrated as best they could, some simply lay down and wept, some prayed and others just shrugged their shoulders. Corporal John Wyatt of the 2 Surreys, in his camp at Nagoya, summed up the reactions of the men imprisoned there on that historic day when he wrote:

'The one-armed-bandit strode into the hut and said to us in broken English "all waru pinish, u men to Englando". He was closely followed by a Japanese interpreter who calmly informed us that two huge bombs had been dropped killing many Japanese people, the Imperial Japanese Army had surrendered and we were to be free to return home. "It is very bad"' he said. "Japan is appealing to the United Nations." He promptly turned his back on us and walked out to much cheering and laughter. After four years of hell it dawned on me that perhaps I might just see my family again, yet I was fearful of such a thought, as it had become so ingrained in my mind over the past three and a half years that a violent and painful death was inevitable. My hopes of survival had been dashed so many times that I simply refused to believe these men for whom I held such hate. Somehow suddenly the air in the hut became fresher and cleaner than it was and it was at this point that many of us knelt to pray. Others were shouting [and] some were crying, some didn't move at all and the lads who were too weak to move just lay there staring up at the ceiling. We were going home. An American doctor came in soon after and said, "Men, your freedom is here. You have suffered much but I beg of you all, do not go out looking for revenge; one bullet or bayonet through you and all the horrors you have suffered will be in vain."'

Even though the Japanese had surrendered, the men in the camps scattered over the Far East were still very concerned for their safety, especially those in Japan. Most of the civilian population there held strong hostile feelings towards them, as many had family members who died in the armed forces and in the US bombing raids. In many cases, guards had to protect the prisoners from a populace who were starving whilst they had large amounts of food shipped into their camps.

Captain Barnard of the 2 Surreys, still on the Thai/Burma railway at the end of the war, summed up his feelings when the Japanese surrendered:

'That same evening we were allowed outside the camp, although kept within certain bounds. I shall never forget those first few steps into the outside world. That funny feeling as we walked past the Japanese soldiers still on guard at the gates into the world outside. Freedom after three and a half endless years.'

Almost immediately after the surrender, the Royal Air Force and American Air Force began dropping food by parachute into the camps in Thailand, Burma and Singapore. Leaflets were also dropped giving them some basic advice:

To all Allied Prisoners of War

The Japanese have surrendered unconditionally and the war is over.
We will get supplies to you as soon as is humanly possible and will make arrangements to get you out but, owing to the distance involved, it may be some time before we can achieve this.

YOU will help us and yourselves if you act as follows:

1. Stay in your camp until you get further orders from us.
2. Start preparing nominal rolls of personnel giving fullest particulars.
3. List your most urgent necessities.
4. If you have been starved or underfed for long periods DO NO eat large quantities of solid food, fruit or vegetables at first. It is dangerous to do so. Small quantities at frequent intervals are much safer and will strengthen you far more quickly. For those who are really ill or very weak, fluids such as broth and soup, making use of

the water in which rice and other foods have been boiled, are much the best. Gifts of food from the local population should be cooked. We want to get you back home quickly, safe and sound, and we do not want to risk your chances from diarrhoea, dysentery and cholera at this stage.

5. Local authorities and/or Allied officers will take charge of your affairs in a very short time. Be guided by their advice.

Of course, such advice was ignored by many of the men, who had not seen proper food for over three years; they proceeded to gorge themselves on the supplies that had been dropped. Quite a few were to pay the price for this, as bloating and stomach upsets stuck with them for some time afterwards. One man was reported to have eaten twelve breakfasts one after the other.

Lieutenant Colonel Swinton of the 2 Surreys was camp commander at Kanchanaburi when the surrender eventually came. He described the situation then as 'delicate', and gave his personal guarantee to the Japanese camp commander that the men would keep their discipline and not attack the guards.

The surviving members of the 2 Surreys, along with thousands of other British prisoners of war, were now scattered across great swathes of South-East Asia. It took many months before they were all able to get back home to Britain or Ireland. The responsibility for getting the men home lay with RAPWI, which stood for Recovery of Allied Prisoners of War and Internees (or, as the prisoners called it, Retain All Prisoners of War Indefinitely), an exercise that was to prove extremely difficult and time-consuming. For the men in camps in Japan, Korea and the Philippines, the Americans took over the task, whilst those in Singapore, Burma and Thailand were repatriated by the British and Australians.

The prisoners released from the camps in Burma, Thailand, Malaya and Singapore were initially put into three categories, A to C, with A being the fittest and released first, B coming next whilst C were the more seriously ill prisoners who would be admitted to hospital for treatment before being sent home. My father was in Chunkai camp near Kanchanaburi, and as far as I am aware he was in the A category. From there he was taken by train to Bangkok, a journey that he said was certainly more enjoyable than that he had embarked on from Singapore to Ban Pong almost three years previously. After arriving in Bangkok, the men were provided with accommodation, food and clothing by the Thais, before being flown in RAF Dakotas to Rangoon in Burma. There, a fleet of ships were waiting to ferry them home to Britain. Tragically, several of the Dakotas crashed en route to Rangoon, killing men who were within a whisper of freedom after three-and-a-half years of hell. These flights were not the most comfortable as the aircraft had been used for supply drops and many had their doors removed. Some men reported having to sit on the floor and fasten ropes around them secured to a part of the plane's structure, but they couldn't have cared less as they were now free.

Twenty-four men, including 2 Surrey bandsman R. Gadd, who had lost a leg during Allied bombings on the railway, embarked on Dakota flight 66 of 117 Squadron on 8 September from Saigon. After landing at Bangkok to refuel, the plane ran into difficulties about 13 miles north-west of Moulmein in Burma, plunging from the air and killing all on board. Local villagers found various articles washed ashore the next day at low tide and recovered several bodies from the wrecked aircraft. It was a particularly sad end for a small group of men who had endured such hardships over the previous few years.

Those men still in Changi in Singapore when the Japanese surrendered became free almost immediately. Before being repatriated, many took up residence in empty houses or with Chinese families, enjoying their freedom.

Captain John Barnard of the 2 Surreys summed up many of the men's feeling as they left Thailand behind for the last time:

'As I looked out of the plane windows at the rice fields and jungles of Thailand, I could not help remembering the thousands of our fellows who lay buried there. They, too, had hoped and prayed for this day as much as we had. They, too, had dreamed of happy reunions with their families, but whoever controls the destiny of man had ruled differently, and they lay instead in unknown graves in a foreign land. Just thousands of wasted lives.'

Upon arrival at Rangoon, the men were all handed a letter from the Indian Red Cross and the St John's War Organization that provided a very welcome friendly touch. It read:

'At last the day has come, three years of darkness and agony have passed and a new dawn is here, bringing with it deliverance for all from danger and anxiety, and for you above all freedom after bondage. Through these long years we have not forgotten you. We of the Red Cross and St John's have tried every way of establishing contact and relieving your hardships. Some provisions have been sent and messages despatched; but we do not know how much has reached you, for the callous indifference of the enemy has made the task nigh impossible.

'But now the enemy is beaten and you are free once more, we are doing all we can to give you the welcome you richly deserve and to make your homeward path a pleasant and joyful one.'

Rangoon was like the promised land to the freed prisoners of war. Proper medical treatment and unlimited western food was readily available, much to my father's relief as he always loved his roast beef, potatoes and two veg. At last he could once again indulge in his favourite meal after more than three-and-a-half years on a diet of rice. Tucking into his first roast dinner for over three years, memories of his Irish childhood came flooding back and he admitted that he openly wept tears of joy and relief. He left Rangoon on 26 September on the SS *Ormonde*, stopping off at Colombo in Ceylon on 2 October. As the ship docked at Colombo, lights flashed, rockets split the sky and sirens blared, welcoming the several thousand men on board. The *Ormonde* arrived at Suez on 12 October before finally reaching Southampton on 22 October, a journey that had taken almost a month.

On the *Ormonde*, just prior to docking in Southampton, my father had been given a copy of the War Office document entitled 'To All British Army Ex Prisoners of War' (see Appendix II), a document I found still amongst his papers after his death in 1991.

The national press at the time reported the homecomings of the PoWs in a low-key way. The *Daily Telegraph* stated simply:

'First of 15 liners with nearly 20,000 former prisoners of the Japanese aboard are racing home to Britain from ports in South-East Asia, it was announced yesterday. Among the many famous liners acting as merch ships are the *Empress of Australia*, the *Chitral*, the *Ormonde* and the *Worcestershire*.'

The returning Far East PoWs had to endure several weeks of medical checks and debriefings before they could return home to their families.

When he was finally debriefed, my father caught a train to Liverpool and then the overnight ferry to Belfast. There he boarded an Ulster Transport Authority bus to his home town of Downpatrick, a journey that had taken him almost two days from Southampton. Arriving at the bus station, his father and mother, along with his six brothers and his sister, were there to meet him. It was an emotional moment for the Lowry family as the last military member was welcomed back into their arms.

For the 2 Surrey men imprisoned in Japan, it was a month after the surrender before American forces could eventually land to release them. They parachuted advisors into the camps, along with supplies of food, clothing and medicines. These drops also included leaflets advising the liberated prisoners not to gorge themselves on the now abundant foodstuffs, including chocolate, tobacco and sweets. They were also warned against drinking the local 'saki', an almost pure wood alcohol named after the Japanese rice wine, but again this was ignored as men celebrated their new-found freedom. In Singapore, a man died after drinking a full tin of evaporated milk.

The 2 Surrey men who spent the latter part of the war in Japan were to take a different route home than those in Singapore and Thailand. The US Navy transported them to Manila in the Philippines, where many waited for up to four weeks, before boarding transport ships for the journey across the Pacific to the west coast of America or Canada.

Corporal John Wyatt, who was released from his camp in Japan, outlines his journey home in his book *No Mercy from the Japanese*:

'It was 5 September 1945, almost a month after the Atomic bomb had been dropped on Hiroshima, when we eventually marched out of the gates of the camp for the final time. Not with the usual feeling of depression and dread about the grind of the day to follow, but with a feeling of unbelievable elation that it was at last all over. We sang and cheered as we marched about two miles along the road towards the small local railway station, waving our home-made Union Jacks[,] where we boarded a train bound for the Port of Yokosuka, another two hours away.

'At Yokosuka, we boarded the *USS Benevolence* a hospital ship where we were given the most modern drugs available at that time. After a few days, we were transferred to an American aircraft carrier the *USS Wagner* that took us from Tokyo Bay to the Philippines where we boarded the *USS Admiral Charles Hughes* bound for San Francisco on the next leg of our long journey back to England[,] a voyage that lasted around two weeks.

'As the ship sailed past Honolulu, the plans had been changed and the ship would now be heading up the coast towards Victoria, Vancouver Island in Canada.

'At Vancouver, we boarded a Pullman train of the Canadian National Railroad service for the 3,000-mile journey across Canada to Halifax[,] Nova Scotia. As the train pulled into Halifax, the sight of the *Queen Elizabeth* lying alongside the docks was one of the most uplifting sights of my life.

'The five-day journey across the Atlantic was smooth and uneventful and it was a typical dark and damp December day when we edged into the Solent and tied up alongside the docks in Southampton.'

The ships bringing the men back from camps in Thailand, Burma and Singapore arrived at either Liverpool or Southampton, where they were greeted by cheering crowds, bands and military representatives. At Liverpool, even though a dock strike was in progress, the dockers, realizing the importance of their new arrivals, helped them disembark and get to Lime Street railway station. One man remembers his arrival at Liverpool:

'We were driven in army trucks through the city. We saw women driving tramcars. We thought it was great. The lassies were all screaming and jumping up on the tailboards and kissing and cuddling the boys.'

Upon arrival home, most of the men were given the choice of remaining in the forces or being demobilized. Many, like my father, who had served nine years in the army, chose demobilization and returned to civilian life and the families they had not seen for many years. But as three-and-a-half years of malnutrition and severe mistreatment had taken its toll on many of the returning 2 Surreys, quite a few found it difficult to adjust to civilian life. They struggled to deal with their experiences during those years of captivity. My own father drank heavily upon his return, often suffering flashbacks to his days fighting or in the camps. My aunt told me that he would often come home drunk late at night, crawling on his hands and knees up the street, shooting at imaginary Japanese soldiers. It was a year after his return from captivity in the Far East that he met my mother, a lady who turned out to be his rock and helped him to overcome the demons in his head. I can recall when I was about 7 years old waking up in the middle of the night and hearing him screaming and running up and down the hallway. My mother would soothe me with the words, 'Go back to sleep, your daddy is just having a nightmare,' – it is only now that I understand why.

Quite a few of the men found it difficult to talk about their experiences as prisoners of war, not even to wives or families, whilst others would only talk about them to fellow ex-prisoners. Some men were told not to discuss their captivity with their families as it might upset them

Many were not able to settle down again into civilian life. Some of those who did not talk about it thought that it was to be kept secret and were concerned about items 3 and 4 of the War Office document they were given (see Appendix II) and the small leaflet 'Guard your tongue', which stated:

'You are free now. Anything you say in public or to the press is liable to be published throughout the world. You have direct or indirect knowledge of the fate of many of your comrades who died in enemy hands as a result of brutality or neglect. Your story, if published in the more sensational press, would cause much unnecessary unhappiness to relatives and friends. If you had not been lucky enough to have survived and had died an unpleasant death at the hands of the Japanese, you would not have wished your family and friends to have been harrowed by lurid details of your death. That is just what will happen to the families of your comrades who did die in that way if you start talking too freely about your experience. It is felt certain that now you know the reason for this order you will take pains to spare the feelings of others. Arrangements have been made for you to tell your story to interrogating officers who will then ask you to write it down. You are not to say anything to anyone until after you have written out your statement and handed it in.'

One man slept on the floor of his house for several years after his return; after years sleeping on rice sacks, he simply could not get used to a bed. Many men remained bitter about their treatment and bore a grudge against the Japanese for the rest of their lives, whilst others simply forgave but could not forget. My father hated the Japanese with a vengeance for the rest of his life and would never buy any product made in Japan.

Whilst jobs were readily available to the returning prisoners after the war, some could not hold down a job for very long as the readjustment to civilian life proved too difficult. Corporal John Wyatt found it very hard to adjust to life again in his native Sydenham when he discovered that the girl he loved and had got engaged to before setting off for the Far East had married another man. John was so in love with her that he had her name tattooed on his arm when he arrived in Singapore in March 1941. When he returned in late 1945, she wept and told him that she thought he had been killed.

When John explained this to me during one of my visits to see him, I had to fight back the tears. He said:

'I was looking forward to seeing my girlfriend Elsie again, but was devastated when my mother told me that she had married another man during the time I was a prisoner. Although things between Elsie and I were over, I felt that I just had to go and see her again, so the next morning I walked around to her house and nervously knocked on the door. She had heard that I was back and looked very sheepish when she opened the front door.

"Hello Elsie, remember me?" I said, feeling rather foolish to ask the question.

"I'm really sorry John, but I heard from the authorities in 1942 that you were reported missing, possibly dead," she sobbed.

'"I'm not bitter, have no regrets and I'm only too pleased that you are happy. I'm just thankful to God that I have survived the horrors of the last four years."

'My heart was heavy as I walked home that day, but there was nothing I could do about it and I just had to try and get on with my life.'

He explained his thoughts to me at his home in Sydenham a year before he died in 2008:

'It became very difficult for me to adapt to life back home in Sydenham and I began to feel trapped in that miserable house in Abingdon Grove. I had forgotten what life was like out of uniform, and it was obvious that the horrific experiences were still playing on my mind. I felt very claustrophobic, possibly because I had spent the last three-and-a-half years out of doors and sleeping in large open huts with many other men. I could not get used to sleeping in a small room, and all I wanted to do was to get out in the fresh air and walk around. I was also not too keen on mixing with people, and of course I had lost touch with most of my original friends whilst away serving my country in the Far East. This suited me, as I did not want to mix with people anyway, preferring my own company.

'Most mornings I would leave the house after breakfast and walk for miles around the streets of Sydenham on my own. This was very therapeutic, and my mother and father were very sympathetic and understanding. They understood how I felt after the horrible experiences of the camps, and just left me alone to try and put my life back in some sort of order.

'For the first few months I just couldn't settle down at all and felt very depressed. I made no effort to get a job and as my back Army pay was about £300 (quite a lot in those days) I was not short of money.

'I eventually managed to get a job as a postman in Sydenham. It really was the best job I could get as I could be out in the fresh air walking around all day – a job that I was very happy doing for the next thirty-seven years.'

Conclusion

When the Second World War broke out, the British Empire covered between a quarter and a third of the globe, representing an area over 150 times the size of Great Britain. Singapore was one of the empire's prime strategically located ports and one of the jewels in the crown. Malaya produced 38 per cent of the world's rubber and its mines produced 58 per cent of the world's tin. It was little wonder that Japan, with its envious eyes on such riches, decided to invade these British possessions in 1941.

Winston Churchill, speaking at the outbreak of the war with Japan in December 1941, said of the British Empire:

'It embodies the enlightenment of western civilisation and therefore is a force for the redemption and generation of mankind. It is integral to that "civilisation" that Britain is defending.'

Such an idealistic principle meant little to the 365 men of the 2 Surreys whose young lives were to be cut short trying to defend this empire against a determined and well-trained enemy. These would have been hollow words in their ears as they gave their lives on the battlefields of Malaya and Singapore, in Japanese prisoner of war camps, drowned at sea enroute to Japan or in escape attempts to avoid captivity. The remains of these patriotic young men lie scattered across great swathes of South-East Asia. Many lie in manicured war cemeteries in Thailand, Singapore, Burma and Japan, whilst others have no known grave.

Despite being consistently warned by his military advisors, Churchill's blinkered bigotry made him blind to the threat posed to British possessions in the Far East by a militarist Japan. He said, 'The Japanese would never dare attack a white power.' Doggedly convinced that his own opinions were right, he went even further and described the Japanese as, 'The Wops of the East, who would shout and threaten but would not move.' These were words that would come back to haunt him.

The loss of the *Prince of Wales* and the *Repulse*, together with 800 of their crews, was a huge blow to the defence of Malaya and Singapore. Had the resources so badly needed been made available then, many lives might not have been lost. In my opinion, Churchill more than anyone else had to take the ultimate responsibility for the fall of Singapore in 1942 and the deaths of many Allied servicemen, including the 365 men from the 2 Surreys.

As prisoners of war, the men of the 2 Surreys, along with thousands of their comrades, were compelled to take a very different mental outlook to that of a free person. With their lives totally in the hands of a harsh and brutal enemy, day-to-day survival was the only thought in their minds. Had the Japanese shown even a degree of compassion and goodwill, or had they possessed the basic principles of supply and organization, many lives could have been saved. The normal rules and regulations of a civilized society regarding the treatment of the sick and injured were in most cases simply ignored. It should be pointed out, however, that the experiences of prisoners at the hands of the Japanese varied considerably depending on when and where they were imprisoned, and universal conclusions are impossible to make. Yet there is no doubt that the vast majority of prisoners were inhumanely treated by their captors.

If one can take just a crumb of comfort from the 2 Surreys' experiences in the Far East, it was the cultivation of a sense of comradeship that remained with them for the rest of their lives. Lord Harewood of the Grenadier Guards, who himself was a prisoner of war at the hands of the Germans, wrote, 'You never really know a man until you have been a prisoner of war with him.'

By the early months of 1945, Japan realized that it was losing the war and an invasion of its home islands by the Americans was likely. The Japanese feared that large numbers of prisoners across the plethora of camps in the Far East might revolt and interfere with their defence. Consequently, an order was sent out to every camp commander that all prisoners were to be annihilated, with all evidence destroyed. A copy of the order was found in US archives after the war:

The Time:

Although the basic aim is to act under superior orders, individual disposition may be made in the following circumstances:

(1) When an uprising of large numbers cannot be suppressed without the use of firearms.

(2) When escapees from the camp may turn into a hostile fighting force.

The Methods:

(1) Whether they are destroyed individually or in groups, or however it is done, with mass bombing, poisonous smoke, poisons, drowning, decapitation, or what, dispose of them as the situation dictates.

(2) In any case it is the aim not to allow the escape of a single one, to annihilate them all, and leave not any traces.

There is some doubt, however, that this edict reached all of the camp commanders and many chose to ignore it anyway for fear of post-war crimes. Eminent historian Norman Stone has described the Japanese at that time in the following way:

'Aa talented people led by maniacs who knew perfectly well that the war would end in disaster but who were determined to keep their honour intact to the final gruesome suicidal point.'

Of course, the dropping of the atomic bombs on Hiroshima and Nagasaki ended the war quickly, saving the lives of many thousands of prisoners, including my father and the rest of his surviving 2 Surrey colleagues.

Three thousand Japanese were put on trial for war crimes when the war ended, a lengthy process that took several years to complete. Many of those tried were sentenced to death and others to terms of imprisonment.

Of the 2 Surrey Regiment's 960 men who prepared to face the Japanese on 8 December 1941 at Jitra, only 260 were accounted for on 14 February 1942 when Lieutenant General Percival surrendered Singapore to General Yamashita. By then, 185 had already lost their lives in the battles of Jitra, Gurun, Kampar and Singapore, with another 400 scattered over the Malaya peninsula or the surrounding seas.

The story of the surrender was made even more difficult to stomach when it was discovered after the war that Colonel Tsuji, commander of the

Japanese forces, admitted that his ammunition for an assault on Singapore was almost exhausted. He said:

> 'We had barely a hundred rounds per gun left for our field guns, and less for our heavy guns. With this small ammunition supply it was impossible to keep down enemy fire by counter-battery operations.'

This book has told the story of incredible bravery in the face of overwhelming odds by the men of the 2 Surrey Regiment during the Second World War. When war broke out, they were one of several well-trained regiments, fully acclimatized to living and fighting in the jungle, who gave a good account of themselves at the battles of Jitra, Gurun, Kampar and Singapore. Some people have accused the Allied troops who fought in Malaya and Singapore of cowardice, but I totally refute that after conducting my own research for this book. It was not the fault of the men on the ground, like my father and his colleagues, that Malaya fell, but the crass arrogance of the politicians in London and the senior officers based in Singapore.

They are truly the 'forgotten army', and more than seventy years on, with very few still alive, it is a privilege to set the record straight and to honour these men for their brave service to their country.

When the 2 Surreys were sent to north Malaya in 1942, their colours, with their distinctive black facings, were hidden in the vaults of a bank in Singapore. There they lay undamaged for almost four years, before being recovered intact when the war ended. They were taken back to England and deposited in the Queen's Royal Surrey Regiment Museum at Clandon Park, near Guildford, Surrey. In April 2015, the building was destroyed by fire and the regimental colours were sadly lost. The colours of the 2 Surreys, however, will live on in the minds of the relatives of these brave men, many of whom gave their lives for their country.

It can be argued that no other period in British military history marked, changed or ended so many people's lives as the Second World War. The memories and experiences, particularly of Far East prisoners of war, were so intense for those who survived that even today, many can vividly remember key wartime moments.

The British media has long been obsessed about the lives of prisoners of war in German camps, the Battle of Britain and the D-Day landings, but from Far East prisoners of war you will only hear stories about beatings, starvation and being worked to death. This book has hopefully gone some way to portray the terrible conditions endured by my father and the rest of the men taken prisoner by the Japanese at the fall of Singapore.

The East Surreys song:

Don't flurry or worry the boys of East Surrey
  will pull you through all right
Midst fun and noise, they're real good boys
And lads that love a fight
Station them here or station them there
In fact you can station them anywhere
They're British lads without a care
And boys that have made the whole world stare
Fearless and bold, like the lads of old
They are born of the bulldog strain
With plenty of grit, they do their bit
And their colours bear no stain
But VALOUR is their motto
And they boast a brave VC
Whilst they pride themselves of honour
On land as well as sea
So we're proud of the East Surrey Regiment

Appendix I

Brothers in Arms

At the outset of the war in the Far East, ten sets of brothers were serving together in the 2 Surreys. Out of these twenty men, eight lost their lives, with the other twelve returning home at the end of the war. One can only imagine the thoughts and feelings of the parents and families of these ten sets of brothers during that dreadful time.

Private Malcolm Riveron and Bandsman Peter Riveron came from a military family, their father serving in the RAF at the outbreak of war. The Riveron brothers were strong swimmers, representing the regiment at swimming competitions on numerous occasions. Peter was the first to be sent from Changi to the Thai/Burma railway on 9 October 1942, with his brother following him six months later on 23 March 1943. It is not known if the two brothers' paths crossed whilst working on the Thai/Burma railway, but both survived and returned home at the end of the war.

Privates A. Sheppard and R. Sheppard from Colliers Wood, south-west London, both lost their lives in the Far East. A. Sheppard was killed at the Battle of Jitra early in the war on 11 December 1941, whilst his brother died when the *Hofuko Maru* carrying him to Japan was sunk on 21 September 1944. R. Sheppard would no doubt have been aware that his sibling had lost his life at Jitra, and must have had that on his mind during the following three years of his captivity before tragedy struck for a second time for the family.

Sergeant Harry Wilson and Private Henry Wilson from Hampton, Middlesex, survived the Malayan campaign, only for both to die as prisoners of war on the Thai/Burma railway. Henry died of dysentery at Kanchanaburi on 25 May 1943, whilst his brother Harry died in the same camp six months later on 5 November 1943, again of dysentery.

Lance Corporal Yewings from Paddington was killed in action around 4 February 1942 in Singapore. His stepbrother, Private Wheeler, had been transferred to Mission 204 (a British military mission to China) a year previously before the Japanese invasion, and survived the war.

Lance Corporal E. Woolard and Private R. Woolard from Bognor Regis were both killed in action during the Malayan campaign. Lance Corporal Woolard was killed on 17 December 1941 during the Battle of Gurun, and his brother three weeks later at the Battle of Kampar on 2 January 1942.

Lance Corporal G.H. McClarty and Bandsman T. McClarty from East Dulwich, south-east London. Both survived the war and the Japanese PoW camps, returning safely home.

Corporal R. Hawkins and Private D. Hawkins from Tolworth, south-west London. Corporal Hawkins was killed in action at Gurun, whilst his sibling survived the war.

Privates A. Hillier and H. Hillier from north London survived the Malayan campaign and were taken prisoner. Both were sent to the Thai/Burma railway on 25 October 1942. The brothers were split up in February 1945 when H. Hillier boarded the *Haruyasa Maru* in Keppel Harbour bound for Japan, leaving his brother in Thailand. Due to the presence of American submarines, the ship only made it to Saigon, where he spent the rest of war in a prison camp. Both brothers survived to return home.

Sergeant J. Craig from Colliers Wood died of beri-beri as a prisoner of war in Kanchanaburi four days before Christmas 1943. His brother, Private C. Craig, survived the Thai/Burma railway and returned home to Colliers Wood at the end of the war.

Privates S. Law and T. Law from Islington, London, survived the Malayan campaign. They were split up soon after arriving in Changi when S. Law was sent to the Thai/Burma railway in October 1942 at the same time as my father. His brother stayed in Changi for another year. In October 1943, S. Law was sent to Japan on board the *Asama Maru*, and spent the rest of the war labouring in a prisoner of war camp at Nagasaki. There is little doubt that he would have witnessed the dropping of the atomic bomb on Nagasaki on 9 August 1945.

Appendix II

Ministry of Defence Return Document, September 1945

RESTRICTED
the information given
in this document is not
to be communicated
either directly of
indirectly to the press
or to any other person
not authorised to
receive it

TO ALL BRITISH ARMY

EX PRISONERS OF WAR

THE WAR OFFICE, D.P.W. September 1945

BRITISH ARMY

STATUS, RANK, SERVICE AND SECURITY

1. RANK. You will retain any paid acting, temporary, or paid local rank or lance appointment you hold for 61 days from the date of your arrival in this country or until you are posted to a specific vacancy in a W.E., whichever is earlier. But if such return to England is held up by admission to hospital overseas under British or Allied control you may not retain your paid acting, temporary or paid local rank or lance appointment beyond a maximum period of four months from the date of your admission to hospital or for more than 61 days from the date of your arrival in England or until you are posted to a specific vacancy in W.E., whichever is the earlier. Any promotion you get later will follow the normal rules for promotion in war. Unpaid acting rank will be retained for 61 days but will not be converted to paid rank, nor will paid acting or temporary rank be converted to temporary or war substantive rank during this period.

2. SERVICE. At the conclusion of your repatriation leave you will be released from the Army unless: –
(a) you are an officer holding a permanent Regular Army commission;
(b) you are a Regular Soldier with Colour Service to complete;
(c) you have applied to defer your release, and your application has been confirmed.
In the above cases, you will be retained in the U.K. for a period of six months and will not be returned to the Far East.

3. SECURITY. You must not grant interviews to press, newsreel or broadcasting representatives unless permission is given.

4. INTELLIGENCE AND CASUALTY INFORMATION OR ANY OTHER CONFIDENTIAL INFORMATION REGARDING P.W. CONDITIONS. You should have had an opportunity of giving information to representatives of M.I. 9, but if you have any further details to give ask to see the M.I. 9 officer in the reception camp. Do not pass any casualty information to next of kin as the responsible authorities will inform them officially after it has been checked against existing records.

5 DISEMBARKATION. On arrival in England those of you who are to go to hospital will go there direct. The rest of you will be taken to a Reception Camp. You will understand that difficulties of transport to, and accommodation at the port of disembarkation or Reception Camp will make it impossible for your relatives or friends to greet you there. If you go to hospital do not expect to be visited by your relatives immediately unless you are seriously ill, because accommodation in the neighbourhood of the hospitals is scanty. The hospital to which you first go will be the nearest suitable military hospital to the port at which you disembark. If you are not seriously ill, you will shortly be going on leave.

6. ARRIVAL TELEGRAMS. Immediately on arrival at the Reception Camp you will be given a telegram, which you can send free of charge to your next-of-kin.

7. MEDICAL INSPECTION. At the reception camp, you will be medically inspected to *ascertain* that you are sufficiently fit to go on leave, and your chest will be X-rayed by mass miniature radiography. You will later be given a full medical examination during your leave (as you will see from paragraph 19) to determine your fitness. Nevertheless, if you are worried about your state of health and wish to have it investigated fully before proceeding on leave, you should say so and arrangements will then be made for you to go to a hospital for the purpose but at the hospital you will have to take your turn with other patients and this may involve a delay of some days.

8. WELFARE—PERSONAL AND DOMESTIC PROBLEMS. There is a welfare centre at the reception camp staffed by welfare officers whom you will be able to consult privately about any personal difficulty.
If by chance, you find that you need help or advice while on leave, ask at a police station or Post Office for the address of one of the following:
Army Welfare Officer.
Soldiers', Sailors' and Airmen's Families Association.
Inc. Soldiers', Sailors and Airmen's Help Society.
Citizens' Advice Bureau.
British Red Cross.
Ministry of Labour and National Service Resettlement Advice Office
You will almost certainly find a representative of one of these organizations near your home who will be only too glad to help you.

9. LEAVE RATION CARDS AND N.A.A.F.I. PERMITS.   You will be given leave ration cards which will entitle you to buy rations at double the civilian scale during the first 42 days of your leave. For any leave you get after that you will be issued like other soldiers with ration cards on the civilian scale. If you have any difficulty in buying the double rations get into touch with the local food officer of the Ministry of Food, who will see that you can get your double rations from a convenient retailer.

N.A.A.F.I. Form 578.E overstamped by Camp Commandant's Office, Military or E.M.S. Hospital will be issued to you. This form, on presentation to the Camp Institute, will entitle you to buy six weeks' ration of privilege price cigarettes (or tobacco) and chocolate and sugar confectionery.

Where, in exceptional cases, an extension of leave is granted in excess of the normal six weeks, N.A.A.F.I. Form 578.B will be sent to you by Officer i/c Records at the same time as he forwards your leave pass and ration card. Officers will obtain Ration Cards from their Holding Units or Depot.

10. PAY AND ACCOUNTS.   (a) Immediately on arrival at the reception camp officers will ' be able to draw one advance of up to ten pounds *(£10)*.   Other Ranks will be issued with one advance of pay of five pounds *(£5)*. In addition, before being sent on leave the following advances of pay will be made: –

Warrant Officers	*£10*
Staff-Sergeants and Sergeants	*£8*
Lance-Sergeants and Corporals and Lance-Corporals	
Privates	*£6*

An R.A.P.C. Officer and staff will be at the reception camp and you will be able to discuss any pay or allowance difficulties with them.

In applying for advances, you should remember that in the cases of officers and protected personnel deductions have been made of the amounts which should have been paid by the detaining power during captivity in respect of pay other than working pay. These deductions are provisional and subject to adjustment in accordance with the facts when full information becomes available.

(6) In order to facilitate any adjustment which may be necessary to your home account, you may be asked to complete a statement showing whether you received any pay or working pay during captivity. You may also be asked to produce any documents in your possession which relate to your account with the Detaining Power, credit balance, or status (including any evidence of recognition by the Detaining Power as a protected person) or any receipt for currency which was surrendered or impounded from you during captivity.

Unissued Credit Balances   *(c)* Owing to difficulties of communication which prevented many prisoners of war in the Far East from handling their own financial affairs and utilising credit balances due to them, authority was granted from the 31st March, 1945, for quarterly deposits to be made in the Post Office Savings Bank in respect of balance of pay due to prisoners of war in the Far East which remained unissued in the absence of any effective instructions from those concerned. The deposits are equal to balances due less the following amounts, which remain credited to the individual's pay account:

Officers (including Nursing Officers)	£25–26
W.Os. and N.C.Os. of the rank of Sergeant or above	£15–16
Soldiers below the rank of Sergeant	£10–11

On repatriation, the deposit remaining due in each case (including interest) will be transferred to a personal accou for the prisoner of war concerned in the Post Office Savings Bank. Further information can be obtained from your Regimental Paymaster.

11. FOREIGN CURRENCY.   Any foreign currency received by you before capture, during captivity or before you came under Allied Control should be retained by you until arrival in England when it will be collected and dealt with in conjunction with the adjustment of your pay account for the period of your captivity.

12. KIT AND CLOTHING CLAIMS—OFFICERS ONLY.   The R.A.P.C. staff at the reception camp will assist in preparing an claims you have for compensation for loss of kit.

13. KIT—OFFICERS ONLY.   Any kit which you left behind when you were captured may have arrived in England. You should make enquiries of the Commandant at the reception camp and also of your next-of-kin.

14. CLOTHING.   Military clothing for officers is obtained from private outfitters and is subject to surrender of clothir coupons. An issue of coupons will be made to enable officers to renew or complete their kits. Battle dress, however can be purchased—without surrender of coupons—at the reception camp.

Officers will also be entitled to draw, at the reception camps, their normal proportionate maintenance allowance of Service clothing coupons for the current clothing rationing year. This includes an element of 21 " Special " coupon valid for the purchase of civilian recreational clothing, e.g., sports jacket and flannel trousers. All service coupons are valid for the purchase of underclothing, pyjamas, handkerchiefs, dressing gowns and footwear in addition to th normal items of uniform.

At the time of your release from the Service all unused Service coupons must be returned to your Commanding Officer for disposal.

Other ranks will be issued with all necessary Army clothing and necessaries, and will also receive 20 coupons which can be used for purchase of pyjamas, and other minor items of civilian attire not included in the Army kit. Facilities exist at the reception camp for issue to other ranks of chits with which handkerchiefs can be purchased without surrender of coupons.

C.R.S.C.I.A.   This is a special form which you can obtain at the reception camp or at your nearest Local Assistance Board (usually located at the local Fuel Office). This form enables you to claim coupons to replace any civilian clothing, which has been destroyed in this country by causes outside your control, e.g., by enemy action.

15. IDENTITY AND LEAVE DOCUMENTS.   The reception camp will issue identity certificates or temporary identity documents, free travel documents and leave passes. Train times for leave destinations will be notified under camp arrangements.

16. MEDAL RIBBONS.   The various campaign stars and medals to which personnel are entitled for service during this war will be explained to you at the reception camp. The ribbons of those to which you appear to be entitled will be issued to you, also any appropriate emblems to wear on the ribbons. These issues are provisional only and will not constitute an award; a proper claim form must therefore be completed by you later, and on this the actual award will be authorized.

If you are released or cease to serve before you can complete the claim form you should apply to War Office (for officers) or the Officer i/c Records (for other ranks) for the forms to be sent to you.

17. ELECTORAL REPRESENTATION.   Special arrangements will be made to provide you with an opportunity of completing the declaration card in order to entitle von to vote at Parliamentary and Municipal Elections.

18. HOSPITAL.   Those of you who are not well enough to go to a reception camp will be admitted to a military hospital.

On leaving hospital the arrangements for pay, clothing, clothing coupons, ration cards, N.A.A.F.I. permits and identity documents will be exactly the same as at the reception camps.

If you require hospital treatment everything possible will be done to arrange for this treatment in a hospital near your home. It must be realized, however, that hospital accommodation so situated may not, in every case, be available, particularly if specialized treatment is required.

You will be sent on leave as soon as you are sufficiently fit; your relatives will be able to visit you at the hospitals.

19 LEAVE   After reporting to a reception camp you will be given 42 days leave during which time you will appear before a medical board. This will not take place during the first 14 days of your leave.

If you are found unfit for further service you will report, at the conclusion of your repatriation leave, to a unit where the medical board proceedings will be confirmed and you will be given 56 day's terminal leave, together with overseas leave on the scale of one day for each month of overseas service since September 1939 provided that at least six months' overseas service has been given.

If, however, you are admitted to hospital immediately on arrival you will, if found to be fit for further service, be granted 42 days leave when discharged from hospital. On the other hand, if at the hospital it is found that you are unfit for further service your discharge procedure will not be initiated earlier than 42 days after arrival in the U.K. and your 56-day's terminal leave will date from the 43rd day. If you are in need of in-patient treatment in hospital, your discharge will be postponed until a later date.

20. EXTENSION OF LEAVE.   (a) If the period of leave is extended, additional ration cards, leave passes and any necessary railway warrants will be issued on request by depots in the case of officers and in the case of other ranks by the Officer i/c Records.

During your leave, you can obtain the reduced concession fares, granted by the Railway Companies, by showing your identity card (officers) or leave pass (other ranks) to the booking clerk; the concessions are applicable whether you are in uniform or civilian clothes.

b) If you are admitted to hospital for treatment whilst on leave you may apply to your Officer i/c Records for an extension of leave, not exceeding 28 days, to cover the period spent in hospital. If, however, after admission to hospital you are found to be unfit for further service and are recommended for a discharge from the Army, you will not be entitled to an extension of leave in respect of the time spent in hospital.

21. ADMINISTRATION.   Officers will be posted to an appropriate depot with effect from date of their disembarkation in the United Kingdom and will be notified accordingly, but they will not report in person unless instructed to do so by the War Office.

Other ranks will be attached by their Officer i/c Records to units near their homes for local administration while on leave.

Other ranks will be informed by Officers i/c Records while on leave of the unit to which they are to be attached and its location. If any advice or help is required, get in touch with the officer in charge of the unit to which you are attached, or if you are spending your leave in Eire where you cannot be attached to-a unit write direct to your Officer i/c Records.

22. CHANGE or ADDRESS.   Officers will immediately notify any change of address both to-the War Office, Hobart House, London, S.W.I, and to the Officer i/c Depot to which they have been posted.

Other ranks who change their address when on leave will immediately complete A.F. W 3045, issued to them at the reception camp, and post it to their regimental paymaster who will inform their Officer i/c Records. If you lose your A.F. W 3045, you must apply to the local police station for the address of your Officer i/c Records and then immediately inform Records of the change of address. If you are attached to a local unit for administrative purposes, you must also inform that unit of your change of address. On hearing of your change of address, the Officer i/c Records will attach you to a unit near your new address.

23. MEDICAL AND DENTAL ATTENTION.   Officers who need medical attendance when on repatriation leave should make their own arrangements for treatment. They must meet the cost of any treatment themselves but a refund of reasonable expenses of treatment will be allowed by the War Office if their disability is regarded as attributable to service. Officers who need hospital treatment when on leave will apply for treatment to the nearest Military or Emergency Medical Services Hospital.

Other ranks who need medical attention or hospital treatment when on repatriation leave will comply with the instructions on the back of their leave passes.

Every endeavour will be made to complete your dental treatment as soon as possible after your return. Should you be discharged or invalided, however, and your dental condition suffered owing to failure of the Detaining Power to provide adequate facilities for treatment, you may apply within six months of your discharge or invaliding from the Army, to the Under Secretary of State, The War Office (A.M.D. 6), London, S.W1 for the treatment necessitated by such neglect to be carried out at public expense.

In your application, you should give the following information: Army Number, Rank, Full Name and Address, Full particulars of your unit, the period of your detention as a prisoner of war, and the date of your repatriation and of your discharge or invaliding from the Army.

In cases where the provision of dental treatment is approved, arrangements will be made for your attendance at the Army Dental Centre nearest to your home or, in the rare cases where this is impracticable, special arrangements will be made by the War Office for any treatment recommended by an Officer of the Army Dental Corps to be carried out by a civilian dental practitioner.

24. INCOME TAX.   If you have income apart from your service pay, or if your wife has an income of her own, you may in certain circumstances have been liable to less tax while serving outside the United Kingdom or while a prisoner of war than you would have been if you had been serving in the United Kingdom. You should, therefore, write to the tax office which deals with your liability (or call there personally) stating the period of your absence from the United Kingdom and asking whether you are entitled to repayment of any tax paid during your absence.

25. LEAVE PETROL   Repatriates may apply for active service petrol allowance in the same way as officers and other ranks on leave from abroad. The car or motor cycle must be registered in the name of the applicant, his wife, father or mother. Coupons for 450 miles for your 42 days leave and a further 75 miles for subsequent 7 days up to a maximum of 600 miles may be obtained on application to Recruiting Offices, T.A. Association Offices or Welfare Offices.

Applicants will apply in person or through a properly authorized representative. Application will not be made by post. The car or motor-cycle registration book and applicant's leave document must be produced.

AFTER LEAVE

26. UNFIT OFFICERS.   For any officers (other than those holding permanent Regular Army Commissions) graded by the Medical Board as permanently unfit for any further military service, there is, of course, no alternative but that they should relinquish their commissions. In relinquishment, the responsibility for any disability award to which they are entitled becomes a matter for the Ministry of Pensions, to which Department their cases are immediately referred subject to the provision that if in-patient hospital treatment is required they will be retained on army pay for up to a maximum of six months from date of admission to hospital before their 56-day's terminal leave begins.

Officers holding permanent Regular Army Commissions graded as permanently unfit for any further military service will be placed on the half pay list unless instead they wish to apply to retire. They may remain on the half pay list for a period of 5 years, at the end of which time they will be retired, but they will be at liberty to apply to retire at any time while on the half pay list. The extent to which an officer may receive half pay while on the half pay list depends on the circumstances of his case. If his disability is due to military service, he is eligible to receive half pay for the full period of 5 years regardless of the length of his service but if his disability is not due to service he will not be eligible to receive half pay unless he has 3 or more years' service, and the period for which he may draw half pay while on the half pay list depends on the length of his service.

Officers graded temporarily unfit for further military service (medical category " D ") will be dealt with according to the Medical Board's recommendation, *e.g.,* medical treatment, sick leave, followed by a further medical board, unless they are eligible for and desire release meantime.

27. FIT OFFICERS AND OFFICER RECEPTION UNITS.   Any regular or non-regular officer who is fit and who volunteers for further service and is therefore not released in accordance with para. 2 above, will go for interview to Special

Officer Reception Units as soon as possible after the end of 42 days leave, and will be able to discuss his future with experienced officers whose job will be to ensure that he is posted wherever his special abilities and qualifications can be most usefully employed. If he does not receive orders by' the end of the 42 days leave, he should report in writing to his Personnel Branch at the War Office, Hobart House, S.W.1. that he is still awaiting instructions and he remains on leave until they are issued.

28. UNFIT OTHER RANKS.   Any other rank graded unfit for further military service will be discharged under arrangements to be made by Officer i/c Records and will be put into touch with the Ministry of Labour and National Service, the Ministry of Pensions and other organizations which will help him in his resettlement in civil life. Subject to the provision that if in-patient hospital treatment is required he will be retained on army pay for up to a maximum of six months from date of admission to hospital before his 56-day's terminal leave begins.
Other ranks graded temporarily unfit will be dealt with in accordance with the Medical Board's recommendations.

29. FIT OTHER RANKS—POSTING AFTER LEAVE, ETC.   Like officers, any other rank of the Regular Army who is not released in accordance with terms of paragraph 2 above, will go to a special unit, where the posting that is best for him will be carefully considered and decided. He will be able to discuss his future with officers whose job it will be to fit him into the most suitable employment, having regard to the needs of the Army at the time as well as his own wishes and abilities. Since July 1942, every man entering the Army has had the benefit of this individual assessment and advice, and he will have the same opportunity of having his special abilities and qualifications taken into account before he is posted.

30. ALL RANKS—RETRAINING.   Any officer and man who is fit and who is accepted for further service will be given whatever refresher course or further training is needed. If you are fit for service in your own arm this training will bring you up-to-date, and make you thoroughly familiar with the most recent weapons and methods in the Army. You may be fit for further service but in another arm, or possibly in a field unit; you will then be given the full training necessary to fit you for the arm and unit for which your medical category is suitable. It is realised that this means your transfer to other regiments or corps; this process has already been carried out on a large scale in the Army and is still being adopted, in order to make the best possible use of all available manpower.
If you are a Regular or T.A. soldier who is transferred, you will have the right of re-transfer at the end of the emergency to your original corps or regiment if you desire it.

31. CIVIL RESETTLEMENT.   For those of you who are to be discharged or released from the Army, a voluntary course is provided of from four to twelve week's duration, during which time you will live under pleasant conditions and have a chance to settle down before returning to civil life.
Whilst on the course you will be brought up to date with current events and be able to make contacts with various civil organizations which will be of assistance to you when you finally leave the Army.
A pamphlet entitled " Settling Down in Civvy Street " which provides information on the course will be sent you whilst on leave by your Officer i/c Records at the same time as he advises you of the local unit to which you are to be attached. B45/357) 50000 10/45 W.O.P. 23617

Appendix III

2 East Surreys Roll of Honour

East Surreys killed in action – Battle of Jitra/Alor Star, 7–13 December 1941
Pte D. Allen from Chertsey: Singapore Memorial
Pte S. Anderson from Clapton: Krangi War Cemetery
Pte E. Berkley: Taiping War Cemetery
Pte C. Brooker from New Cross, 11/12/1941: Singapore Memorial
Pte J.A. Brown from London, 11/12/1941: Singapore Memorial
Pte W. Budge from Somerset, 12/12/1941: Singapore Memorial
Sgt F. Burgess from Long Ditton: Singapore Memorial
L.Cpl A. Cant from West Ham, 11/12/1941: Singapore Memorial
CSM G. Cason from Harwich, 13/12/1941: Singapore Memorial
Cpl S. Cooper from Tolworth, 12/12/1941: Singapore Memorial
Pte J. Corbett from Bromley, Yorkshire, 10/12/1941: Singapore Memorial
Pte H. Fluin from North London, 11/12/1941: Singapore Memorial
Pte E. Hefferman from Rotherhithe, 11/12/1941: Singapore Memorial
Cpl R. Hillier from Sutton, 11/12/1941: Singapore Memorial
L.Sgt F. Humphreys from Mitcham, 11/12/1941: Singapore Memorial
Pte R. Jeffrey from Weybridge, 12/12/1941: Singapore Memorial
Pte S. Parker: Kranji War Cemetery
Lt L. Sear from Walthamstow: Taiping War Cemetery
Pte A. Shepherd from Colliers Wood, 12/12/1941: Singapore Memorial
Pte W. Simkin from Battersea, 11/12/1941: Singapore Memorial
Pte K. Swansbury from Kingston, 12/12/1941: Singapore Memorial
Pte H. Turner from Ilford, 12/12/1941: Singapore Memorial
Pte J. Whittal from Fulham: Taiping War Cemetery
Pte G. Williams from Dalston
Pte G. Willingdale from Kensington, 11/12/1941: Singapore Memorial
Cpl F. Young from Maida Vale

East Surreys killed in action – Battle of Gurun, 15–22 December 1941
Pte D. Alexander from Ottersham, 22/12/1941: Singapore Memorial
Pte S. Ball from Hammersmith, 15/12/1941: Singapore Memorial
Pte G. Bannatyne from Boroughbridge, 15/12/1941: Singapore Memorial
L.Cpl F. Barling from Shanghai, 22/12/1941: Singapore Memorial
Cpl J. Bartram from Addlestone, 15/12/1941: Singapore Memorial

Pte E. Beckett from Liverpool, 15/12/1941: Singapore Memorial
Pte B. Bobbins from East Molesey, 22/12/1941: Singapore Memorial
Capt. K .Bradley from London, 17/12/1941: Singapore Memorial
2Lt R. Bradford from Ashford, 17/12/1941: Singapore Memorial
Pte L. Britchford from Cape Town, 15/12/1941: Singapore Memorial
Pte J. Brown from Brockley
Pte A. Brumby from Fulham, 15/12/1941: Singapore Memorial
Pte B. Chapman from Brixton, 15/12/1941: Singapore Memorial
Pte J. Clark from Wimbledon, 17/12/1941: Singapore Memorial
WO T. Clarke from Goodmayes, 17/12/1942: Singapore Memorial
Dmr W. Corlett from Walsall, 17/12/1941: Singapore Memorial
Maj. F. Dowling from Winchester, 17/12/1941: Singapore Memorial
L.Sgt S. Ferris: Taiping War Cemetery
Pte C. Greenwood from Islington
Pte J. Haggis from Battersea
Sgt W. Hall from Edmonton: Taiping War Cemetery
Pte A. Harris from Stratford, 19/12/1941: Singapore Memorial
Cpl R. Hawkins from Tolworth
Pte A. Hayes from Wandsworth, 17/12/1941: Singapore Memorial
Pte W. Hewitt from Chertsey, 17/12/1941: Singapore Memorial
Pte L. Hickey from Wandsworth, 17/12/1941: Singapore Memorial
Pte P. Huzzey from East Ham, 22/12/1941: Singapore Memorial
Sgt F. Jowett from Dunton Green, 15/12/1941: Singapore Memorial
Capt. J. Kerrich: Taiping War Cemetery
L.Cpl J. Leonard from Holloway, 15/12/1941: Singapore Memorial
Pte R. Livermore from Sidcup, 15/12/1941: Singapore Memorial
Pte E. McAuliffe from Thornton Heath, 17/12/1941: Singapore Memorial
Cpl M. Mason from Catford, 15/12/1941: Singapore Memorial
L.Sgt H. Meddle from Worcester Park
2Lt W. Meyers from Richmond, Surrey, 15/12/1941: Singapore Memorial
Pte J. Mitchell from Teddington, 13/12/1941: Singapore Memorial
Pte A. Paget from Folkstone, 15/12/1941: Singapore Memorial
Pte G. Penfold from Merton Park, 17/12/1941: Singapore Memorial
Rev. P. Rawsthorne, 14/12/1941: Singapore Memorial
Cpl J. Reynolds
Sgt S. Roche from Tunbridge Wells, 15/12/1941: Singapore Memorial
Sgt A. Rudd from Stoke Newington, 15/12/1941: Singapore Memorial
L.Cpl W. Seaton from South Norwood, 15/12/1941: Singapore Memorial
Pte B. Sherfield from Norbiton, 22/12/1941: Singapore Memorial
2Lt D. Smith from Bromley, 20/12/1941: Singapore Memorial
Pte L. Smith from Battersea, 25/12/1941: Taiping War Cemetery
Pte T. Smith from Thannington, Kent, 15/12/1941: Singapore Memorial

Pte J. Stanford from New Malden, 15/12/1941: Singapore Memorial
Pte A. Steel from London, 30/12/1941: Singapore Memorial
Pte A. Stephens from Shoreham, 15/12/1941: Singapore Memorial
Pte C. Stiles, 15/12/1941: Singapore Memorial
Pte O. Stock, 16/12/1941: Singapore Memorial
Capt. H.B. Thomson from Belfast, 15/12/1941: Singapore Memorial
Pte C. Warn from Devon, 17/12/1941: Singapore Memorial
C.Sgt V. Wildman from Hunslet, Leeds 17/12/1941: Singapore Memorial
Pte G. Williams from Dalston: Taiping War Cemetery
L.Cpl E. Woolard from Bognor Regis, 17/12/1941: Singapore Memorial
Pte S. Wright from New Zealand, 17/12/1941: Singapore Memorial

East Surreys killed in action – Battle of Kampar, 1–10 January 1942
Capt. A. Hill from Sydney, 01/01/1942: Singapore Memorial
Pte H. Arnold: Taiping War Cemetery
Pte J. Blackman: Taiping War Cemetery
Pte F. Burkett, 06/01/1942: Taiping War Cemetery
Cpl D. Boyce from Chertsey: Taiping War Cemetery
L.Sgt R. Deadman from Wimbledon, 10/01/1942: Singapore Memorial
Pte W. Dougherty from Wandsworth: Taiping War Cemetery
Pte W. Douglas
Pte F. Dyne: Taiping War Cemetery
Pte W. Field from Chertsey: Taiping War cemetery
CSM J. Foley from Birmingham
Pte G. Greenwood, 02/01/1942: Singapore Memorial
Pte A. Holloway: Taiping War Cemetery
Pte W. Jenkins from Streatham: Taiping War Cemetery
Sgt C. LeClair: Taiping War Cemetery
L.Cpl R Long: Taiping War Cemetery
Pte E. Marsh: Taiping War Cemetery
L.Sgt H. Meddle from Worcester Park, 06/01/1942: Singapore Memorial
Cpl L. Milner from Northampton, 08/01/1942: Singapore Memorial
Pte W. Pearce from Wimbledon: Taiping War Cemetery
Cpl J. Reynolds from Margate: Taiping War Cemetery
Pte L. Rance from Surrey: Taiping War Cemetery
L.Cpl E. Samuels, 10/01/1942: Singapore Memorial
Pte K. Wilks from Devon: Taiping War Cemetery
L.Cpl E. Woolard from Bognor Regis: Taiping War Cemetery
Pte R. Woolard from Bognor Regis: Taiping War Cemetery

East Surreys killed in action – Batu Pahat, 16–29 January 1942
Sgt M. Abery from London, 21/01/1941: Singapore Memorial
Pte S. Beesley from Peckham, 21/01/1942: Singapore Memorial

Pte W. Dobson from Islington, 16/01/1942: Singapore Memorial
Pte N. Lamb from Bow, 21/01/1942: Singapore Memorial
Cpl J. Maynard from Carshalton, 21/01/1942: Singapore Memorial
L.Cpl G. Mitchell from Northampton, 29/01/1942: Singapore Memorial
L.Cpl A. Musgrave
Cpl O. Riddle from Darlington, 21/01/1942: Singapore Memorial
L.Cpl E. Samuels from Richmond
Pte L. Smith
Pte A. Webster from East Prenton, 21/01/1942: Singapore Memorial

East Surreys killed in the Battle for Singapore 1–14 February 1942
Pte F. Atkins from Lambeth, 07/02/1942: Singapore Memorial
Cpl C. Austin from Kingston Hill, 10/02/1942: Kranji War Cemetery
Pte D. Bagnaro, 10/02/1942: Kranji War Cemetery
Pte C. Ballard from Holloway, 07/02/1942: Singapore Memorial
Pte W. Batt from East Ham, 10/02/1942: Krangi War Cemetery
Pte C. Beckness, 14/02/1942: Kranji War Cemetery
Cpl J. Belham from Aldershot, 12/02/1942: Singapore Memorial
Lt R. Bobe, 10/02/1942: Kranji War Cemetery
Pte L. Brandon from Kensington, 10/02/1942: Singapore Memorial
L.Cpl J. Bray from Dagenham, 14/02/1942: Singapore Memorial
Pte F. Brown from Homerton, 03/02/1942: Singapore Memorial
Pte T. Burkett from Hammersmith, 07/01/1942: Singapore Memorial
Pte H. Constable from Shepherds Bush, 05/02/1942: Singapore Memorial
Pte D. Coombs from Herne Bay, 13/02/1942: Singapore Memorial
Pte H. Cooper, 10/02/1942: Kranji War Cemetery
Pte K. Cottle from Swindon, 15/02/1942: Singapore Memorial
Pte R. Daniels, 10/02/1942: Kranji War Cemetery
Pte T. Davies from Port Talbot, 05/02/1942: Singapore Memorial
Pte R. Davis from Glamorgan, 14/02/1942: Singapore Memorial
Pte H. Deakin from Walton-on-Thames, 12/02/1942: Singapore Memorial
Pte W. Dougherty from Wandsworth, 01/02/1942: Taiping War Cemetery
Pte C. Duffy from Monmouth, 10/02/1942: Kranji War Cemetery
Pte S. Dye from Fulham, 14/02/1942: Kranji War Cemetery
Pte V. Edgson from Millwall, 13/02/1942: Singapore Memorial
Lt M. Edmonson from Perth, Australia, 10/02/1942: Singapore Memorial
Pte A. Fennell from Nottingham, 05/02/1942: Singapore Memorial
Pte B. Fitzpatrick, 07/02/1942: Kranji War Cemetery
WO J. Foley from Birmingham, 13/02/1942: Kranji War Cemetery
Pte E. Gosling from Nottingham, 10/02/1942: Singapore Memorial
Pte N. Grinter from Amesbury, 10/02/1942: Kranji War Cemetery
L.Sgt J. Gunn from Stoke Newington, 10/02/1942: Kranji War Cemetery
Pte J. Hall, 13/02/1942: Singapore Memorial

Cpl G. Henty, 10/02/1942: Kranji War Cemetery
Pte S. Hobbs from Grimsby, 05/02/1942: Singapore Memorial
Pte R. Holmes from Dorset, 14/02/1942: Singapore Memorial
Pte E. Horwood from Milford Haven, 05/02/1942: Singapore Memorial
Pte H. Howes from London, 05/02/1942: Singapore Memorial
Pte J. Hubbard from Camberwell, 10/02/1942: Kranji War Cemetery
Pte A. Hunt from Hammersmith, 10/02/1942: Kranji War Cemetery
Pte G. Hardy from Hayes, 05/02/1942: Singapore Memorial
Pte D. Jenkins from Sunbury, 14/02/1942: Singapore Memorial
Pte R. Kingsley from Canada, 10/02/1942: Singapore Memorial
Pte A. Loraine from Sunderland, 13/02/1942: Singapore Memorial
Pte J. McLeary from Glasgow, 05/02/1942: Singapore Memorial
Pte A. Mace from Clapton, 05/02/1942: Singapore Memorial
Pte J. Marman from Colliers Wood, 10/02/1942: Kranji War Cemetery
Pte J. Matthews from West Ham, 10/02/1942: Kranji War Cemetery
Pte A. May from West Molesey, 08/02/1942: Singapore Memorial
Pte T. Meddings from West Norwood, 07/02/1942: Singapore Memorial
Pte J. Minihane from Cork, 14/02/1942: Kranji War Cemetery
L.Cpl D. Mitchell from Northampton, 10/02/1942: Kranji War Cemetery
Pte A. Morris from Islington, 10/02/1942: Singapore Memorial
Pte H. Morton from Morden, 10/02/1942: Kranji War Cemetery
Pte P. Noad from Kensington, 14/02/1942: Singapore Memorial
Pte C. Nobbs, 10/02/1942: Kranji War Cemetery
L.Cpl A. Nuthall from Richmond, Surrey, 10/02/1942: Kranji War Cemetery
Cpl W. Paul, 10/02/1942: Kranji War Cemetery
Sgt W. Perkins from Weston-super-Mare, 10/02/1942: Singapore Memorial
Sgt G. Potter, 13/02/1942: Singapore Memorial
Cpl A. Robinson from Lambeth, 13/02/1942: Singapore Memorial
Pte E. Rowlands from Loughborough, 05/02/1942: Singapore Memorial
Pte E. Russell from Tooting, 13/02/1942: Singapore Memorial
2Lt H. Russell from Ealing, 13/02/1942: Kranji War Cemetery
Pte J. Salter from Laindon, Essex, 05/02/1942: Singapore Memorial
Pte T. Sampson from Sutton, 11/02/1942: Kranji War Cemetery
Pte L. Seymour from Sutton, 10/02/1942: Kranji War Cemetery
Pte A. Shrimpton from Cheltenham, 15/02/1942: Singapore Memorial
Pte A. Smith from Kensington, 05/02/1942: Singapore Memorial
Pte F. Stallwood from London, 14/02/1942: Singapore Memorial
Pte R. Strong from Hampton, 10/02/1942: Kranji War Cemetery
Pte R. Swain from Glamorgan, 05/02/1942: Singapore Memorial
Pte H. Tame from Kensington, 05/02/1942: Singapore Memorial
L.Cpl F. Tonnison from South Woodham, 10/02/1942: Singapore Memorial
Pte R. Tooth from Christchurch, Hampshire, 05/02/1942: Singapore Memorial

Sgt J. Vaughan from Leeds, 14/02/1942: Singapore Memorial
L.Cpl F. Wells from Cheam, 10/02/1942: Singapore Memorial
Pte R. Wilmhurst from Kensington, 05/02/1942: Singapore Memorial
L.Cpl F. Wilson from Croydon: 10/02/1942: Kranji War Cemetery
L.Cpl C. Yewings, 10/02/1942: Kranji War Cemetery
Cpl F. Young from Perak, Malaya, 05/02/1942: Singapore Memorial

Evacuated on the hospital ship *Talamba* on 2 February 1942

Pte F. Beach	Cpt. J. Gilbody
Pte F. Bergeman	Pte T. Girdler
L.Sgt J. Bird	Pte A. May
2Lt B. Boothby	Pte G. Mulberry
Pte J. Carroll	Pte A. Park
Pte A. Caston	Pte F. Salter
Pte L. Cochran	Pte P. Simpson
Sgt F. Croft	Pte W. Taylor
Pte G. Dimond	Lt J. Quarrell
Pte A. Field	Lt P. Wilkinson
Pte W. Gardiner	

The men chosen by Captain Gingell to escape on the *Dragonfly* from East Surrey ranks were:

Pte R. Ambler from Newark	Pte D. Jenkins from Sunbury
Sgt T. Baldwin from Moseley, Surrey	Pte A. Leatherland from Chertsey
L.Cpl J. Bray from Dagenham	Pte P. Noad from Kensington
Sgt T. Cahill from Bath	Pte M. Ray from Surrey
Pte W. Carpenter from Kingston	Pte R. Robinson from Leatherhead
Cpl V. Clothier from Kennington	Pte S. Stallwood from Edmonton
Pte R. Holmes from Mitcham	C.Sgt J. Vaughan from Leeds

Six of the above East Surrey men were killed in the attack or subsequently drowned. These men were:

L.Cpl J. Bray from Dagenham	Pte P. Noad from Kensington
Pte R. Holmes from Mitcham	Pte S. Stallwood from Edmonton
Pte D. Jenkins from Sunbury	C.Sgt J. Vaughan from Leeds

East Surrey men on the Hellships, 1942–1945
(D) = died

Lt S. Abbott from Wimbledon	Pte W. Adamswaite from North
Pte G. Abery from Plastow (D)	Kensington

Pte J. Addison from Colliers Wood

Pte W. Arlett from Camberwell (D)

Pte R. Ashton from Holloway

Cpl L. Barber from Chertsey

Pte Bateman from Kingston

Sgt J. Beach from Colchester

Pte H. Blackman from Epsom (D)

L.Cpl F. Blake (D)

L.Cpl A. Bone from Chichester

L.Cpl R. Booker from Sutton (D)

Sgt D. Boorer from Morden

Pte D. Brewer from Stroud Green

Pte W. Brice from New Barnet

Pte Bridgewater from Ilford (D)

Cpl D. Brightman from Ruislip (D)

Pte G. Broom from Ipswich (D)

Pte C.H. Brown from Fulham (D)

Pte H. Brown from Mortlake (D)

Pte J. Brown from Norbiton (D)

Pte C. Browning from London

Pte V. Buckle from Kingston upon
   Thames (D)

Pte W. Carleton from Wexford

Pte R. Cattermole from Mitcham

Pte P. Chalcroft from Kingswood

Pte J. Chennell from Chertsey (D)

Pte L. Chernin from Bow

Pte C. Chidwick from Twickenham

Pte E. Chittey from Ashstead

Sgt M. Cleary (D)

Sgt W. Collier

Pte C. Connelly from Romford

Pte R. Constable from Croydon

Pte N. Coombe from Worley (D)

Pte Coughlan from Tipperary

Pte S. Cove from Mitcham

Pte S. Cox from London

Pte B. Crane from Edmonton

L.Cpl R. Cranston from Harringay

Pte G. Cudd from Balham (D)

Pte W. Currey

Pte F. Dade from Ilminster

Pte H.G. Dance from Addlestone

Pte H. Darby from Hammersmith (D)

Pte G. Davies from Liverpool

Pte F. Davis from Wimbledon

Pte G. Deane from Virginia Water (D)

Pte R. Dedman from Battersea (D)

Pte J. Dennis from Reigate

Pte W. Dobson from Barking (D)

Pte W. Dobson from Islington

Pte C. Donaldson (D)

Sgt A. Eatwell from Sydenham

Pte D. Evans from Morden (D)

Pte J. Evans from North London

Pte N. Finlay from Durham

Pte D. Forshaw from Bognor Regis

Pte A. Freeland from North London (D)

Pte A.D. Freeman from Wandsworth

Pte R. Gadd from Tolworth (D)

Sgt W. Gallagher from Brisbane

L.Sgt R. Glazier

Pte W. Greenaway from Acton (D)

Pte J. Griffin from Dungarvan, Ireland

L.Cpl J. Griffiths from Twickenham

Sgt J. Hastell from Sutton (D)

Pte J. Hawkins from Teddington (D)

Pte S. Hayes from Gloucester

Pte C. Hibbert from Kentish Town

Pte H. Hicks from Bushy Park

Pte A. Hilliard from Canning Town

Pte H. Hillier from North London

Pte R. Himsworth from East Belfort

Pte D. Hodgson from Crayford

Pte S. Holman from Cobham (D)

Pte W. Howard from Richmond

Pte C. Howlett from Garfield (D)

Pte S. Hughes from Durham

Pte J.J. Ions from Thames Ditton

Pte A. Irwin from Egham

Pte A. Jeffra from Brixton (D)

Pte E. Johnson from Foots Cray,
   London (D)

Pte T. Jones

Pte J. Keenan from Durham
L.Cpl J. Lackenby
Pte R. Lake from Blackfriars
Pte S. Law from Islington
Pte A. Lawrence from Fulham
Sgt W. Lazard from Herne Hill
Pte H. Leeding from Kingston
Pte R. Leigh from Warrington (D)
RQMS F. Livermore from Sidcup
Pte J. Logan Ayrshire
Pte D. Lomasey from Balham
Pte W. Lord from Brisbane
Pte M. Lyons from Dublin
Sgt E. Manley from Shaford (D)
Pte W. Marks from Belfast
Pte W. Marley from Monmouthshire
Sgt C.G. Martin from Bow
Cpl N. Martin from Rhonda
Sgt D. McClean from Thames Ditton
L.Sgt H. McDonough from Carlan,
  Donegal
Pte A. Metcalfe from Earlsfield
Pte R. Miles from Hanwell
Pte G. Mills from Battersea
Pte W. Monteith from Sydney
Pte D. Moore from Wimbledon
Pte R. Moralee from Durham
Cpl G. Mordecai (D)
Pte A. Morris from Islington
Pte P. Murphy from Wexford
Pte A. Musgrave from Newcastle
L.Cpl J. Naulls from Wellingborough
Pte P. Neithersoot from Bow
L.Cpl V. Newman from Bristol
Pte A. Nuttall
L.Cpl E. Oatley from Earlsfield
Pte P. Osborn from Colliers Wood
Pte L. Pardoe from Herne Hill (D)
Cpl L. Parfett from Stoke Newington
Pte S. Peel from Notting Hill (D)
Pte D. Poole from Kentish Town
Pte W. Quinnell from Brisbane

Pte W. Reeves from Nunhead
Cpl P. Robertson from Newcastle (D)
Pte R. Robinson from Leatherhead (D)
Pte C. Ross from North London
Pte H. Ruoff from Herts
LtCol M. Russell from Horsell,
  Surrey (D)
L.Cpl R. Russell from Streatham
Pte F. Sanger from Blackheath
Pte G. Saschekin from London
CSM R. Shemmings from Folkstone (D)
Pte R. Sheppard from Colliers Wood (D)
Pte M. Shiels from Dublin
Sgt F. Shipton from Colchester
Pte R. Simmons from Shanghai
Pte A. Slade from Islington (D)
Pte W. Slade from Reading
Pte H. Snowden from Hartlepool (D)
Pte L. Sorge from the Wirral
Pte J. Spike from Stepney
Pte H. Squires from Richmond
Pte A. Stanbury from Barnet
Pte A. Staplehurst from Devon
Pte G. Street from Mitcham
Pte A. Thomas from London
Pte D. Thomson from Farnborough (D)
Pte J. Thomson from Wandsworth (D)
L.Cpl H. Tugwell from Tatfield
Pte D. Turner from Stocksbridge
Pte W. Turnham from East Preston
Pte C. Vause from Morden (D)
Pte G. Wallace from Stanwell Moor
Pte G. Walters from Effingham
Pte R. Warren from Balham
Pte V. Watson from Highbury
Pte R. Webley from London
Pte R. Webster from London
Pte F. Williams from Tottenham (D)
L.Cpl H. Wilson from Walton-on-
  Thames
Pte W. Wiltshire from Roehampton
Pte J. Woods from Renfrewshire (D)

Pte W. Woolton from Oxshott
Pte J. Wright from Battersea

Cpl J. Wyatt from Sydenham

East Surreys In PoW camps Korea:
Pte W. Howard from Richmond
Pte D. Lomashey from Balham
Pte G. Mills from Battersea

Pte G. Poole from Kentish Town
Pte J. Spike from Stepney

East Surreys in PoW camps Borneo:
Pte A. Bridgwater from Ilford
Cpl C.H. Brown from Fulham
Pte R. Cattermole from Mitcham
Pte P. Chalcroft from Kingswood
Pte R. Constable from Croydon
L.Cpl C. Donaldson from Epsom
Pte C. Hibbert from Kentish Town
Pte J. Keenan from Durham
Sgt C.G. Martin from Bow

Pte W. Monteith from Sydney
L.Cpl A. Musgrave from Newcastle
Pte A. Nuttall
Pte L. Selly from New Malden
Pte H.G. South from Richmond
L.Cpl A. Staplehurst from Tenton
Pte G. Walters from Effingham
Pte J. Wright from Surrey

East Surreys in PoW camps Taiwan:
Pte W. Curry

Pte J. Hill from Holloway

East Surreys in PoW camps Japan:
Lt S. Abbott from Wimbledon
Pte G. Abery from London
Pte G. Bateman from Kingston
Cpl A. Bone from Chichester
L.Cpl R. Booker from Sutton (D)
Sgt D. Boorer from Morden
Cpl D. Brightman from Ruislip (D)
Pte J. Brown from Norbiton (D)
Pte W. Carleton from Wexford
Pte P. Chalcroft from Kingswood
Pte L. Chernin from London
Cpl C. Chidwick from Twickenham
Pte E. Cleaver from Hanwell
Pte C. Connelly from London
Pte R. Constable from Croydon
Pte N. Coombs from Worley
Pte D. Coughlan from Tipperary
Pte S. Cove from Mitcham
Pte S. Cox from South-East London

L.Cpl R. Cranston from Harringay
Pte H. Cussell
Pte F. Dade from Ilminster
Pte H.G. Dance from Addlestone
Pte F. Davis from Wimbledon
Pte G. Davis from Wimbledon
Pte G. Deane from Virginia Water
Pte N. Dellow from Wandsworth
Pte W. Dobson from Barking (D)
Sgt A. Eatwell from Sydenham
Pte D. Forshaw from Bognor Regis
Pte A.D. Freeman from Wandsworth (D)
Sgt W. Gallagher from Brisbane
L.Cpl J. Griffith from Twickenham
Pte J. Hawkins from Reigate
Pte S. Hayes from Gloucester
Pte H. Hicks from Bushy Park
Pte R. Himsworth from East Belfort
Pte D. Hodgson from Crayford

Pte S. Holman from Cobham (D)
Pte W. Howard
Pte S. Hughes from Durham
Pte J.J. Ions from Thames Ditton
Pte A. Irwin from Egham
Pte T. Jones
Pte J. Keenan from Durham
L.Cpl J. Lackenby
L.Cpl R. Lake from London
Sgt W. Lamport from Sittingbourne
Pte G. Law from Islington
Pte A. Lawrence from Fulham
Pte H. Leeding from Kingston
RQMS F. Livermore from Sidcup
Pte W. Lord from Brisbane
Pte M. Lyons from Dublin
Sgt E. Manley from Shaford
Pte E. Marks from Belfast
Pte G. Marley from Cwmbran
Sgt C. Martin from London
Cpl N. Martin from Rhonda
L.Sgt H. McDonaugh from Carlan
Pte A. Metcalf from Earlsfield
Pte R. Miles from Hanwell
Pte W. Monteith from Sydney
Pte D. Moore from Wimbledon
Pte R. Moralee from Durham
Pte A. Morris from Islington
Pte P. Murphy from Wexford
L.Cpl J. Naulls from Wellingborough
Pte P. Neithersoot from Bow
L.Cpl V. Newman from Bristol
Pte A. Nuttall

Pte P. Osborn from Colliers Wood
Cpl L. Parfett from Stoke Newington
Pte G. Poole
Pte W. Quinell from Brisbane
Pte W. Reeves from Nunhead
Cpl P. Robertson from Newcastle upon Tyne
Pte H. Ruoff from Herts
L.Cpl R. Russell from Streatham
Pte F. Sanger from Blackheath
Pte G. Saschekin from London
Pte L. Selly from New Maldon
Pte M. Shiels from Dublin
Sgt F. Shipton from Colchester
Pte H. Snowden from Hartlepool (D)
Pte L. Sorge from Wirral
Pte H. South from Richmond
Pte A. Stanbury from Barnet
Pte G. Street from Mitcham
Pte A. Thomas from London
Pte W. Turnham from East Preston, Sussex
Pte C. Vause from Morden
Pte G. Wallace from Stanwell Moor
Pte R. Warren from Balham
Pte V. Watson from Highbury
Pte R. Webster from London
L.Cpl H. Wilson from Walton-on-Thames
Pte W. Wiltshire from Roehampton
Pte J. Wright from Battersea
Pte J. Wyatt from Sydenham

East Surreys in PoW camps Ubon, north-east Thailand:
Pte J. Ainslie
Pte B. Alywin from Kingswood
Pte F. Austin from Bromley
Pte J. Barnett from Brixton
Pte H. Beer from Hanwell
Pte T. Bell from Greenford
Pte H. Bennett from Tooting

Pte L. Blackhurst
Pte C. Bone from Belfast
Pte W. Boxell from Battersea
Pte H. Cowell from Plymouth
Cpl C. Easton from London
Pte W. Edser from Willesden Green
Pte G. Edwards

Pte C. Finch from Hounslow
Pte T. Fisher from London
Pte H. Franklin from Addlestone
L.Cpl G Frost from South-West London
Pte G. Garrett from Kennington
Pte H. Grant
Pte A. Graves
Pte Green
L.Cpl E. Gregory
Pte J. Guy
Pte J. Hale
Pte W. Hall
Pte S. Hawkins from Shepherds Bush
Pte P. Hornsby from Staines
Pte L. Howes from Deptford
Pte B. Hudson from Ascot
Pte R. Hutchins from Surbiton
Pte L. Jelley from Earlsfield
Pte F. Johnson from Worcester Park
Pte A. Lambert from West Croydon
Pte T. Lucas from Battersea
Pte L. Manning from Manor Park

Pte E. Mansfield from Herne Bay
Pte E. Marshall from Nunhead
Pte E. Maslyn from South Benfleet
Pte R. Millward from Camberwell
Cpl G. Morris from Sutton
Cpl H. Murray from Welwyn
Cpl J. Nall
Pte J. Noon from London
Pte J. Perry from Twickenham
Pte L. Phillips from Enfield
Pte A. Plant from London
Pte E. Sewell from Enfield
Pte J. Smith from Battersea
Pte A. Stenning from York
Pte V. Stiff from Bury St Edmunds
Pte W. Sutton from Twickenham
Pte J. Thompson from Wimbledon
Pte D. Turner from Sutton
Pte G. Tuson from Kilburn
Pte B. Williams from Welwyn
Pte F. Wilson from Hammersmith
RSM Worsfold from Carshalton

East Surreys who died as prisoners of war – February 1942–August 1945

1942

Pte W. Dougherty from Wandsworth: Singapore, 02/1942 (dysentery), Krangi War Cemetery

Pte D. Allen from Chertsey: Changi, 25/02/1942, Singapore Memorial

Lt L. Bingham: Singapore, 26/02/1942 (wounds), Taiping War Cemetery

Pte E. Hatt from Kew: Changi, 01/03/1942, Taiping War Cemetery

Cpl S. Cooper from Tolworth: Changi, Singapore, 04/03/1942 (septicaemia), Taiping War Cemetery

Sgt H. George from Beckenham: Singapore, 11/03/42 (tropical ulcer), Taiping War Cemetery

Pte W. Shaw from London: Changi, 09/04/1942 (shot by guards), Taiping War Cemetery

Pte C. Holliday from Tottenham: Singapore, 13/04/42 (MT accident), Taiping War Cemetery

Pte G. Bragg from Hoxton: Changi, 01/05/1942, Singapore Memorial

Pte S. Foulger from Wandsworth: 01/05/1942, Taiping War Cemetery

Pte H. Leach from Morden: Singapore, 10/05/1942 (dysentery), Taiping War Cemetery

Cpl A. Hunt from Hammersmith: Hindat, 10/08/1942, Hindat Cemetery

Pte H. Waters from Birmingham: Singapore, 02/09/1942 (shot escaping), Taiping War Cemetery

Pte E. Carr: Changi, 01/10/1942, Singapore War Memorial

Pte W. Tobin from Erith, Kent: Kami Songkurai, 19/10/42 (dysentery), Chungkai War Cemetery

Sgt V. Osborn from London: 15/11/1942, Kanchanaburi War Cemetery

1943

Pte C. Richardson from Liverpool: Kanchanaburi, 04/02/1943 (executed), Chungkai War Cemetery

Pte E. Cleaver from Hanwell: Kanchanaburi, 04/02/43 (executed), Chungkai War Cemetery

Pte J. Croker from Bournemouth: Kanchanaburi, 04/02/43 (executed), Chungkai War Cemetery

Pte N. Dorval: Kanchanaburi, 04/02/43 (executed), Chungkai War Cemetery

Bsman J. Arnold from Dagenham: Chungkai, 18/02/43, Chungkai War Cemetery

WO F. Bullard from Croydon: 19/02/1943, Chungkai War Cemetery

Pte J. Sinclair from Clapham: Singapore, 25/03/1943 (of wounds), Taiping War Cemetery

Pte G. Gove from Chadwell Heath: Chungkai, 10/04/43 (dysentery), Chungkai War Cemetery

Pte J. Harvey from Ilford: Kanchanaburi, 18/04/1943, Kanchanaburi War Cemetery

Pte R. Vincent from Thorpe: Tonchan, 26/04/1943 (cerebral malaria), Kanchanaburi War Cemetery

Pte T. Johnson from Southend: Kannyu, 26/04/1943 (dysentery), Kanchanaburi War Cemetery

Cpl R. Moore from Crowborough: Kanchanaburi, 28/04/1943, Kanchanaburi War Cemetery

Pte S. Foulger: Taiping, 05/1943 (dysentery), Taiping War Cemetery

Pte W. Bevan from Woodbridge: Hindat, 09/05/43, Chungkai War Cemetery

Pte E. Jenn from Bromley: Kannyu, 18/05/1943 (undergoing operation), Kanchanaburi War Cemetery

Pte W. Sharp from London: Kanchanburi, 22/05/1943 (shot by accident), Kanchanaburi War Cemetery

Pte H. Wilson from Hanworth: Kanchanaburi, 27/05/1943 (dysentery), Kanchanaburi War Cemetery

Lt Col M. Russell from Horsell, Surrey: Labuan Borneo, 05/06/1943 (tropical ulcer), Labuan War Cemetery

Pte R. Dennis from Farnborough: Tonchan, 12/06/43 (cholera), Kanchanaburi War Cemetery

Cpl J.S. Gray from Dover: Tha Makham, 12/06/43 (dysentery), Kanchanaburi War Cemetery

Pte L. Anderson from London: Tha Sao, 22/06/1943 (beri-beri), Kanchanaburi War Cemetery

Cpl L. Nunn from Twickenham: Kanchanburi, 25/06/1943 Kanchanaburi War Cemetery

Cpl D. Booker from Welling, Kent: Kui Yae, 07/1943, Kanchanaburi War Cemetery

Pte R. Pope from Weybridge: Kannyu, 02/07/1943 (malaria), Kanchanaburi War Cemetery

L.Cpl L. Young from Mitcham: Tha Khanun, 04/07/1943 (dysentery), Kanchanaburi War Cemetery

Pte J. Burroughs from Carshalton: Chunghai, 05/07/43 (avitaminosis), Chungkai War Cemetery

Pte R. Abrahams from Chelmswood: Chungkai, 27/07/43 (beri-beri), Chungkai War Cemetery

Pte A. Brown from Reading: Kanchanaburi, 08/07/43, Kanchanaburi War Cemetery

Pte H. Etches from Earlsfield: Kanchanaburi, 08/07/43, Kanchanaburi War Cemetery

Pte R. Wheeler from Paddington: Kannyu, 08/07/1943, Kanchanaburi War Cemetery

Pte F. King from Reigate: Tha Khanun, 10/07/1943 (dysentery/beri-beri), Kanchanaburi War Cemetery

Pte S.J. Holman from Cobham: Japan, Yokohama War Cemetery

Pte D. Day from Belmont, Surrey: Kinsaiyok, 19/07/43, Kanchanaburi War Cemetery

Pte A. Parr from Chelmsford: Kui Yae, 20/07/1943, Singapore War Memorial

Pte Ayres from Grantham: Kinsaiyok, 22/07/43, Kinsaiyok Dutch Cemetery

Pte H. Read from Tooting: Hin Tok, 01/08/1943 (dysentery), Kanchanaburi War Cemetery

Pte T. King from Brixton: Nam Chon, 05/08/1943 (cholera), Kanchanaburi War Cemetery

Pte F. Hunt from Walton-on-Thames: Tha Sao, 09/08/1943 (dysentery), Kanchanaburi War Cemetery

Cpl A. Hunt from Middlesborough: Hindat, 10/08/1943, Hindat War Cemetery

Pte J. Driscoll: Kinsaiyok, 10/08/1943, Singapore War Memorial

Pte J. Gray from West Croydon: Kanchanaburi, 11/08/43 (avitaminosis), Kanchanaburi War Cemetery

Pte E. Warman from London: Kami Songkurai, 16/08 1943 (cholera), Thanbyuzayat War Cemetery

Pte J. Pugh from Monmouth: Kanchanaburi, 17/08/1943 (dysentery), Kanchanaburi War Cemetery

Pte W. Hornsea from Brixton: Kanchanaburi, 19/08/1943, Kanchanaburi War Cemetery

L.CplV. Garrard from Epsom: Prang Kasi, 23/08/43, Kanchanaburi War Cemetery

Pte G. Broom from Ipswich: Kurikonta, Japan, 03/09/43, Kanchanaburi War Cemetery

Pte C. Lock from London: Chungkai, 06/09/1943 (avitaminosis), Chungkai War Cemetery

Pte L. Gadson from Wandsworth: Chungkai 09/09/43 (avitaminosis), Chunghai War Cemetery

Pte S. Russell from Streatham: Chungkai, 16/09/1943 (avitaminosis), Chungkai War Cemetery

Pte F. Williams from Tottenham: en route to Japan (drowned), 21/09/1943

Pte K. Smith from Hornsey: Chungkai, 25/09/1943 (avitaminosis/dysentery), Chungkai War Cemetery

Cpl J. Hawkins from Reigate: Songkurai, 02/10/1943 (beri-beri/ulcers), Thanbyuzayat War Cemetery

Pte W. Payne from Littlehampton: Chunghai 04/10/1943 (dysentery), Chungkai War Cemetery

Pte G. Reed: Thanbaya, 09/10/1943 (dysentery), Thanbyuzayat War Cemetery

Pte W. Tobin from Rhodesia: Songkurai, 09/10/1943, (dysentery), Thanbyuzayat War Cemetery

Pte S. Law from Islington: at sea 12/10/1943 (drowned), Singapore War Memorial

QMS W. Lawrence from Fulham: Kui Yae, 12/10/1943 (malaria), Singapore War Memorial

Pte J. Warren from Sutton: Chungkai, 16/10/1943 (dysentery), Chungkai War Cemetery

Pte S. Lunny: Chungkai, 16/10/1943 (amoebic dysentery), Chungkai War Cemetery

L.Cpl A. Stephens from Hampshire: Songkurai, 20/10/1943 (dysentery), Thanbyuzayat War Cemetery

Pte H. Upfold from Walworth: Kanchanaburi, 23/10/1943 (beri-beri), Kanchanaburi War Cemetery

Pte C. Wall from Kingston: Nong Pladuk, 23/10/1943 (beri-beri), Chungkai War Cemetery

L.Cpl C. Reeves from London: Chungkai, 31/10/1943 (tropical ulcers), Chungkai War Cemetery

Pte V. Heckett from Wood Green: Nam Chon Yai, 03/11/1943 (malaria), Kanchanaburi War Cemetery

Sgt H. Wilson from Chessington: Kanchanaburi, 05/11/1943, Kanchanaburi War Cemetery

Pte H. Miller from Wimbledon: Kanchanaburi. 12/11/1943, Kanchanaburi War
 Cemetery
Pte F. Mercer from Hull: Thanbaya, 14/11/1943 (tropical ulcers), Thanbyuzayat
 War Cemetery
Sgt V. Osborn from Colliers Wood: Tha Makham, 15/11/1943, Kanchanaburi War
 Cemetery
Pte H. Robertson from Kennington: Tha Sao, 18/11/1943 (oedema), Kanchanaburi
 War Cemetery
L.Cpl W. Newman from London: Thanbaya, Burma, 04/12/1943 (dysentery),
 Thanbyuzayat War Cemetery
L.Cpl S. Lewin from Kent: Kanchanaburi, 08/12/1943 (beri-beri/ulcers),
 Kanchanaburi War Cemetery
Pte F. Craig from Colliers Wood: Kanchanaburi, 08/12/43 (beri-beri),
 Kanchanaburi War Cemetery
Pte H. Leonard from London: Kanchanaburi 10/12/1943 (pleurisy), Kanchanaburi
 War Cemetery
Pte S. Seymour from Cobham: Chungkai, 12/12/1943 (pellagra), Chungkai War
 Cemetery
Pte R. Harrison from Oxford: Kanchanaburi, 16/12/43 (beri-beri), Kanchanaburi
 War Cemetery
Cpl J. Craig from Colliers Wood: Kanchanburi, 21/12/43 (dysentery),
 Kanchanaburi War Cemetery

1944

Pte A. Stone from Streatham: Chungkai, 06/02/1944 (dysentery), Chungkai War
 Cemetery
L.Cpl A. Carter from Sheffield: Tha Sao, 12/02/44 (dysentery), Kanchanaburi
 War Cemetery
Sgt C. Friday from Epsom: Chungkai, 10/04/44 (pneumonia/malaria), Chungkai
 War Cemetery
Pte F. Smith from Southwark: Chungkai, 24/04/1944 (bombing), Chungkai War
 Cemetery
Pte R. Chaston from Leyton: Ni Thea, 23/06/1944, Singapore War Memorial
Cpl D. Keats from Morden: en route to Japan, 26/06/1944 (drowned), Singapore
 War Memorial
Pte L. Jennings from St Leonards: Nakhon Pathom, 12/07/1944, Kanchanaburi
 War Cemetery
Pte F. Williams from Tottenham: Singapore War Memorial
Pte R. Webley from London: en route to Japan, 04/09/1944 (drowned), Singapore
 War Memorial
Pte S. Short from Battersea: Non Pladuk, 07/09/1944, Kanchanaburi War
 Cemetery

Pte A. Foyster from London: Nong Pladuk, 07/09/44 (in air raid), Kanchanaburi War Cemetery

Pte R. Spencer from Worcester Park: Nong Pladuk, 07/09/1944, Kanchanaburi War Cemetery

Pte H. Blackman from Epsom: en route to Japan, 12/09/1944 (drowned), Singapore War Memorial

Pte W. Arlett from Camberwell: en route to Japan, 21/09/1944 (drowned), Singapore War Memorial

Pte J. Brown of Norbiton: en route to Japan, 21/09/1944 (drowned), Singapore War Memorial

L.Cpl L. Blake: en route to Japan, 21/09/1944 (drowned), Singapore War Memorial

Pte J. Chennell from Chertsey: en route to Japan, 21/09/1944 (drowned), Singapore War Memorial

Sgt M. Cleary: en route to Japan, 21/09/1944 (drowned), Singapore War Memorial

Pte G. Cudd from Balham: en route to Japan, 21/09/1944 (drowned), Singapore War Memorial

Pte H. Darby from Hammersmith: en route to Japan, 21/09/1944 (drowned), Singapore War Memorial

Pte R. Dedman from Battersea: en route to Japan, 21/09/1944 (drowned), Singapore War Memorial

Pte D. Evans from Morden: en route to Japan, 21/09/1944 (drowned), Singapore War Memorial

Pte A. Freeland from London: en route to Japan, 21/09/1944 (drowned), Singapore War Memorial

Sgt R. Shemmings from Folkstone: en route to Japan, 21/09/1944 (drowned), Singapore War Memorial

Pte R. Shepherd from Merton: en route to Japan, 21/09/1944 (drowned), Singapore War Memorial

Pte W. Greenaway from Acton: en route to Japan, 21/09/1944 (drowned), Singapore War Memorial

Pte J. Woods from Renfrewshire: en route to Japan, 21/09/1944 (drowned), Singapore War Memorial

Sgt J. Haskell from Sutton: en route to Japan, 21/09/1944 (drowned), Singapore War Memorial

Pte A. Slade from Islington: en route to Japan, 21/09/1944 (drowned), Singapore War Memorial

Pte D. Thomson from Farnborough: en route to Japan, 21/09/1944 (drowned), Singapore War Memorial

Pte J. Thomson from Esher: en route to Japan, 21/09/1944 (drowned), Singapore War Memorial

Pte E. Johnson from Foots Cray: en route to Japan, 21/09/1944 (drowned), Singapore War Memorial

Pte E. Leigh from Warrington: en route to Japan, 21/09/1944 (drowned), Singapore War Memorial

Cpl G. Mordecai: en route to Japan, 21/09/1944 (drowned), Singapore War Memorial

Pte L. Pardoe MM from Herne Hill: en route to Japan, 21/09/1944 (drowned), Singapore War Memorial

Pte S. Peel from Notting Hill: en route to Japan, 21/09/1944 (drowned), Singapore War Memorial

Cpl J. Roper from Hampstead: Formosa, 29/09/1944 (malaria), Yokohama Cemetery

Pte A. Bridgewater from Ilford: Kutching, Borneo, 30/09/1944, Singapore War Memorial

Pte A. Jeffra: Changi, 01/10/1944, Singapore War Memorial

Cpl T. Rogers from Dover: Nakhon Pathom, 01/10/1944 (dysentery), Kanchanaburi War Cemetery

Pte A. Jeffra: Changi, 01/10/1944, Singapore War Memorial

Pte L. Pritchard from Islington: Tha Mayo, 16/11/1944 (malaria), Kanchanaburi War Cemetery

L.Cpl A. Staplehurst from Devon: Borneo, 19/11/1944, Singapore War Memorial

1945

Bmn E. Manley from Shafford: Amagasaki, Japan, 15/01/1945, Yokohama War Cemetery

L.Cpl A. Musgrave: Singapore, 20/01/1945, Singapore War Memorial

Pte E. Jenkins from Glamorgan: Nakhon Pathom, 05/02/1945, (dysentery), Kanchanaburi War Cemetery

L.Cpl J. Heath from Richmond: Nong Pladuk, 05/02/1945 (cholera), Chungkai War Cemetery

Pte E. Hookey: Wang Pho, 09/02/1945, Kanchanaburi War Cemetery

L.Cpl C. Donaldson from Epsom: 24/02/1945 (drowned at sea), Singapore War Memorial

Pte C. Howlett from Garfield: Borneo, 26/02/1945, Singapore War Memorial

Pte H. Snowden from Hartlepool: Tukuoka, Japan, 03/03/1945, Yokohama War Cemetery

L.Cpl S. Sanders from Walthamstow: Kachu, 25/03/1945, Kanchanaburi War Cemetery

Cpl C.H. Brown from Fulham: Kutching, Borneo, 28/03/1945, Singapore Memorial

Dmr V. Buckle from Kingston: Saigon, 07/04/1945 (in air raid), Taiping War Cemetery

Pte D. Brightman from Ruislip: Japan, 03/05/1945, Yokohama War Cemetery

Pte A. Cooke: Changhai, 08/06/1945, Kranji War Cemetery

Sgt G. Cast from Walthamstow: Mergui Burma, 08/06/45 (dysentery), Kanchanaburi War Cemetery

Pte L. Anderson from London: Tarsoe, 22/06/1945, Kanchanaburi War Cemetery

Pte P. Treasure: Kuala Lumpur, 24/06/1945, Labuan War Cemetery

Pte R. Simmons from Shanghai: Sarawak, 16/08/1945, Labuan War Cemetery

Pte D. Mardlin from Stroud: after release, 02/09/1945 (dysentery), Kanchanaburi War Cemetery

Pte R. Gadd from Tolworth: over Saigon, 07/09/1945 (air crash), Singapore War Memorial

Pte L. Merry from Hanwell: Changi, 03/10/1945, Kranji War Cemetery

Appendix IV

Nominal Roll of the 2 East Surreys as of 7 December 1941 (outbreak of hostilities)

(K) killed in action Malaya/Singapore campaign (D) died as a prisoner of war

Commanding Officer:
Lieutenant Colonel G.E. Swinton MC

Majors:

R. Chidson	Harvey	C. Poole
F. Crafter	F. Magee	M.C. Russell (D)
F.B.B. Dowling MC (K)	D. Orme	

Captains:

E. Andrews	W.A.C. Edwards	A.J.H. Martin
Rev. H.C. Babb OBE CF	W.G. Gingell MBE MM	C. O'Neil Wallis MC
K. Bradley (K)	A. Hill (K)	Rev. R. Rawsthorne (K)
P. Bruckman	E.A.F. Howard	Dr H.B. Thomson (K)
W.A.C. Cater	J. Kerrich (K)	

Lieutenants:

J.T. Barnard	R. Bowden	E.J. Peel-Yates
E.W. Bateman	H.R. Cross	L. Sear (K)
S. Bishop	R. Daniel	D.K. Smith (K)
R.H.V. Bobe (K)	M.G.D. Edmondson (K)	
T.R. Bond	R.C. Humphries	

2nd Lieutenants:

S S Abbott	D H League	J Whittaker
L B Bingham (D)	W Meyers (K)	F Wilkinson
B F Boothby	J Quarrel	RQMS F. Barnard
R Bradford (K)	R J Randolph	Warrant Officer F.
J D Carter	H Russell (K)	Bullard (D)
R P Cave	H P Sharland	ORQMA E.G. Camp
G G Falkner	R D Thompson	G. Cason (K)

T. Clark (K)
R.H. Colls
J. Foley (K)

RQMS Lewington
RQMS E.A. Livermore

B/Master E.E. Manley
  (D)
RSM E. Worsfold MBE

CSMs:

F. Bullard (D)
E. Croot
J. Ives

T.W. Johnson
R. Shemmings (D)
W.G. Swanson

J. Vaughan (K)
L. Weston

Colour Sergeants:

J.W. Beach
T. Cahill
G. Cason (K)
G.W. Cast

T. Clark
A.H.T. Eatwell
W.J. Lawrence (D)
W.A. Lazard

Moffatt
V. Osborn (D)
L. Sorge
V. Wildman(K)

Sergeants:

M. Abery (K)
C. Austin (K)
P. Baker
F. Baldwin
J. Beach
D. Boorer
B. Brown
F. Burgess (K)
G. Cast (D)
T. Cahill
C. Challis
M. Cleary (D)
C. Clue
W. Collier
J. Craggs DCM
J. Craig (D)
F. Croft
J. Dermody
E. Dickenson
A. Eatwell

J. Filby
G. Forman
W. Gallagher
H. George (D)
J. Gunn (K)
W. Hall (K)
W. Harrison
J. Hastell (D)
J. Ives
A. Jackson
F. Jowett (K)
J. Kaye
J. Killick
W. Lamport
F. Laverack
J.C. Le Clair (K)
D. MacLean MM
C. Martin
W. McPherson
E. Miles

W. Perkins (K)
G. Potter (K)
C. Roberts
S. Roche (K)
A. Rudd (K)
F. Searles
F. Shipton
W. Simper
A. Stening
A. Stratford
S. Stutley
A. Thomas
N. Turner
White
Wildman
J. Williams
W. Williams
H. Wilson (D)

Lance Sergeants:

L. Avery
J. Bird
G. Frost

R.J. Glazier
D. McDonough
R. Deadman (K)

S. Francis
S. Humphries
A. Levey

H. Meddle (K)
O. Riddle

C. Roberts
C. Wise

C. Friday (D)

Corporals:

E. Armstrong
L. Barber
J. Bartram (K)
J. Belham (K)
A. Bone
R. Booker (D)
D. Boyce (K)
A. Bradfield
H. Braim
D. Brightman (D)
C.H. Brown (D)
M. Brown
G. Buckley
C. Chidwick
D. Clemens
W. Collier
A. Connor
A. Cook
D. Coombs
E. Cooper (D)
J. Craig (D)
C. Easton
J. Fletcher
A. Garvey (D)
D Gavin

J. Gray (D)
L. Harding
J. Hawkins (D)
R. Hawkins (K)
G. Henty (K)
F. Hewes
A. Hillier (K)
J. Hocking
F. Humphries (K)
A Hunt(D)
D. Keats (D)
T. Kerslake
M. Mason (K)
J. Maynard(K)
L. Milner (K)
G. Mordecai (D)
G. Morris
J. Nall
L. Nunn (D)
E. Oatley
L. Parfitt
H. Parker
F. Parsons
W. Paul (K)
R. Pederson

J. Perkin
J. Pike
E. Polfrey
J. Rea
J. Reynolds (K)
O. Riddle (K)
W. Riley
P. Robertson (D)
A. Robinson (K)
T. Rogers (D)
J. Roper (D)
J. Sampson
B. Sherman
H. Sleight
G. Smith
W. Smith
A. Sumner
T. Tamplin
R. Thompson
A. Tipping
H. Tugwell
F. Young (K)
R. Young

Lance Corporals:

W. Abbott
J. Arthur
F. Baldock
F. Bardhill
F. Barling (K)
E. Berkeley (K)
F. Blake (D)
R. Booker (D)
A. Bradfield
J. Bradshaw
J. Bray (K)

C. Brown (K)
J.P. Brown
C. Browning
G. Buckley
J. Cain
A. Cant (K)
A. Carter (D)
S. Chaplin
V. Clothier
F. Colley
A. Cooke (D)

D. Coughlan
R. Cranston
C. Donaldson (D)
V. Garrard (D)
H. Heath (D)
S. Lewin (D)
G. Mitchell (K)
R. Moore (D)
A. Musgrave (D)
E. Musk
V. Newman

W. Newman (D)
A. Nuthall (K)
L. Page
A. Parris
G. Potter (K)
C. Reeves (D)
R. Russell
E. Samuels (K)
S. Sanders (D)
W. Seaton (K)

J Seymour
S. Simmons
F. Skelton
A. Staplehurst (D)
A. Stephens (D)
G. Thirtle
F. Tonnison (K)
H. Tugwell
F. Turner
A. Webber

F. Wells (K)
F. Wilson (K)
H. Wilson
E. Woolard (K)
J. Wyatt
J. Yates
C. Yewings (K)
F. Young (K)
H. Young
L.L. Young (D)

Privates:

G. Abery (K)
L. Abery
R. Abrahams (D)
W. Adamswaite
J. Addison
J. Ainslie
D. Alexander (K)
L. Alexander
A. Allen
A.B. Allen
D. Allen (D)
R. Ambler
L. Anderson (D)
S. Anderson (K)
W. Arlett (D)
E. Armstrong
J. Armstrong
H. Arnold (K)
J. Arnold (D)
S. Arnold
R. Ashton
J. Askham
G. Asprey
F. Atkins (K)
F. Austin
B. Aylwin
A. Ayres (D)
W. Bacon
D. Bagnaro (K)
J. Bainbridge

A. Baker
F. Baker
W. Baker
S. Ball (K)
C. Ballard (K)
A. Banks
T. Bannatyne (K)
A. Barber
J. Barnett
A. Barton
C. Barton
C. Barton
G. Barton
A. Bartram
G. Bateman
J. Bates
W. Batt (K)
W. Batten
H. Beer
A. Beesley
S Beesley (K)
F. Beach
J. Beach
E. Beckett (K)
C. Beckness (K)
T. Bell
J. Bellsham
F. Bennett
H. Bennett
H. Betts

W. Bevan (D)
R. Bird
L. Blackhurst
H. Blackman (D)
J. Blackman (K)
T. Blyde (K)
B. Bobbins (K)
H. Boland
C. Bone
P. Bowry
W. Boxall
A. Bradley
A. Bradley
J. Bradshaw
G. Bragg (D)
L. Brandon (K)
W. Brevington
D. Brewer
W. Brice
G. Bridger
A. Bridgewater (D)
L. Britchford (K)
G. Britton
C. Brooker (D)
G. Broom (D)
A. Brown (D)
H. Brown (D)
F. Brown (K)
J. Brown (D)
J.A. Brown (K)

P. Brown
A. Brumby (K)
C. Bryce
V. Buckle (D)
W. Buckle
W. Budge (K)
H. Bull
T. Burberry
F. Burkett (K)
T. Burns
J. Burrows (D)
J. Butler
W. Carleton
W. Carpenter
E. Carr (D)
J. Carroll
A. Carter
F. Carter
A. Caston
R. Cattermole
P. Chalcroft
C. Challice
S. Chaplin
A. Chapman
B. Chapman (K)
R. Chaston (D)
J. Chennell (D)
L. Chernin
C. Chessman
J. Childs
E. Chittey
W Chivers
W. Church
J. Clark (K)
R. Clarke
S. Cleall
E. Cleaver (D)
L. Cochran
W. Cockroft
A. Coleman
F. Coleman
H. Colgate

C. Connelly
H. Constable (K)
R. Constable
R. Cook (K)
A Cooke
C. Coombs
D. Coombs (K)
N. Coombs
H. Cooper (K)
J. Corbett
J. Corlett (K)
K. Cottle (K)
S. Cove
H. Cowell
E. Cowles
W. Cowles
H. Cox
S. Cox
C. Craig
F. Craig (D)
B. Crane
R. Cranston
J. Crocker
J. Croker (D)
A. Cross
A. Crowhurst
G. Cudd (D)
P. Currie
W. Curry
C. Cushing
H. Cussell
D. Da Costa
F. Dade
H. Dance
R. Daniels (K)
W. Daniels
H. Darby (D)
G. Davies
G. Davies
J.C. Davies
N. Davies
T.J. Davies

W. Davies
F. Davis
F. Davis
J.C. Davis
R. Davis (K)
D. Day (D)
P. Day
H. Deakin (K)
G. Deane
R. Dedman (D)
N. Dellow
E. Deluce
J. Dennis
R. Dennis (D)
E. Denyer
H. Dimmock
G. Dimond
J. Dines
W. Dobson
W. Dobson (D)
W. Doherty (D)
N. Dorval (D)
D.J. Douglas
J. Driscoll (D)
G. Drury
C. Duff
C. Duffy (K)
S. Dye (K)
F. Dyne (K)
F. Earle
V. Edgson (K)
G. Edwards
J. Edwards
R. Edwards
C. Emerson
H. Etches (D)
D. Evans (D)
J. Evans
W. Farrell
A. Fennell (K)
A. Field
W. Field (K)

C. Finch
N. Finlay
L. Fisher
T. Fisher
J. Fitzgerald (K)
B. Fitzpatrick (K)
H. Fluin (K)
C. Flynn
D. Forshaw
S. Foulger (D)
A. Foyster (D)
H. Franklin
W. Franklin
A. Freeland (D)
H. Freeman (D)
J. Freeman
G. Fullbrook
P. Furderer
R. Gadd (D)
L. Gadsden (D)
W. Gardiner
C. Garrett
A. Garvey
J. Gavin
R. George
S. Gillan
T. Girdler
L. Glendenning
W. Golden (D)
F. Gosling (K)
G. Gove (D)
H. Grant
P. Graves MM
J. Gray (D)
H. Green
R. Green
W. Greenaway (D)
C. Greenwood (K)
J. Griffiths
J Grifin
N. Grinter (K)
C. Gunton

J. Guy
J. Hall (K)
J. Hall
S. Hall
J. Haggis (K)
W. Harbroe
G. Hardy (K)
C. Harmer
G. Harmer
A. Harris (K)
R. Harrison (D)
J. Harvey (D)
R. Harvey
E. Hatch
E. Hatt (D)
C. Hawkins
D. Hawkins
S. Hawkins
A. Hayes (K)
S. Hayes
H. Heard
S. Hearne
V. Heckett (D)
E. Hefferman (K)
D. Helder
T. Henbury
F. Herbert
P. Heron
C. Hewer
W. Hewitt (K)
C. Hibbert
L. Hickey (K)
H. Hicks
J. Higgins
C. Hill
J. Hill
P. Hill
B. Hills
A. Hilliard
H. Hillier
R. Hillier
R. Himsworth

D. Hines
S. Hobbs (K)
A. Hocking
D. Hodgson
B. Holden
J. Holden
J. Holland
C. Holliday (D)
A. Holloway (K)
S. Holman (D)
R. Holmes (K)
F. Holt
E. Hookey (D)
A. Hornblow (K)
P. Hornsby
W. Hornsey (D)
E. Horwood (K)
W. Howard
H. Howes (K)
L. Howes
C. Howlett (D)
J. Hubbard (K)
B. Hudson
S. Hughes
A. Hunt (K)
F. Hunt (D)
W. Hurst
R. Hutchins
P. Huzzey (K)
J. Ions
A. Irwin
A. Jeffra (D)
R. Jeffrey (K)
L. Jelley
R. Jelly
D. Jenkins (K)
E. Jenkins (D)
W. Jenkins (K)
E. Jenn (D)
G. Jennings
L. Jennings (D)
P. Jewell

E. Johnson (D)
F. Johnson
G. Johnson
T. Johnson (D)
E. Joyce
J. Keenhan
F. King (D)
T. King (D)
R. Kingsley (K)
J. Kinsella
J. Knight
J. Lackenby
R. Lake
N. Lamb (K)
A. Lambert
A. Lambert
W. Lamport
A. Latchford
C. Laver
S. Law
T. Law
A. Lawrence
H. Leach (D)
H. Leeding
R. Leigh (D)
H. Leonard (D)
L. Leonard (K)
A. Letherland
D. Lewcock
J. Lewis
R. Livermore (K)
E. Livesby
F. Loates
C. Lock (D)
J. Logan
C. Long
D. Lomasney
V. Loomes
A. Loraine (K)
W. Lord
H. Lowry
T. Lucas

S. Lunny (D)
M. Lyons
E. McAuliffe (K)
R. McCarthy
T. McClarty
J. McLeary (K)
A. Mace (K)
G. Maker
L. Manning
E. Mansfield
D. Mardlin (D)
W. Marks
W. Marley
T. Marman (K)
E. Marsh (K)
A. Marshall
E. Marshall
L. Marshall
H. Martin
L. Martin
R. Maslyn
J. Matthes
J. Matthews (K)
A. May (K)
T. Meddings (K)
H. Mellows
F. Mercer (D)
L. Merry (D)
D. Mesha
A. Metcalf
F. Miles
R. Miles
H. Millar (D)
G. Mills
R. Millward
J. Minihane (K)
J. Mitchell (K)
G. Mitchess
W. Monteith
R. Moon
D. Moore
G. Moore

M. Moore
R. Moralee
A. Morris
A. Morris (K)
H. Morton (K)
G. Mulberry
D. Mullins
P. Murphy
H. Murray
J. Naulls
P. Neithercott
G. Nethercott
B. Newman
S. Newman
H. Nicholls
E. Nickless
P. Noad (K)
C. Nobbs (K)
G. Noon
A. Nuttall
J. Offord
D. O'Leary
H. O'Looney
J. Orchard
P. Osborn
A. O'Shea
A. Paget (K)
L. Pardoe MM (D)
A. Park
S. Parker (K)
A. Parkins
A. Parr (D)
J. Pascoe
E. Pate (K)
J. Pavlick
A. Payne (D)
W. Pearce (K)
S. Peel (D)
G. Penfold (K)
J. Penfold (K)
W. Penfold (D)
J. Pepper

J. Perkin
J. Perry
H. Pettitt
A. Phillips
J. Phillips
L. Phillips
C. Peverett
W. Pickett
R. Pike
A. Plant
D. Poole
R. Pope (D)
T. Powell
L. Pritchard (D)
J. Pugh (D)
C. Purcess
P. Pythian
W. Quinell
L. Rance (K)
A. Randolph
M. Ray
N. Ray
A. Read
H. Read (D)
C. Reader
A. Redford (K)
A. Reece
G. Reed (D)
W. Reeves
D. Regan
S. Reid
E. Reilly
E. Restall
C. Richardson (D)
D. Richardson
G. Richardson
J. Rivers
M. Rivron
P. Rivron
S. Roberts
H. Robertson (D)
S. Robertson

P. Robinson
R. Robinson (D)
W. Robinson
F. Roper
C. Ross
E. Rowlands (K)
G. Ruler
H. Ruoff
E. Russell (K)
S. Russell (D)
L. Ryan
B. Salmon
F. Salter
J. Salter (K)
T. Sampson (K)
J. Samways
F. Sanger
D. Saskechin
R. Scarborough
L. Sear (K)
L. Selley
E. Sewell
F. Seymour
L. Seymour (K)
S. Seymour (D)
J. Sharp
W. Sharp (D)
W. Shaw (D)
A. Shepherd (K)
R Shepherd (D)
B. Sherfield (K)
F. Shettle
M. Shiels
S. Short (D)
A. Shrimpton (K)
S. Shury
W. Simkins (K)
R. Simmons (D)
V. Simpson
J. Sinclair (D)
A. Skelton
A. Slade (D)

C. Slade
W. Slade
A. Smith (K)
A. Smith
D. Smith (K)
F. Smith (D)
F. Smith
H. Smith
J. Smith
J. Smith
K. Smith (D)
L. Smith (K)
T. Smith (K)
W. Smithers
H. Snowden (D)
H. Solly
H. South
R. Spencer (D)
T. Spike
J. Spurdle
H. Squires
S. Stallwood (K)
A. Stanbury
J. Stanford (K)
A. Starr
A. Steel (K)
E. Steer
A. Stephens (K)
V. Stiff
C. Stiles (K)
G. Stirling
O. Stock (K)
A. Stone (D)
G. Street
G. Strohm
R. Strong (K)
D. Surman
A. Sutton (K)
R. Swain (K)
K. Swansbury (K)
T. Taburn
H. Tame (K)

S. Tatum
S. Taylor
W. Taylor
T. Tegg
J. Thompson (D)
J.H. Thompson
D. Thompson (D)
R. Thomson
W. Tinkler
W. Tobin (D)
R. Tooth (K)
F. Travers
P. Treasure (D)
S. Tredrea
F. Truesdale
D. Turner
F. Turner
H. Turner (K)
J. Turner (K)
W. Turner
W. Turnham
J. Tuson
H. Upfold (D)
D. Upton
V. Vale
C. Vause (D)

R. Vincent (D)
T. Walker
W. Walker
C. Wall (D)
G. Wallace
G. Walters
E. Warman (D)
C. Warn (K)
J. Warren (D)
R. Warren
H. Waters (D)
R. Watson
V. Watson
R. Webley (D)
A. Webster (K)
R. Webster
J. Welch
C. Wells
E. Wells
J. Wells
J. Wells
W. Weston
S. Wheatley
A. Wheeler (D)
R. Wheeler (D)
H. White

L. White
J. Whittal (K)
E. Whitten
J. Wilcox
J William
F. Williams (D)
G. Williams (K)
G. Willingdale (K)
R. Willoughby
W Wilks (K)
R. Wilmhurst (K)
F. Wilson
H. Wilson (D)
H. Wilson (D)
K. Wiltshire
F. Woodrow
H. Woods
J. Woods (D)
R. Woolard (K)
W. Woolton
A. Wright
H. Wright
J. Wright
S. Wright (K)
J. Young

Bibliography

Abbot, S., *And All My War Is Done*, Pentland, Durham, 1992.

Arnold, M., *The Sacrifice of Singapore*, Marshall Cavendish, Singapore, 2001.

Arthur, M., *Forgotten Voices of the Second World War*, Random House, London, 2004.

Barber, N., *Sinister Twilight*, Cassell, London, 1968.

Barnard, J., *The Endless Years*, Chantry, London, 1950.

Barwick, I., *In the Shadow of Death*, Pen and Sword, Barnsley, 2003.

Bayley, C., and Harper, T., *Forgotten Armies*, Penguin, London, 2005.

Beattie, R., *The Death Railway*, TBRC, Kanchanaburi, 2015.

Braddon, R., *The Naked Island*, Birlinn, Edinburgh, 2005.

Bradley, J., *Towards the Setting Sun*, Fuller, Wellington, 1982.

Brooke, G., *Singapore's Dunkirk*, Pen and Sword, Barnsley, 2014.

Bruton, P., *British Military Hospital Singapore*, self-published.

Chung, O., *Operation Matador*, East University Press, Singapore, 2003.

Churchill, W., *The Second World War*, Pimlico, London, 2002.

Clandon Museum, *Malaya 1941-42*, booklet.

Clarke, H., *A Life for Every Sleeper*, Allen and Unwin, Sydney, 1986.

Clarke, H., *Last Stop Nagasaki*, Allen and Unwin, London, 1984.

Coogan, A., *Tomorrow You Die*, Mainstream, Edinburgh, 2013.

Cosford, J., *Line of Lost Lives*, Gryphon, Northants, 1988.

Craigie, Sir Robert, *Behind the Japanese Mask*, Hutchinson, London, 1945.

Daniels, D.S., *History of the East Surrey Regiment 1920–1952*, Ernest Benn, London, 1957.

Davies, P., *The Man Behind the Bridge*, Athlone, London 1991.

Daws, G., *Prisoners of the Japanese*, Robson, London, 1995.

Dear, I., *Escape and Evasion*, Cassell, London, 1997.

East Surrey Regiment, *The Final Years*.

East Surreys, *Malaya 1941-1942*.

Farrell, B., *The Defence and Fall of Singapore*, Tempus, Stroud, 2005.

Felton, M., *The Final Betrayal*, Pen and Sword, Barnsley, 2010.

Frank, R.B., *Downfall*, Penguin, New York, 2001.

Fyans, P., *Conjuror on the Kwai*, Pen and Sword, Barnsley, 2011.

Gavin, D., *Quiet Jungle, Angry Sea*, Lennard Publishing, Oxford, 1989.

Gillies, M., *The Barbed-Wire University*, Aurum Press, London, 2012.

Glover, E.M., *In 70 Days*, Fredrick Muller, London, 1946.

Hack, K., and Blackburn, K., *Did Singapore Have to Fall?*, Routledge, London, 2003.

Hammond, R., *The Flame of Freedom*, Leo Cooper, London, 1988.

Harmsen, P., *Shanghai 1937*, Casemate, Oxford, 2013.

Hastain, R., *White Coolie*, Hodder and Stoughton, London, 1947.

Hastings, M., *Nemesis*, Harper, London, 2007.

Holmes, R., and Kemp, A., *The Bitter End*, Bird Publications, Chichester, 1982.

Horner, R., *Singapore Diary*, Spellmount, Stroud, 2007.

Hotta, E., *Japan 1941*, Vintage, New York, 2014.

James, L., *Churchill & Empire*, Phoenix, London, 2013.

Kennedy, J., *Andy Dillon's Ill-Fated Division*, United, Cornwall, 2000.

Kinvig, C., *Death Railway*, Pan/Ballantine, London, 1973.

Lane, A., *Lesser Gods, Greater Devils*, Lane Publishing, Stockport, 1993.

Lane, A., *Seventy Days to Hell*, Lane Publishing, Stockport, 2011.

Lane, A., *When You Go Home*, Lane Publishing, Stockport, 1993.

Langley, M., *The East Surrey Regiment*, Leo Cooper, London, 1972.

Lewis, D., *Judy: A Dog in a Million*, Quercus, London, 2014.

Lewis, J., and Steele, B., *Hell in the Pacific*, Ch4 Books, London, 2001.

Lockwood, S., *Unbelievable But True*, Vanguard, Cambridge, 2006.

Lomax, E., *The Railway Man*, Cape, London, 1995.

Loong, C., *The British Battalion in Malaya*.

Low, N., and Cheng, H., *This Singapore, Our City of Dreadful Nights*, Singapore, 1945.

McArthur, B., *Surviving the Sword*, Time Warner, London, 2005.

McEwan, A., and Thomson, C., *Death Was Our Bedmate*, Pen and Sword, Barnsley, 2013.

McEwan, J., *Out of the Depths of Hell*, Pen and Sword, Barnsley, 2005.

Michno, G., *Death on the Hellships*, Leo Cooper, Barnsley, 2001.

Mitchell, R., *Baba Nonnie Goes to War*, Coombe, 2004.

Moffatt, J., and McCormick, A.H., *Moon Over Malaya*, Tempus, Stroud, 2002.

Moore, A.W., *Writing War*, Harvard University Press, 2013.

Partridge, J., *Alexandra Hospital Singapore*, Singapore Poly, 1998.

Peek, I., *One Fourteenth of an Elephant*, Transworld, London, 2004.

Pike, F., *Hirohito's War*, Bloomsbury, London, 2015.

Rees, L., *Horror in the East*, BBC Books, 2001.

Richards, R., *The Survival Factor*, Costello, Tunbridge Wells, 1989.

Russell, Lord, *Knights of Bushido*, Corgi, London, 1960.

Saddington, S., *Escape Impossible*, Lane, Stockport, 1997.

Searle, R., *To the Kwai and Back*, Collins, London, 1986.

Sergeant, H., *Shanghai*, Cape, London, 1991.

Sherwood, J., *Lucky Johnny*, Hodder and Stoughton, London, 2014.

Skinner, H., *Guest of the Imperial Japanese Army*, Skinner, Littlehampton, 1993.

Smith, C., *Singapore Burning*, Viking, London, 2005.

Spencer-Chapman, R., *The Jungle is Neutral*, Reprint Society, London, 1949.

Summers, J., *The Colonel of Tamarkan*, Simon and Schuster, London, 2005.

Taylor, E., *Faith, Hope and Rice*, Pen and Sword, Barnsley, 2015

Thompson, P., *Pacific Fury*, Heinemann, Sydney, 2008.

Thompson, P., *The Battle for Singapore*, Portrait, London, 2006.

Trukhanovsky, V., *British Foreign Policy During World War II*, Progress, Moscow, 1970.

Tsuji, M., *Japan's Greatest Victory, Britain's Worst Defeat*, Spellmount, Kent, 1997.

Urquhart, A., *The Forgotten Highlander*, Little, Brown, London, 2010.

Wasserstein, B., *Secret War in Shanghai*, Profile, London, 1998.

Wavell, Sir A., *Speaking Generally*, Macmillan, London, 1946.

Woodburn Kirby, S., *The War Against Japan*, Naval and Military Press, Uckfield, 2004.

Wyatt, J., and Lowry, C., *No Mercy from the Japanese*, Pen and Sword, Barnsley, 2008.

Index